Mishap or Malpractice?

CLIFFORD HAWKINS

Mishap or Malpractice?

PUBLISHED FOR

THE MEDICAL DEFENCE UNION

FOR ITS CENTENARY IN 1985 BY

BLACKWELL SCIENTIFIC PUBLICATIONS

OXFORD   LONDON   EDINBURGH

BOSTON   PALO ALTO   MELBOURNE

© 1985 by
Blackwell Scientific Publications
Editorial offices:
Osney Mead, Oxford, OX2 0EL
8 John Street, London WC1N 2ES
23 Ainslie Place, Edinburgh, EH3 6AJ
52 Beacon Street, Boston
    Massachusetts 02108, USA
667 Lytton Avenue, Palo Alto
    California 94301, USA
107 Barry Street, Carlton
    Victoria 3053, Australia

First published 1985

Set, printed and bound
at The Alden Press, Oxford

DISTRIBUTORS

USA
    Blackwell Mosby Book Distributors
    11830 Westline Industrial Drive
    St Louis, Missouri 63141

Canada
    Blackwell Mosby Book Distributors
    120 Melford Drive, Scarborough
    Ontario M1B 2X4

Australia
    Blackwell Scientific Publications
    (Australia) Pty Ltd
    107 Barry Street
    Carlton, Victoria 3053

British Library
Cataloguing in Publication Data

Hawkins, Clifford
    Mishap or malpractice?
    1. Medical laws and legislation
    I. Title
    342.4′41   K3601

ISBN 0-632-01414-8
ISBN 0-632-01415-6 Pbk

Contents

Preface

The invitation to write a book to celebrate the centenary of the Medical Defence Union was a daunting challenge: a single-author publication was wanted and I was not versed in medico-legal matters. Fortunately the subject soon fascinated me.

Three phases were needed before the manuscript was ready for the publisher. First, to learn; apart from the extensive literature on the law concerning doctors, much historical material was available in the archives of the Medical Defence Union. Secondly, to write the book. Thirdly, the text was studied by the experts listed under 'Acknowledgements' in order to check its factual accuracy. Opinions and advice are mine and do not necessarily reflect those of the Medical Defence bodies.

Medicine is a highly emotive subject and disagreements between patients and doctors receive the floodlight of publicity. Litigation against doctors is increasing. This book aims to give an account of the problems that hinder harmonious doctor–patient relationships, and perhaps the suggestions made for avoiding them may help to prevent the emergence of 'defensive medicine' in the United Kingdom and elsewhere, for this is as bad for the patient as it is for the doctor.

The book is aimed primarily at doctors and dentists, and others who provide health care; and I hope it will interest lawyers. If a lay person should read it and be horrified because of the book's necessary concentration on what has gone wrong rather than what is going right, it will reassure him or her to consider that the risks of most mishaps and malpractice are no greater than those accepted as part of daily living.

Clifford Hawkins

Acknowledgements

I doubt whether the book would have been completed without the special help of two members of the staff of the MDU: Mrs Gladys McLeod MA, who acted as research assistant, and gave me help of outstanding value as well as checking carefully each new version of the typescript as it came off the word processor; Dr Brian Rhodes, retired Deputy Secretary with twenty years of experience of medico-legal matters, was my mentor and also painstakingly ferreted out historical and other material from the Annual Reports and law libraries. Library searches were aided by the Librarians Mr S. R. Jenkins of the Medical School library and Mrs Gail Smyth in the University of Birmingham. Dr J. M. H. Moll drew the caricatures and cartoons. A discussion with Dr Peter Ford, Secretary of the Medical Protection Society (MPS), was much appreciated and he kindly gave me some of the publications of the MPS. Dr John Reckless of North Carolina supplied me with data concerning insurance premiums paid by American doctors. The word-processor operators, Mrs Jacky Dench and Mrs Sylvia Witney, patiently and efficiently produced draft after draft. Mr John Bright-Holmes provided helpful and professional editorial advice.

I am most grateful to the following who read the text, commented on it, and checked its factual accuracy: Dr J. W. Brooke Barnett, the Secretary of the Medical Defence Union (MDU) and Mr C. H. H. Butcher, the senior partner of Hempsons, solicitors to the MDU. Mr William L. Thorp, American attorney who specializes in civil litigation concerning doctors, read the chapter on litigation in the United States of America, and Dr C. E. Newman CBE, medical historian, approved of the accuracy of Chapter 1. Others who commented on sections were Dr W. D. Wylie, President of the MDU and Dr A. L. Gwynne, Principal Secretary. Dr Philip Addison, Honorary Consulting Secretary to the MDU, provided me with historical data that he had assembled. Mrs Bridget Kirkham DipFAA (Otago) supplied me with computer print-outs which gave the data used in this book.

My wife supported me by searching the newspapers and hardly a day went by without something connected with this subject being reported; she also read and commented upon the typescripts. My son Dr M. J. Hawkins, a general practitioner, was also inflicted with it to avoid any impractical advice being given. My thanks are due to Caroline Richards, sub-editor at Blackwell

Acknowledgements

Scientific Publications, for the painstaking and intelligent care with which she prepared the manuscript for publication. Finally I regret that many who have helped will have to join that anonymous group 'et al.', particularly those whom I have provoked into argument and discussion in order to learn.

1

A century of change

On 31 July 1884, Dr David Bradley MD MCh was making up a bottle of medicine in his surgery for Eliza Swetmore, wife of a coalminer living at Whittington Moor near Chesterfield, when he heard a peculiar sound, and turning, found that she was about to have a fit. Having nothing else at hand he held the stopper of the bottle containing liquor ammoniae fortior (sal volatile) to her nose; this provoked a faint murmur of 'Oh doctor don't!'. The fit was arrested by the stimulant and he went into the next room for assistance. While his back was turned, Mrs Swetmore walked into the street, called at a neighbour's house and said that the doctor had raped her; and that she had screamed, cried, fought and struggled, but had failed to attract attention, though numerous persons were within sight and earshot.' This, on the face of it, seemed unlikely as she was not in Dr Bradley's surgery for more than five minutes, and the door which opened on to the street was at least six inches ajar during the whole time; nor were her dress or hair disarranged as was later stated for the prosecution; and there were no marks of violence on her person, nor stains upon the linen, which undoubtedly would have been the case if intercourse had taken place, either with or without consent. Furthermore, she had been subject to epileptic fits, more or less severe, since eleven years of age.

Dr Bradley's person and dress showed no marks of resistance, or any evidence of struggling, and his conduct throughout appeared to have been glaring proof of his innocence; for, firstly, he allowed the woman to walk out of the surgery without any attempt to detain her; then, secondly, he remained in the neighbourhood though he might have at any time forfeited his bail; thirdly, he sternly forbade any attempts at compromise! [2]

However, he was found guilty of attempted criminal assault and served eight months of a two-year prison sentence. There was considerable pressure from the medical profession to get him released and Mr Lawson Tait, a distinguished surgeon, wrote a letter to the *British Medical Journal* stating that at a meeting of the Birmingham and Midland Counties branch of the British Medical Association the following resolution was passed 'that this meeting, having heard a statement of the case of Dr David Bradley, recently convicted of a felonious assault at the Leicester Assizes, desires to express its opinion that this case is eminently one in which a reconsideration of the verdict of the jury is demanded. This opinion is based upon the consideration of the following facts: (1) that the complainant had been admittedly the subject of epileptic fits since childhood; (2) that such persons are specially liable to be subject to erotic delusions during and after a seizure. It is, therefore, of the utmost importance that the corroborative evidence in such a case should be decisive, whereas in the case of Dr Bradley it seems to be singularly defective' [3]. The Home Secretary eventually granted a free pardon because he felt sufficient doubt about the conviction was present to warrant this. It was generally believed that a conviction would never have been secured if expert evidence had been submitted on Dr Bradley's behalf.

An editorial in the *British Medical Journal* commented that 'the dangers in this type of case are obvious, the attack was insidious, and the means of defence imperfect and not always at hand. The mysterious conditions under which they arise cannot easily be explained to any jury; for to appreciate them requires a great deal of medical knowledge, a belief in medical records and opinions, which to the stolid intelligence of the average jury person may seem superstitious and absurd. There remained', it continued, 'the inevitable consideration of how such incidents can best be warded off by the private action of the individual, or how far collective action can be taken to assist those who are threatened with such calamities' [4].

As a result of this case and of others that had occurred over the previous twenty years, the pressure for some form of collective action brought about the creation of the Medical Defence Union (MDU). At first this was an inward-looking, parochial and protective body, but from 1887 it evolved, initially under the leadership of its first president Mr Lawson Tait, into a world-wide organization that served doctors and dentists by supporting them, morally and financially, in medico-legal matters, and, indirectly, it also benefitted their patients by promoting measures to prevent mishap and malpractice.

Before this development is described, however, it is useful to consider briefly the medical scene in the mid-1880s and how patients were being looked after at that time. This will enable the reader to appreciate the contrast with the situation today. No century passes without change but it is the speed of this change over the last hundred years that has been unusual—indeed phenomenal—especially in those areas that concern the practice of medicine: science, society and technology.

Medical practice in 1885

The art of medicine in 1885 mainly consisted of 'amusing the patient while nature cures the disease' as Voltaire had cynically remarked in a previous century. No drugs were curative and only a handful had any beneficial effect, in contrast to the 250 drugs and vaccines that are listed as necessary by the World Health Organization today. The distinguished American physician and man of letters, Oliver Wendell Holmes, wrote in 1883 that 'if the whole materia medica as now used, could be sunk in the bottom of the sea, it would be all the better for mankind and all the worse for the fishes.' . . . 'Furthermore', he continued, 'part of the blame of over-medication must, I fear, rest with the profession for yielding to the tendency to self-delusion, which seems inseparable from the practice of the art of healing' [5]. Lest we feel smug, over-prescribing is still a problem today and many drugs are merely expensive placebos.

The modern doctor could look back with nostalgia to a time when legislation affecting the practice of medicine hardly existed—whereas now he is surrounded by a plethora of regulations. Physicians were the oldest and most respected members of the profession, men who had the reputation of using their heads and not hands—displaying skills of learning and not technology. To be successful, a cynic jestingly remarked, the physician needed a top hat to give authority, a paunch for dignity, and piles to cause an anxious caring expression. Their high status in society was perhaps due to their priestly origin and to their former habit of only speaking in Latin before the patient—an approach that was hardly likely to improve communication! The paternalistic approach was the usual one and the idea of informed consent had not arisen for, as Holmes again remarked, 'your patient has no more right to all the truth you know than he has to all the medicine in your saddlebags . . . he should get only just so much as is good for him' [6].

Surgeons developed from barber surgeons; barbers entered the medical field in medieval times when the clergy treated illness as, due to a religious scruple about shedding blood, barbers were called in to bleed people, for this was then considered a therapeutic measure. The Barber Surgeons' Company was formed in 1540 but they were refused a doctorate by the Royal College of Physicians as their training and education were not considered to have reached a satisfactory standard. When this was later remedied and the Royal College of Physicians offered a doctorate, the surgeons took insult and kept to the term Mister rather than Doctor; they have cherished this almost as a superior degree ever since—often to the confusion of the public in the United Kingdom and elsewhere where all are called 'doctor'.

For centuries, operations had been confined to opening abscesses, amputat-

3

ing limbs (mortality rate 25–60%), excising some tumours and operating for stone in the bladder, but a new era had developed in the 1880s due to anaesthesia and the antiseptic technique of Lord Lister with his carbolic spray. The spray made surgery much safer but was replaced by asepsis when the importance of cleanliness of the hands and clothes was realized; hitherto an old frock coat, blood-stained and often used in the dissecting room as well, was considered by eminent surgeons to be the correct wear for the operating theatre. As a result, elective operations as well as emergency surgery were now filling the theatre lists and it was becoming commonplace for the abdomen to be opened (laparotomy), a technique pioneered by Lawson Tait, the architect of the Medical Defence Union.

Dentistry had suffered an unhappy history ever since the barbers and surgeons had split in 1745 when the Company of Surgeons was formed, but a new and better phase was begun by an Act in 1878 which made it illegal for an unqualified person to call himself a dentist; then a dental register was set up under the control of the General Medical Council. Nevertheless, tooth-pulling was often done by a doctor's unqualifed assistant and anyone could still open a 'surgery' for the extraction of teeth, or for supplying guinea dentures from a shop displaying giant signboards [7].

General practitioners evolved from apothecaries in the early nineteenth century. George Eliot (1819–1880) in her novel *Middlemarch* accurately described the contemporary scene (see Figure 1) and the emergence of this new kind of doctor and the controversies provoked by jealousy from the surgeon apothecaries who practised in the same district. The GPs' status was more on the footing of servants and their income usually low, which explained the opposition to unqualified persons practising medicine. Rounds were carried out with a horse and gig, or a hansom cab might be hired; patients could only be visited within range of a horse, so it was not always easy for them to obtain treatment. Motor cars began to come in only in 1896 and some doctors were then able to speed up their mode of transport to about 25 mph, a fact—as Sir Ronald Gibson remarked in his book *The Family Doctor*—that was responsible for the gradual disappearance of the top hat and frock coat; it was difficult to keep the hat on in an open car and not easy to change a tyre in a frock coat [8]. Although that newfangled instrument, the telephone, was invented in 1876, rare was the doctor who possessed one in 1885, in order that it would not disturb his night nor harass his wife by day.

So the life of GPs then was probably less exacting than that of many today. Not so, however, for the city doctor who would be disturbed by the night bell and often be dependent for his livelihood on the poor patients who subscribed 3d a week to the sickness benefit club. George Bernard Shaw (1856–1950), who was no respecter of doctors and lampooned them in his satirical play *The*

FIGURE 1. 'The Doctor' by Sir Luke Fildes, 1891 (by kind permission of the Tate Gallery). A crisis in a country cottage is depicted: a small girl is perhaps dying, and in the background the mother hides her head and the father stands, frightened, trying to comfort her. The half-consumed bottle of medicine would have had no beneficial effect and all that the doctor could do was to provide TLC—a term used by doctors to acknowledge that the best which could be done in the circumstances was to provide tender loving care.

Doctor's Dilemma, suddenly struck a note of sympathy when he wrote in its preface 'The real woes of the doctor are the shabby coat, the wolf at the door, the tyranny of ignorant patients, the work-day of 24 hours, and the uselessness of honestly prescribing what most of the patients really need: that is, no medicine, but money'. Since then, conditions have improved immeasurably and no one need be concerned as Shaw was when he reflected 'One wonders why the impatient doctors do not become savage and unmanageable, and the patient ones imbecile. Perhaps they do, to some extent'.

Novelists like Mary Ann Evans were not the only ones who had to assume a pseudonym—in her case George Eliot—to be accepted in a man's world. It was shocking enough for women to study law or theology but it was quite beyond the understanding of those Victorians that any respectable woman could desire to study medicine [9], and some doctors were shocked at the mere thought of a 'doctress'. Yet, as Dame Albertine Winner described in her lecture 'Women in Medicine' [10], the history of women in this role goes far back in time to Ancient Egypt when women surgeons were skilful with their stone knives, performed caesarean section and removed carcinomatous breasts.

In recent times, the first woman doctor was the remarkable Dr James Barry, who, after qualifying in Edinburgh in 1812, had a distinguished though tempestuous career in the army; she finished up as an inspector general of hospitals, the highest rank given to a doctor and equivalent to a major general. A biography of her [11] makes fascinating reading: she anticipated Florence Nightingale in her efforts to reform military hospitals and the living conditions of servicemen, she fought a duel, and her deception was only discovered when she died (around the age of seventy)—the charwoman who laid her out found that she was a woman and, noticing the striae gravidorum in the lower abdomen, thought that she had probably borne a child early in life.

In 1881, there were twenty-one registered women doctors [12], and this success was largely due to the activities of two women: Elizabeth Garrett Anderson who founded a new hospital for women which later grew into the Elizabeth Garrett Anderson Hospital in London, and Sophia Jex Blake who founded the London School of Medicine for Women in 1874 with fourteen students. The frustrations of these women were great: students at the Middlesex Hospital petitioned for Miss Garrett to be removed after a year and Miss Blake's admission at Edinburgh with four other women caused a students' revolt leading to a riot at Surgeon's Hall—perhaps because the five did brilliantly—and, after a High Court action, they lost their permit to study. Separate teaching classes had to be held for men and women, and Charles Newman in *Medical Education in the 19th Century* [13] described the opposition to women in medicine: many thought it impossible to lecture on venereal disease to a mixed audience and the teachers who were most vocal were the anatomists, for they wanted to teach indecent mnemonics and were incapable of imagining any other way of implanting meaningless details. He wrote of the contribution that women have made to medicine and pointed out that the medical profession was not completely opened to women until half way through the twentieth century.

At this time medical technology had just begun. Dr John Bradbury, physician to Addenbrooke's Hospital, Cambridge, lectured on 'Modern Scientific Medicine' to the 48th Annual Meeting of the British Medical Association in 1880 [14]. He described the new instruments of precision: the microscope, ophthalmoscope, laryngoscope, spectroscope, and electricity which was of value (faradism and galvanism) in diagnosing diseases of the nervous system (e.g. upper and lower motor neurone lesions). He gave much space to his work on the thermometer during the previous ten years and of its use in diagnosing fevers and other conditions; the small clinical thermometer, invented by Sir Clifford Allbutt in his youth, had just replaced the cumbersome one which was ten inches long and took five minutes to record. The sphygmograph had opened up a new field of discovery about cardiovascular disease; the pattern of the pulse wave led to the diagnosis of valvular lesions of the heart but, most important to the speaker, was that it established the diagnosis of high blood pressure, and he described the conditions where this occurred. Finishing with a word of caution to the younger doctors he advised them 'not to rely too exclusively upon the information derived from the use of these instruments, to which perhaps there is a great temptation . . . we must not ignore the aids which stood our predecessors in such good stead—the information for which the physiognomy furnishes us—the estimation of the nervous element in patients, and the other features of disease recognisable by our senses . . . we must still, therefore, be contented in some measure to cultivate that "tact" upon which our ancestors mainly relied.' The editorial in the *British Medical Journal* praised this lecture highly but mentioned that the older practitioners were apt to think that these new methods of making accurate observations were 'but ingenious and beautiful toys; that the "tactus eruditus" [meaning feeling the pulse] gives better information than the sphygmograph, the facies [face] of the patient than the surface-thermometer, and the general diathesis safer indications for treatment than analysis and examination of the fluids and excretions of the body; that medicine, in fact, is wandering away from her mission to cure a disease to become engrossed in interesting investigations into phenomena, forgetting the patient while the disease is studied' [15]. History repeats itself.

Roentgen, the German physicist, had not yet demonstrated his remarkable flesh-penetrating process—the X-ray; this came later in 1896. So doctors had no anxiety from possible actions in negligence because of failure to X-ray patients. This was an era when discoveries could be made solely by clinical observation without research teams equipped with electronic and other devices. Eponyms have made their authors immortal: Hutchinson's teeth (1861) after Sir Jonathan Hutchinson who later became the first President of the Medical Protection Society; Paget's disease (1882) by Sir James Paget, and the Koplik spots of measles (1896) by Dr Henry Koplik. Research rarely took place and could be disastrous: Mr Braxton Hicks, a gynaecologist at Guy's Hospital, thought that blood transfusion might be possible and in 1884 transfused four patients using sodium phosphate as a possible anticoagulant but all died due to this [16]—blood groups were only discovered in 1907. Such disasters caused no litigation and research ethical committees were unknown. The present age of investigative medicine then started, led by Sir James McKenzie who pioneered knowledge of cardiovascular disease.

Specialism was in its infancy, having been born earlier in the USA; a leader in the *British Medical Journal* (1887) entitled 'Lessons from Specialists' supported its development but gave a warning that 'specialism no doubt is open to great evils . . .' [17]. Surgical specialties were diseases of the eye, ear, nose and throat, ovarian diseases and dentistry; and medical ones consisted of diseases of women, infectious conditions and diseases of the skin. Geriatricians, however broad the definition, would have had little work as the average age of death was around forty years (compared with the length of life in 1982 being seventy-one years for men and seventy-seven years for women). Pulmonary tuberculosis caused many deaths, and bronchitis, pneumonia and influenza were rife; fevers like scarlet fever and diphtheria were common and often mortal—these, together with whooping cough and measles, killed the young; smallpox and infections of the ear, pharynx and larynx caused most of the rest of the deaths [18]. The infant mortality rate was high, being 150 per 1000 live births compared with about ten today.

Obstetricians had plenty of work because there was no question of birth control. Indeed, E. S. Turner (1958) noted in his book *Call the Doctor* that 'in Queen Victoria's reign, any doctor who set out to popularise knowledge of birth control risked summary removal from the Register' [7]. Indeed this happened in 1887 to Dr Arthur Allbutt, a consulting physician in Leeds who was internationally known; he had, amongst other achievements, received awards in Paris and been elected a member of the Society of Medicine in Athens and the Medico-Legal Society of New York. In 1887 he wrote a booklet called *The Wife's Handbook* and in the introduction stated that 'this little work was undertaken at the suggestion of several friends who have always had sympathetic hearts for the sufferings of women and children, and who advised me to write a book which could be understood by most women, and at a price [sixpence] which would ensure a place in even the poorest household.' The sub-title was 'How a Woman should order herself during Pregnancy, in the Lying-in Room, and after Delivery, with Hints on the Management of the Baby, and on other Matters of Importance, necessary to be known by married Women' [19]. It was this last sentence that condemned him for it referred to a short chapter 'How to Prevent Conception'; in it he debunked methods such as sitting up in bed and coughing after intercourse to expel semen from the vagina or the taking of arsenic by the husband in small doses to lessen male sexual vigour and thus produce impotence—instead he discussed the so-called 'safe period', mentioned the possible nervous effect of coitus interruptus and recommended the use of douches, pessaries, or the 'Letter' worn by the husband. Because of this reference to contraception, he was brought before the General Medical Council. Perusal of the minutes of the meetings of the General Medical Council, held in secrecy to consider his case, showed how intensely seriously the matter was taken; it was argued that the booklet was dangerous because it might get into the hands of the unmarried, and he was struck off the

Register. So there were no medico-legal problems concerned with failed sterilization or prescribing the Pill for girls under sixteen years. Women were just expected to have children and that was their function; the idea was that women did not enjoy sex but had to put up with it. Dr J. M. Duncan, in his Gulstonian lecture delivered at the Royal College of Physicians in 1883, must have shocked Victorian minds for he stated that 'the desire for offspring may be intense while there is neither desire nor pleasure, and the desire to avoid pregnancy may be intense while there is desire and pleasure' [20]. He regarded the sexually active woman to be the norm; it was no longer the monopoly of men. Then, the law of England legitimized marriage at a very early age—too early an age, Duncan thought, though a girl rarely did marry at the age of twelve or a boy at fourteen years.

The state of doctor–patient relationship is impossible to assess for there were no audits, no Gallup polls, and no working parties organized by the Government or State Department to obtain statistical information. Most doctors seemed to occupy an authoritative position; suffering and death were the 'will of heaven' and disasters an act of God rather than a medical mistake. Most, especially the poor, were grateful for any attention and put up with conditions that would be considered intolerable today. A leader in the *Lancet* (1932) entitled 'A Casualty Department Forty Years Ago' [21] reported a lecture given by Sir D'Arcy Power where he described the surgical side of the casualty department at St Bartholomew's Hospital, London, in 1898. Patients began to assemble on the steps outside at half past eight but, whatever the weather, there was no shelter and the doors were kept locked until the last stroke of nine o'clock; a queue or rather a crowd had assembled by this time on the steps and pavement. At the last stroke of nine each door was held ajar to admit one patient at a time. The porter on the male and the nurse on the female side asked each patient what he or she complained of and referred them to the physician or surgeon as was thought fit. The hall was usually filled by ten minutes past nine and the junior assistant surgeon made a rapid diagnosis, asking a few pertinent questions, and sorted patients roughly into three categories—trivial, teaching, and serious. Patients with minor complaints were handed over to the house surgeon who alloted them amongst his dressers; cases useful for teaching were sent to the out-patient room, there to await the arrival of the assistant surgeon of the day at half past twelve; those who were seriously ill were taken straight into a ward. A fresh batch of patients was admitted from the street as often as the benches in the hall were empty, until the clock struck ten. The outer doors were then closed though the morning's work often continued till midday or even later; by this time on a damp and foggy morning the atmosphere of the hall was poisonous and the odour pungent. It was, however, worse on the medical side: Dr Robert Bridges, who later became Poet Laureate, said that he saw and prescribed for 7,735 persons during his year of office in 1877 and that 5,530 of these were new patients; the average time spent on each case was 1·28 of a minute and he congratulated himself on having given a separate audience to the troubles of 150 talkative women in three and a quarter hours. The dispensary so closely resembled the bar of a public house that any drunken man was usually persuaded to take a double dose of house physic thinking it was a last glass before going home—one for the road.

The public must have been less sensitive, for visiting lunatic asylums to watch the inmates was apparently a popular entertainment for Londoners—and the Elephant Man, a poor fellow with severe deformities due to neurofibromatosis, was exhibited at freak shows and circuses throughout the country. A critical approach which leads to complaints depends partly upon education; many had been uneducated but according to G. M. Trevelyan 'between 1870 and 1890 the average school attendance rose from one and a quarter million to four and a half millions, while the money spent on each child was doubled' [22].

The reader may now wonder why a medical defence body was born at a time when doctors were free from most of the now familiar medico-legal hazards of practice. One explanation is that the nineteenth century was an era of social organization of groups: the trade unions, the British Medical Association itself (founded in 1832) and medical societies which were being developed throughout the country—their objects were education, the development of professionalism with a code of ethics, and the formation of assemblies of those with a common interest. Two other reasons for forming a body to safeguard the interests of doctors are illustrated by two problems: competition from the unqualified and the threat of litigation against doctors.

COMPETITION FROM THE UNQUALIFIED

Unqualified persons practising medicine abounded. They threatened the livelihood of doctors who depended upon fees and did not yet enjoy a regular income from a National Health Service. Attempts to persuade Parliament to legislate against quacks usually met with little encouragement, for 'the law-makers and the intellectuals of the day held no high opinion of orthodox medicine and, as a rule, were quick to suspect attempts by its warring branches to enrich themselves at each other's expense. A little quackery, they thought, was no bad thing if it helped to ginger the gentry with the gold-headed canes' [7]. So quacks were prospering and there were even curious instances of some who impersonated doctors who had died or emigrated.

Treatment of the sick by the unqualified has indeed nettled doctors since early times although, in truth, this was often necessary for the care of many of the population who otherwise would have received no attention. The Royal College of Physicians, when it was founded in 1518, was determined to campaign against the unqualified 'doctor', as was the British Medical Association in 1832. In fact, it is common in the evolution of all professions that a time comes when the distinction is made between the qualified and unqualified. This, in England, was brought about by the Medical Act of 1858 which led to a minimum standard of medical education being laid down for the qualification of the 'safe doctor'; it also set a standard which was needed by the profession and provided the public with a general medical practitioner who could be recognized as competent. Once legally qualified, he was able to practise anywhere within the United Kingdom and perform any medical or surgical treatment without either further qualification or training. Clause 40 of the Act stated:

> Any person who shall wilfully and falsely pretend to be, or take or use the name or title of a physician, doctor of medicine, licentiate in medicine and surgery, bachelor of medicine or surgeon, general practitioner or apothecary, or any name, title, addition or description implying that he is registered under this Act, or that he is recognized by law as a physician or surgeon, or licentiate in medicine and surgery, or a practitioner in medicine, or an apothecary, shall upon summary conviction for any such offence pay a sum not exceeding £20.

The General Medical Council (GMC) was then established; it was made responsible for determining the minimum qualification for the new general register and it published for the first time a national pharmacopoeia.

Quacks may be sincere and have almost a religious faith in their treatments, though some are like 'con artists', whose motivation is greed: flashy equipment impresses and the characteristic clichés 'Thank goodness you've come to me in time' or 'If only you had come to me before, I could have done far more' elevates them in the patient's opinion and denigrates the doctors previously consulted; unfortunately these statements sometimes are used by doctors themselves and encourage a patient to take legal action. Patients have been harmed by the unqualified (see Chapter 2), but safeguarding his own interest rather than protecting the patient probably lay behind the doctor's desire to prosecute them.

In spite of the Medical Act of 1858 and the formation of the GMC, quacks still flourished and two medical societies were formed because of this [23]. The Medical Alliance Association devoted itself 'chiefly to preserving the medical domain against the encroachment of unauthorized intruders'; it more than once promoted Parliamentary bills aimed at protecting doctors but these shared the fate of other bills on the subject. According to Forbes [24], it gave its support to the Medical Defence Union (MDU) from the beginning and its officers became members of the General Council.

The Medical Defence Association was another society formed 'for the purpose of suppressing the practice of medicine and surgery by persons not legally qualified'; it aimed also at 'suppressing the publication of indecent so-called medical works and advertisements relating thereto, and for procuring the amendment of the laws relating to the sale of quack medicines'. Interestingly, it considered the subject of out-patient hospital reform and 'any matters of a medico-ethical character' but its work was hampered by lack of funds. At first it existed concurrently with the Medical Defence Union and protested that its name had been virtually copied, but in 1889 it became defunct and the Honorary Secretary was elected a member of the Council of the MDU.

THE THREAT OF LITIGATION AGAINST DOCTORS

A search of the legal literature has failed to discover more than a few examples of legal actions against doctors in the Law Reports (1892) [25] but important legal cases only were included. Horace Smith, in his *Treatise on the Law of Negligence* (1880), confirmed the paucity of cases by writing that 'the cases in which mere negligence has been established against professional persons, such as solicitors, doctors, etc., do not appear to be very numerous and two reasons may be given for this. In the first place, the taking of care is almost their *raison d'être*, while to many other persons the duty to take care is an impediment to their business; and in the second place, and as a consequence from the above mentioned reasons, when they are negligent, such negligence amounts in general to fraud or intentional neglect. In the case of doctors such matters have become the subject of investigation in the criminal courts where death has ensued' [26]. Probably the ordinary person could not afford to go to law (no legal aid was available), and was unlikely to question a professional man because of lack of education. Respect for authority was general in these days and the egalitarian age had not begun.

Surgeons were more liable than physicians to litigation, no doubt because their alleged negligence could be seen, such as the failure of a wound to heal, whereas physicians' mistakes could easily be attributed to nature. 'Physicians of all men are most happy; what good successe soever they have, the world proclaimes, and what faults they commit, the earth covers', wrote Francis Quarles (1592–1644). Furthermore the surgeon undertook 'to cure wounds and other ailments of the human system'—an optimistic endeavour in the days before antibiotics and other therapy. Some legal cases related to fractures uniting badly or, for example, to a dislocated shoulder treated negligently.

What probably worried doctors was not so much the frequency of medico-legal cases but that these hit the headlines and were discussed prominently in daily newspapers and medical journals. In addition to that of Dr Bradley, there were other dramatic and public cases.

Doctor falsely accused of murder. Miss Banks died after a three-week illness of abdominal pain and diarrhoea. Sir Samuel Wilks, a distinguished physician, wrote a letter to the *Medical Times and Gazette* (1859) describing the post-mortem which he had performed on this young woman: it showed inflammation of the ileum with ulceration in the proximal colon. No cause was found and tuberculosis was excluded. He mentioned 'idiopathic dysentry' though his final opinion was that the girl had died due to a 'vegetable irritant given to cause abortion, but that death unintentionally resulted' [27]. Because of this, he nearly caused a colleague to be wrongly convicted of murder.

Isabella Banks was the young mistress of Thomas Smethurst MD and he was brought to trial for wilful murder and bigamy. It was a *cause célèbre* [28]. The evidence concerning the cause of her death was conflicting but with famous doctors appearing for the prosecution, and a damning summing up from the judge, he was found guilty and sentenced to death. However, the trial stirred up a passionate controversy and letters poured into *The Times* newspaper in support of Dr Smethurst. Ten men, including Wilks, had given evidence for the prosecution that she had died from poison; seven had supported the defence stating that she died from dysentry.

As a result of the conflicting medical evidence and the public outcry, he was given a free pardon from Queen Victoria. Otherwise, he might have been hanged—though totally innocent—because his mistress died from an acute inflammation of the bowel which nowadays would be recognized as Crohn's disease and which has nothing to do with any form of poisoning.

Doctors accused of negligence in failing to diagnose diphtheria.
Dr E. Bower and Mr W. C. Keates were doctors practising in East Dulwich, London, and were called to see a child suffering from what was at first supposed to be croup but turned out to be diphtheria. They felt it necessary to operate and inserted a tube into the windpipe (tracheotomy) and told the father to suck the tube and so

remove the matter from the child's throat. He did so, and himself became infected with diphtheria.

The child died and the father at first prosecuted the doctors for manslaughter, but the prosecution failed. A civil action was then instituted to recover damages: the plaintiff's case was that the defendants ought to have warned him of the danger he ran by sucking the tube, so as to give him the opportunity of refusing to do so, or at any rate of taking immediate precautions, so as to obviate the risk of infection. At the first trial, Mr Justice Field left four questions to the jury, namely (1) did the defendants know at the time of the operation, or ought they to have known, that the child was suffering from diphtheria? (2) did they know, or ought to have known, that suction from the tube would be dangerous? (3) was the plaintiff's illness caused by sucking the tube? and (4) could his illness have been prevented or diminished by warning or precautionary measures? Unfortunately the jury could not agree about the answers and were discharged without a verdict. When the second trial came on, the plaintiff was without the assistance of counsel and the jury gave a verdict for the defendants but an application to the court was granted for a new trial on the ground that the plaintiff's case had not been properly put before the jury. At the third trial the doctors were successful but they incurred costs amounting to over £1,000 (equivalent to about £32,000 today) and had to endure the anxiety of long drawn-out proceedings.

Several interesting points arise from this case. It received great publicity and sympathy for the doctors from the public. For example, a large meeting of their patients, friends and neighbours was held and was presided over by the Vicar of East Dulwich [29]. On opening the proceedings, he congratulated them

> that the wrong which had been done them had been completely redressed. The great sting of that wrong was that it was ungenerous and ungrateful; circumstances which ought to have elicited gratitude were turned into grounds of accusation and attack. A child lay ill, and Dr Bower was sent for. He saw at once that the only chance of life was performance of a critical and delicate operation. The probability of that operation succeeding was very problematical, and a cold and selfish man would have declined to have anything to do with the case. But Dr Bower, with the hand of duty strong upon him, determined to perform the operation, leaving his professional character to take care of itself . . . but the attempt to save a life so

dear to the parents, instead of exciting gratitude, was met with an ungenerous wrong.

The case was taken up by Sir William Jenner, President of the Royal College of Physicians, who appealed in the medical journals for funds, and a special committee was formed to defray the expenses of the defendants. The leading physicians and surgeons of the country gave their full support, and so many contributions flowed that the list was abruptly closed.

Every case has to be judged in the context of its time but in retrospect one wonders whether this was a just decision. Even if the two doctors had had an out-of-date textbook, such as *The Practice of Medicine* by T. H. Tanner (1875), they should have known how to diagnose diphtheria, as the grey membrane covering the back of the throat was clearly described, and this would almost certainly have been visible if respiratory obstruction was so severe that tracheotomy was necessary. The secretions were known to be highly contagious. Reports in the *British Medical Journal* of 1885 show a mortality rate of at least 60% in children. Incidentally, treatment then consisted of abundant brandy and frequent emetics so nothing was lost by the failure to diagnose it. The behaviour to the plaintiff was autocratic: a magistrate described the case as one of 'persecution not prosecution' and the indignation of the profession was aroused with no sign of sympathy for the father of the child who died. Even the *British Medical Journal* wrote that it was a case 'very little on the hither side of vexatious litigation'. Fortunately the attitude of doctors and lawyers is different today.

In 1885 the doctor had to arrange his own defence and bear the cost himself, perhaps with the aid of public appeals made in newspapers and journals. If a victim of slander or libel, he had to sue his prosecutor himself or suffer in silence—and lack of expert advice might prejudice his case; even if successful in court, he would be in severe financial straits due to the costs of the action. Raising funds *after* the event was not a rational approach nor an ideal solution. Hence arose the idea of forming a defence body to protect the interests of doctors.

References

1 Tawney R.H. *Religion and the Rise of Capitalism* (Holland Memorial Lectures given in 1922). Middlesex, England: Penguin Books, 1948.
2 The case of Dr Bradley. *British Medical Journal*. 1 (1885): 448.
3 Tait L. The case of Dr Bradley (letter). *British Medical Journal* 1 (1885): 403.
4 Dr David Bradley (editorial). *British Medical Journal* 2 (1885): 1170–1.
5 Holmes O.W. Medical Essays. In *The Young Practitioner*. Boston: Houghton, Mifflin & Co, 1883, p. 388.
6 Holmes O.W. Medical Essays. In *Currents and Counter-currents*. Boston: Houghton, Mifflin & Co., 1883, p. 203.

7 Turner E.S. *Call the Doctor: A Social History of Medical Men.* London: Michael Joseph, 1958.

8 Gibson, Sir Ronald. *The Family Doctor.* London: George Allen & Unwin, 1981.

9 Shyrock R.H. *The Development of Modern Medicine.* London: Victor Gollancz, 1948.

10 Winner, Dame Albertine. Women in medicine. *Journal of the Royal Society of Arts* 123 (1975): 337–47.

11 Rae, Isobel. *The Strange Story of Dr James Barry.* London: Longman, 1958.

12 Lutzker, Edithe. *Women Gain a Place in Medicine.* New York: McGraw Hill, 1969.

13 Newman C. *Medical Education in the 19th Century.* Oxford: Oxford University Press, 1957.

14 Bradbury J.B. Modern Scientific Medicine. *British Medical Journal* 2 (1880): 244–252.

15 Editorial. *British Medical Journal* 2 (1880): 274–5.

16 Williams G. *The Age of Miracles.* London: Constable, 1981.

17 Lessons from specialists (editorial). *British Medical Journal* 2 (1887): 1226.

18 McKeown T. *The Modern Rise of Population.* London: Edward Arnold, 1976.

19 Allbutt H.A. *The Wife's Handbook.* London: R. Forder, 1887.

20 Duncan J.M. *On Sterility in Woman.* Gulstonian lecture delivered at the Royal College of Physicians, 1883. London: Churchill, 1884.

21 A casualty department forty years ago. *Lancet* 1 (1932): 1000.

22 Trevelyan G.M. *English Social History.* London: Spottiswoode Ballantyne, 1947, p. 581.

23 Laffan T. *The Medical Profession in the Three Kingdoms in 1887.* The essay for the Carmichael Prize awarded by the Council of the Royal College of Surgeons, Ireland. Dublin: Fannin & Co, 1888.

24 Forbes R. *Sixty Years of Medical Defence.* London: The Medical Defence Union Ltd, 1948.

25 Law Reports: *Digest of Cases 1865–90.* London: William Clowes & Sons Ltd, 1892.

26 Smith H.A. *Treatise on the Law of Negligence.* London: Stevens, 1880.

27 Wilks S. Morbid appearances in the intestines of Miss Banks. *Medical Times and Gazette* 2 (1859): 264–5.

28 Stanford, Elspeth. Thomas Addison and his times. *History of Medicine and Allied Sciences* 5 (1973): 3–10.

29 Bower and Keates case (editorial). *British Medical Journal* 1 (1884): 128 and 2: 73–4.

2

The development of medical defence

'All professions are conspiracies against the laity' [1]
BERNARD SHAW

The accusation that all professions are conspiracies against the public is true to some extent, though conspiracy is too strong a word; but the Medical Defence Union can plead 'not guilty' for it was conceived not by the profession but by the laity. Two solicitors and five gentlemen started it; incidentally, the use of the term gentleman was no reflection upon the characters of the lawyers, for it was then an accepted label to define someone of a certain income or property and appears in Registers of Births of that period: the father is listed, for example, as labourer, carpenter, lawyer, or gentleman. Whose original idea the Union was is impossible to tell as no existing documents reveal it, but the leader was Mr Charles F. Rideal, and he no doubt invited some friends to form the quorum needed to start a Company Limited by the guarantee of its members to provide one pound if necessary to keep it solvent (Figure 2). This was registered under the Companies Act 1862 as The Medical Defence Union on 23 October 1885, with offices at Messrs Cridland and Paget, solicitors of Bedford Row, London. The seven men formed themselves into an executive committee, which appointed Rideal as Secretary, Mr John Cridland as Solicitor, and a Mr Ogle as Acting Counsel. Steps were then taken to appoint legal representatives in provincial towns and to form local Councils. A circular was sent to all members of the medical profession and was welcomed by Dr Francis Bond of Gloucester in a letter he wrote to the *British Medical Journal*:

> *The Medical Defence Union*
>
> Sir,—I have received a circular inviting me to join an association which has been formed under the above name for the purposes of defending, or assisting in defending, its members in cases where actions involving questions of principle to the profession, or cruel and groundless charges, are brought against them; of suppressing unauthorised practitioners, and of offering its assistance, as far as may be deemed judicious, in promotion or modification of any Bill or movement initiated for the benefit of the medical profession. These objects appear to be excellent, and the former two of them, at any

17

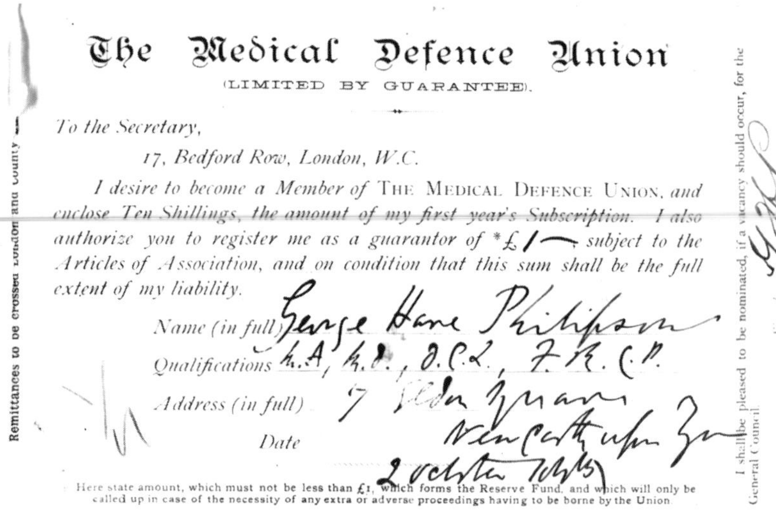

FIGURE 2. Application form completed by an early member of the Medical Defence Union.

rate, fulfil entirely the condition which alone justifies them being made the excuse for establishing a new association, namely, that they are, at the present time, a decided 'want'... these are matters which touch most nearly the interests of every member of the profession, for they affect the question of his self-preservation, which, in medicine, as in other cases, is Nature's first law [2].

He then went on to ask why the British Medical Association could not provide this service but Mr Rideal wrote back to the *British Medical Journal* stating that the BMA did not represent the whole of the profession (as Dr Bond stated) but that it was an association, which like other associations, simply represented the members belonging to it [3].

The object of the company—The Medical Defence Union (Ltd)—covered a broad front as shown in the original memorandum:

* To support and protect the character and interests of medical practitioners practising in the United Kingdom.

* To promote honourable practice and to suppress or prosecute unauthorized practitioners.

* To advise and defend or assist in defending members of the Union in cases where proceedings involving questions of professional principle or otherwise are brought against them.

∗ To consider, originate, promote and support (so far as is legal) legislative measures likely to benefit the medical profession and to oppose all measures calculated to injure it: and for the purposes aforesaid to petition Parliament and take such other steps and proceedings as may be deemed expedient.

Criticism of the circular came from Mr George Brown, the Medical Secretary of the Medical Defence Association:

> Sir,—Within the last few days my attention has been directed to a circular which is now being sent to the members of the profession— and which appears to have emanated from a solicitor's office in Bedford Row—inviting them to subscribe to a new society called 'The Medical Defence Union'. While I have not a word to say against enterprising solicitors or others in these depressed times doing their best to push business, in this particular instance I cannot admire the action of the promoters . . . [4].

Charles Rideal wrote in reply:

> I beg most respectively to state that this gentleman's assertion, that 'the Medical Defence Union emanated from a firm of solicitors in Bedford Row' is incorrect. I am solely responsible for the institution and formation of the Union, and I sought the assistance and cooperation of an able and energetic solicitor, who is as much respected, and whose connections in the legal profession were known long before Mr Brown or his association ever came into existence. Mr Brown's protest against this society adopting the title of the Medical Defence Union comes a little late, for the reason that quite three months ago, before the Union was incorporated and registered, the President and four Vice Presidents of his association received proof prospectuses, with invitations to join; why, then, was not the objection raised before? [5].

Rideal also wrote later that

> Mr Brown admits (though not very graciously) one mis-statement, 'that the Medical Defence Union emanated from a firm of solici- tors' . . . he says that the Union emanated outside the profession. I'm not disposed to call myself an outsider, although I'm not a member . . . but if it had thus emanated, I have yet to learn, Sir, that the profession is so narrow-minded that it would reject a feasible solid project simply because one of itself did not originate it. The proposal to form the Union was submitted to at least a dozen very prominent men before a line of the prospectus was printed. Their opinions coupled with the cordial support the movement is receiving, con- vinced me that it is a necessity, and can be successfully carried out;

therefore, I shall continue to do my utmost until its objects are fully attained.

The Medical Defence Association had been hampered by a lack of funds and it operated in the narrow field of prosecuting unqualified practitioners; it was wound up and George Brown was elected a member of the Council of the Medical Defence Union in 1889. The officers of a similar group, the Medical Alliance Association, co-operated at the start and joined the Executive and General Councils of the Union 'for the sole purpose of effecting a united and thorough system of defence'. Retrospective judgement is as fallible as retrospective diagnosis but it would probably be fair to describe Charles Rideal as an entrepreneur: he gave himself a salary of £250 a year (worth about £4,000 in 1984) and, although instructed by his colleagues to reduce it to £50 a year, continued to take out the same amount though his work as Secretary was unlikely to have been burdensome. He also spent the funds in an improper manner and misappropriated certain sums, so that after two years he was forced to resign and steps were taken to make him bankrupt.

From lay to medical parentage

A most important meeting of local doctors was held in May 1886 at the Medical Institute, Birmingham, organized by an eminent and extroverted surgeon, Mr Lawson Tait, who can be regarded as the true architect of the Medical Defence Union. A leader in the *British Medical Journal* entitled 'Proposed Medical Defence Union' went as follows:

> Mr Lawson Tait occupied the chair, and moved the first resolution [on the advisability of forming a medical defence union], remarking that in the comparatively short period over which his own exper-ience ran—20 years—he had been engaged [presumably as a wit-ness] in no fewer than 21 cases in which charges, sometimes of a criminal kind, and others which formed the basis of civil action, had been made against gentlemen of the medical profession, and, in every one of these instances, the charge had broken down, and a successful result had been obtained. He alluded, in particular, to three cases. The first was that of Mr Croft, of Snitterfield, in which, 12 or 14 years ago, he had to undertake, almost single-handed, the defence of a gentleman who was most unjustly accused of having falsely signed a certificate. In spite of the discharge of the Bill by the Grand Jury, at Warwick, a very large sum, for one in Mr Croft's position, had to be raised to meet legal expenses. In the case of O'Leary, which had only recently occurred, that gentleman had

practically been ruined by a charge which had been most improperly brought against him. For the part which Mr Tait took in the
defence, he had to bear the brunt of a threatened action for libel. In
the recent, and still more painful case of Dr Bradley [see Chapter 1],
a conviction had been secured, and a sentence of hard labour passed
upon an innocent man. The expenses of defending such cases had to
be met by contributions obtained with much trouble, and it seemed
to him (the Chairman) that it was time to put an end to such a state
of affairs when men who were poor, or who were timid, were left
practically helpless, unless some one or two of their professional
brethren would stand forward to their help. If it were known that a
body were in existence charged with the duty of defending such
men, and possessed of sufficient money to secure a competent
defence, these improper actions would become necessarily much
rarer, and, even when entered upon, they would fall with much less
terror on those against whom they were directed . . . and in answer
to a question as to whether such cases were really sufficiently
numerous to make such an institution as the Union necessary, he
would say that, since the circulars had been issued calling the
meeting, he had received applications from four sufferers, who each
hoped that his case might be taken up . . . the resolution that a
committee for the purpose of arranging the details of the establishment of the Midland Branch of the Medical Defence Union should be
formed was passed unanimously and about 60 at once joined the
Union [6].

Lawson Tait's personality and the prowess which he displayed in defending
colleagues no doubt accounted for him being elected Chairman at the Annual
Meeting in February 1887, where he was also elected as the first President—
the office being transferred to Birmingham in 1888. The seven original
signatories then gave way to doctors and various officers were elected. In the
course of the year, however, the MDU was nearly wrecked because its affairs
were in such disorder due to irregularities of the original Secretary, Mr Rideal;
an annotation in the *British Medical Journal* (1887) states that 'not only are the
whole of the subscribed funds dissipated without any good result, but at the
present moment the unfortunate persons who have joined this society are
being threatened with actions at law for arrears of subscriptions, and for the
sums which they guaranteed' [7].

The first Annual Report of 1888 states 'the amount of labour, both in
organising and detail, required by these actions was enormous, and the
profession cannot be too grateful to Mr Lawson Tait for having attacked, dealt
with, and brought to a successful issue such a matter'. This Report continued

that the forces of the MDU had not yet been called into play to defend an action at Law brought against a member on professional grounds but stated that it had helped in the case of a member being libelled (charged unfairly with improper conduct) and that it had reported unqualified practitioners though it referred to 'the great difficulties which the Union had met in its efforts to check quackery and purge the register of unworthy holders of medical qualifications. The machinery which is required to be set in motion before a man can be 'struck off' is most cumbersome, and it is almost impossible to get some licensing bodies to even consider the cases brought before them . . . quackery and unqualified practice is enormously on the increase, and it is high time that the medical profession should look carefully after its own interests. What we require is a central body like the Incorporated Law Society, which should be able to protect the profession from the abuse of unqualified practice and also act as a Censor Board for those qualified'.

One person described as a 'pest of the most objectionable kind' was sent to trial and received a sentence of five years' penal servitude: he had been lecturing as a spiritualist and faith healer in Birmingham and the police had been watching him; he had a diploma from an American college and was carrying out a medical practice under the guise of his alleged spiritual teaching but during the course of this indecently assaulted a young girl.

History, it is said, is the story of people and this especially applies to medical progress. Mr Lawson Tait FRCS (1845–1899) was a remarkable character (Figure 3): he made the MDU but, ironically, he could have destroyed it. He was aggressive, unconventional, dogmatic and original; he made many friends but also many enemies. According to his biographers [8–10], the three qualities responsible for his outstanding success were that he wrote well, talked well, and as a surgeon he was a brilliant operator. He pioneered abdominal surgery and attracted patients from all over the world; he lectured in the USA and received several honorary degrees. He made many contributions to surgery: he was the first to remove successfully an inflamed appendix (1880)—appendicitis then being called typhlitis—though he failed to convince others. He was also the first to operate successfully for tubal (ectopic) pregnancy and by his teaching he established the absolute necessity for this life-saving procedure. He pioneered gynaecological surgery, performing hysterectomy for myoma (1872) and removing ovaries for inflammatory disease (1872) and for other reasons. His influence in advancing biliary and renal surgery in the UK was very great: he did a cholecystotomy for gallstones (1879) and operated on the liver by doing a partial hepatectomy for hydatid cysts or tumours. Trained in Edinburgh, then the centre of medical education, he came to Birmingham and was appointed to the staff of the Women's Hospital at the age of twenty-six and later as Professor of Gynaecology at Queen's College, Birmingham.

FIGURE 3. Mr Lawson Tait FRCS (1845–1899). He was the architect of the Medical Defence Union and its President from 1887–93.

At thirty-two years, he had published 200 papers and books and in 1884 produced his 1,000 cases of laparotomy [11], more cases than any other surgeon in the entire world, and with a mortality rate of 9·3 per cent remarkable at that time especially as seriously ill patients were included; conditions dealt with included 307 appendicectomies, fifty-four hysterectomies and thirteen cholecystotomies, eleven ectopics and many operations upon the Fallopian tubes and ovaries. Ovariotomy where both ovaries were removed caused controversy and he was accused of spaying women; from a study of the letters in the *Lancet* in 1886 it seems likely that there was nothing really wrong with the ovaries—an example of non-disease. If so, he would not be the only surgeon guilty of removing healthy organs: colons were removed later by an enthusiast who believed in the now discredited theory of septic foci and lately unnecessary operations like tonsillectomy have been carried out; new operations are seldom subjected to critical assessment like controlled trials for new drugs.

Opposed to Lister's antiseptic surgery with the carbolic spray, Tait believed that simple cleanliness such as washing the hands and wearing clean clothes was sufficient, thus anticipating asepsis. He was on the Council of the BMA, worked hard for medical reform, and won the Hastings Medal. In a biography of the American doctors William and Charles Mayo [12], he was described as the English Titan and it stated that 'Billroth and Tait boldly led the way in abdominal surgery'. He had many other interests: taking part in municipal and political affairs, standing as a Liberal in the Election of 1887, working as a journalist and being President of a Press club. He showed a wide interest in natural history, wrote on archaeology and was a friend of Darwin. His achievements, especially as he died at fifty-four years from a kidney disease, were great.

'The Union spent the first decade of its life in fighting for its existence', wrote Dr Robert Forbes, a former Secretary of the MDU, in his *Sixty Years of Medical Defence*: 'viewed with suspicion by many members of the profession on account of its lay origin, nearly wrecked by a peccant Secretary, narrowly escaping liquidation before its reconstruction under medical direction, convulsed by internal crisis and opposed by a new body formed by seceding members (the Medical Protection Society), the Union in its early years passed through great tribulation' [13]. Although many doctors joined with enthusiasm, others were doubtful about its intentions. Robert Saundby, Professor of Medicine at the University of Birmingham, who later became one of the leaders of the MDU, at first declined membership because, while he would 'gladly join an association of medical men formed to defend or assist in defending its members against cruel and groundless charges or wanton actions brought against them' he feared that the new organization was meant to be a crusade against unauthorized practitioners; this, he believed, would be troublesome and expensive and lead to little practical result—and this is exactly what did happen. Saundby was ahead of his time in giving a series of lectures to medical students on ethical problems, which were later published as a book on medical ethics [14]. His academic approach to the subject may have been responsible for the suggestion that a library should be created for the use of members with books on medical ethics and jurisprudence, but this never succeeded because of lack of money.

Another problem in these early years was that Lawson Tait himself was the subject of litigation and expected the MDU to fund him. In 1889 he contravened a treasured bylaw of the Royal College of Surgeons when trying to organize a meeting of members and was threatened with loss of the privileges of membership and fellowship, and in 1892 he was sued for libel. This was the *Denholm* v. *Lawson Tait* case [15]; it was brought by a Dr Denholm who had been in practice in Manchester for many years. One of his patients, a Mrs Payne, had a large uterine fibroid and he called into consultation two of the consultant staff of Manchester Royal Infirmary who agreed that operation was inadvisable and suggested that the fibroid might be reduced in size by the double faradic current, an orthodox treatment at that time. Unfortunately a vesico-vaginal fistula next occurred and this was operated on twice without success, so Mrs Payne then consulted Mr Lawson Tait. Tait felt certain that the fistula could not be dealt with effectively until the large fibroid had been removed so he operated, finding that the tumour was very adherent to the peritoneum due to inflammation; the operation took over an hour. The husband called soon afterwards and was told that Mrs Payne was 'going on splendidly' but within forty-eight hours she died. Tait was unable to see him but wrote a letter which tactlessly went as follows: 'the immediate cause of this unfortunate result is the rupture of a blood vessel at or near the spot where the electrical needles caused so much damaging inflammation and sloughing. Had she never been submitted to that treatment the case would have been a straightforward one and her recovery almost certain'.

Her husband—not surprisingly—thought that the letter blamed her death on improper treatment by Dr Denholm, who said that the charge was unfounded and untrue and arranged for a post-mortem examination. This was somewhat inconclusive as to whether the death was due to peritonitis resulting from the operation or connected with the previous electrical therapy; on cross-examination, it was revealed that the body had been examined by gaslight while in the coffin but it was reported later that the gaslight had been augmented by candlelight and that the cause of death was definitely peritonitis [16].

Tait impressed the court and his evidence could not be shaken; 'he made such an imposing witness, impressively opening a big case book and reading extracts from it about the case in question, that he scored with the jury against the Manchester man' [17].

Tait had applied to the MDU for assistance and the Council decided to defend the case and employed eminent Counsel. According to Forbes, when the plaintiff's case had been heard and the defendant's partly heard, the plaintiff's Counsel made overtures for a settlement. The MDU's solicitor and the Secretary, Dr Leslie Phillips, were opposed to a settlement but Tait on the advice of his Counsel accepted the settlement without costs. The solicitor's opinion was that in less than another half hour the case would either have been thrown up in court by the plaintiff's Counsel or stopped by the jury in favour of the defendant. Costs would have been forthcoming from the plaintiff or his friends and if otherwise they would have been collected. As to the plaintiff's ability to pay costs, the solicitor had stated at the court that Denholm himself would be unable to do so. This case illustrated the mistake of writing a libellous letter and letting down a colleague, the importance of the witness (Chapter 6), and is an early example of settling out of court.

Unfortunately the matter did not end with the libel case. It had aroused ill feeling in the MDU and in the profession generally and a growing antagonism developed towards Tait and what it termed 'an autocracy of directors'; as one member put it, 'Tait *is* the Medical Defence Union, surrounded by puppets'. Letters also began to appear in the medical press asking questions about the payment of the College of Surgeons' case and the costs in the *Denholm* v. *Tait* libel action: some correspondents condemned the payment of Tait's costs by the MDU, some suggested a fund to cover these and some maintained that the Union should not have decided to support one side without the fullest enquiry into both sides, and others thought that 'it would have been more desirable in view of Tait's social and professional position for the costs to have come from his own pocket than from the coffers of a young and struggling association'.

On 9 January 1893, Tait offered the Council his resignation, one of his reasons being that 'my Presidency brings trouble on the Union which another man might avoid'—though without him the MDU could have been stillborn. The MDU was in debt, largely due to the costs of the libel case, and Tait was reluctant to provide a cheque for this partly because he was owed out-of-pocket expenses in connection with the bankruptcy of Charles Rideal; he also regarded the MDU as an insurance society. However, one of the results of the *Denholm* v. *Tait* case (where both plaintiff and defendant were doctors) was a resolution 'that this society being a medical defence union it is undesirable that finances should be used to defend or support any action made against another member of the profession and that this be a recommendation to Council'. This policy has been followed ever since and disputants are today advised, if feasible, to submit their differences to arbitration and the costs incurred may be met if a question of professional principle is involved.

The crisis of 1893, which resulted in the resignation of Lawson Tait, also caused the MDU office to be moved from Birmingham; new headquarters had to be found and London was chosen because of its convenience to members who came personally and knocked on the door to seek advice (the twenty-four-hour telephone service was only started in 1975). The new President was Mr (later Sir) Victor Horsley (1857–1916) who had been a member of the Council in 1892 (Figure 4) and he held the office until 1897 when he was elected to the General Medical Council. He was described as an enthusiast being incapable of

FIGURE 4. (*left*) Mr (later Sir) Victor Horsley (1857–1916), President from 1893–97.

FIGURE 5. (*right*) W. E. Hempson Esq. was the lawyer to the Medical Defence Union, from 1894–1920, and the same firm has been consulted ever since.

luke-warmness in any cause. Apart from his work for the Medical Defence Union, British Medical Association and General Medical Council, he achieved world-wide fame as a physiologist, neurologist and surgeon for which he was elected a Fellow of the Royal Society [18]. He pioneered surgery and his first operation on the brain was done in 1886; he was described as the father of modern brain surgery. He, like Tait, had many other interests and his photographs were apparently real works of art. He stood for Parliament as an advanced Liberal and Democrat. He held his opinions very strongly and was ahead of his time in supporting votes for women and opposing the smoking of tobacco.

Hardly had the storm caused by the *Denholm* v. *Tait* case blown over when another arose in *Bloxham* v. *Collie, Collie* v. *Bloxham,* and *Bloxham* v. *The Medical Defence Union* [13]. This case also concerned two doctors, both members of the MDU, and it raised matters of principle which caused friction in the Council. Dr Collie, a general practitioner and a Vice-President of the MDU, alleged that his assistant, Bloxham, had violated his undertaking not to practise within a prescribed radius of Collie's practice, and Bloxham alleged a breach by Collie of an oral partnership agreement. Bloxham first applied to the MDU for assistance. The Secretary, Dr Leslie Phillips, refused the application on the ground that the matter was a business dispute in which the MDU could not intervene and Bloxham withdrew his request; but two months later when the Council received an application for assistance from Dr Collie, this was overruled and it was decided to defend the action as a 'distinctly exceptional case'. It was also decided to change the solicitors to the London firm of Messrs Hempsons & Elgar who had already been acting for Dr Collie. The firm of Hempsons, run then by Mr W. E. Hempson (Figure 5) have acted as lawyers to the MDU from 1893 to the present day.

The case caused much schism; critics at the Annual Meeting in 1894 made it the subject of a motion of censure but this was lost; Dr Collie resigned his seat on the Council to avoid it being said that the Council was influenced by him being on it. Then a writ was received from Bloxham to restrain the MDU from assisting Collie, and Mr Hempson was instructed to defend the action. Bloxham next applied for an injunction restraining the MDU from applying its funds to the costs and expenses of a member in litigation with another member, such action being beyond the scope of the Memorandum and Articles; this was refused but Bloxham appealed to the Court of Appeal where judges entered a new point relating to the interpretation of the Articles; they held that when two members were involved in an action the Union ought to obtain statements from both sides before deciding to defend the action on behalf of one member. Eventually Bloxham's Counsel made overtures for a settlement: Collie agreed to forgo Bloxham's debt and Bloxham agreed to fulfil the covenant he had violated. [13].

Human affairs seldom advance without controversy. This certainly applied to the newborn MDU where the controversy was unfortunately more often destructive than constructive. The *Bloxham* v. *Collie* case and other matters caused Dr Leslie Phillips to resign: he was a young dermatologist in Birmingham and, whereas Lawson Tait as President and figurehead had received the glory for getting the MDU going, Phillips had done much of the hard work—as is the lot of secretaries. The other secretary, Dr A. G. Bateman (Figure 6), continued until his death in 1919. The result of these disagreements was the birth of the Medical Protection Society.

THE MEDICAL PROTECTION SOCIETY (MPS)

Dissatisfaction, especially about the new constitution which Mr Tait had drawn up, had been caused in the Council of the MDU. Although revised

FIGURE 6. (*left*) Dr A. G. Bateman was joint honorary secretary from 1888 to 1894 and became the first paid medical secretary, an office which he held until his death in 1919

FIGURE 7. (*right*) Mr (later Sir) Jonathan Hutchinson (1828–1913), the first President of the Medical Protection Society.

Articles confirming these changes were supported by the special general meeting on 15 January 1892, there was one dissenter—Dr Hugh Woods—who was supported by two postal votes; his criticism was that the new constitution would enable a small group of persons to retain control of the Union's affairs so that Council might deteriorate into an autocracy [19]. He also objected to the introduction of a section into the new Articles to prevent the Annual Meeting from petitioning against legislation injurious to the profession (apparently connected with the Midwives Act). He gathered other dissatisfied members and, on 14 March 1892, a rival organization, the London and Counties Medical Protection Society Ltd, held its first general meeting. (The title was changed to the Medical Protection Society (MPS) after the Second World War.) The new society gained some members at the expense of the MDU; its propaganda emphasized the value of autonomous branches, a system of peripheral organization which the Union was then discarding. Dr Woods was plainly concerned that the voice of the membership would not be heard loudly enough.

Informal negotiations were started shortly afterwards to repair this public disruption and the first step was a letter from Dr Hugh Woods, the Secretary of the new society, asking whether the Council of the Medical Defence Union would receive a deputation from the new society with a view to starting negotiations about amalgamation. Such discussions continued over the years but were never successful. A leading article in the *Lancet* dealt with the reasons for the failure to rejoin. One problem was the difficulty in finding a suitable name for the new joint body. The MDU regarded its name as a valuable part of its goodwill and was worried that another organization might steal one of the two names if combined in any joint title. As the leader writer wrote, 'how can the registration of the compound name protect the separate title of one body from piracy yet make the separate title of the other body of less value as an asset? Again, if the two bodies amalgamate and have henceforth joint interests, what does it matter if one of them loses a valuable asset if it is the other that reaps the resulting advantage? We are utterly at a loss to see why this matter of the registration of a name should prove a serious stumbling block' [20]. Doctors are no different from others—indeed perhaps worse—in failing to agree (as anyone experienced in medical committee work would endorse), but there were no doubt other factors—for example neither seemed prepared to give up its independence—which, up to the present day, have blocked reunion of the two bodies.

Dr Hugh Woods was the real father of the new society. The President, like Lawson Tait, was a distinguished surgeon, Mr (later Sir) Jonathan Hutchinson (Figure 7) who was on the staff of the London Hospital and also had much interest in the welfare of the profession. When he died at the age of 85 in 1913, his achievements were recorded in a detailed obituary in the *Lancet* [21]. Apart from describing the characteristic teeth of congenital syphilis, he was an operating surgeon, an ophthalmologist, a dermatologist, syphilologist and a neurologist, and a follow-up short obituary also recorded his excellence as a gynaecologist.

Today there is little difference between the two London-based bodies and this has been so for many years; indeed, before it was compulsory for all doctors in NHS hospitals in the UK to join a defence body or take out commercial insurance, some failed to join one or the other because they could not decide which was the better. Both are world-wide: the MPS had about 100,000 members in 1984 and the MDU 113,000 members. A joint committee was set up in 1921 to discuss matters of mutual concern and the co-ordinating committee formed in the early 1950s provides co-operation and a common policy. The secretariats work closely together and so share their 'know-how'. Each may support a member on the opposite side in a court case but only when this concerns possible negligence and not when personal matters are involved.

Critics, ever since the birth of the MPS, have suspected a wastage of money and effort due to having two separate bodies; both have staffs of doctors and dentists (nineteen in the MDU and fourteen in the MPS), trained in medico-legal affairs so that many cases can be handled without the cost of legal fees; but all are fully occupied and even if a new building could be found to accommodate them, calculations have shown that any reduction in the annual subscription of members would be minimal. Many feel that it is useful to have a choice, though the competition is slight; it is mainly concerned with enrolling new members (but not with taking members from each other) and this is an incentive to keep improving the service.

THE MEDICAL AND DENTAL DEFENCE UNION OF SCOTLAND (MDDUS)

The MDDUS was formed in 1902. A perusal of notes from the minutes and early annual reports provided by the Secretary, Dr J. Patterson, suggested no particular reason for starting the new body apart from the advantage of this being established in Scotland because of the distance from London. The model for its constitution was the MDU and both bodies have co-operated ever since; its annual subscription is smaller because its activities are less. It has retained a Scottish flavour: graduates of Scottish universities and overseas graduates who take up their first hospital appointment in Scotland are the only doctors who can join.

THE BRITISH MEDICAL ASSOCIATION (BMA)

Doctors belonging to the British Medical Association have to pay three subscriptions: to the BMA, to the General Medical Council, and to a medical defence body. So, not surprisingly, its members have suggested that the BMA takes over the function of medical defence. This was, in fact, first suggested by Dr Francis J. Bond when writing to the *British Medical Journal* in 1885 after receiving the circular suggesting membership of the MDU: he praised the ideas put forth in the circular but wrote 'We have in the British Medical Association a body which represents the whole profession, framed in a powerful organisation, and possessing large funds. Surely it is to such a body that the individual members of the profession should look for the protection . . .' [2]. Also a resolution, adopted by the East Anglian branch of the BMA in January 1886 and approved by fourteen of the Association's twenty-six branches, went as follows:

> That, as medical men may at any time become liable to false and
> groundless charges of a ruinous nature, it is most desirable that a

medical defence fund be formed and administered in connection with the British Medical Association, and that its members should be asked to contribute a small sum annually to this fund, those who do so becoming entitled, should occasion arise, to legal advice and assistance [22].

The Council of the BMA considered this, but rejected it a year later, as such work could not, apparently, be legally supported from BMA funds. Indeed the MDU's foundation in the previous year had been held up while the BMA decided whether or not to take part in the new enterprise [13]. Ten years later, an annotation in the *Lancet* stated 'It is very doubtful, indeed, whether the British Medical Association would add to its strength by attempting the work done now so well by the Medical Defence Union and its sister society. It certainly could not do the defence work better than it is done. And if this work came to be added to the work of the Association, already multifarious enough, the chances are it would be worse done' [23].

The BMA in 1920 asked for a reduction in subscription for its members, and has done so from time to time since then; the reply is that the medical defence bodies owe a duty to members of a similar calibre whether belonging to the BMA or not, and to those the world over. The BMA has always enjoyed a close and mutually helpful relation with the medical defence bodies, although the smooth water was ruffled in 1977 due to the suggestion of a 'Proposed professional indemnity insurance scheme for BMA members' linked with CT Bowring Professional Indemnity Ltd which would have provided cover through the Crusader Insurance Company [24]. This might also have boosted the membership of the BMA. The three defence bodies made a statement in reply [25]. It was discussed by the BMA Council who reported 'not only are there far-reaching financial implications for the Association in sponsoring such a scheme, but it would have to be supported by a personal counselling and advisory service in a wider field than that which the Association also covers', and the annual representatives' meeting eventually turned it down. A leader 'Medical Defence' in the *British Medical Journal* (1977) stated, 'Already harassed by troubles in the NHS and by incomes policies, many doctors have wondered why on earth the long-established defence organisations cannot be left to get on with their job of protecting individual doctors, work which most will agree has been done with diligence, compassion, and an eye for the profession's wider interest' [26]. Also the BMA's annual representative meeting in 1977 decided to suspend consideration of a professional indemnity scheme for BMA members and to seek closer co-operation with the medical defence bodies [27].

Membership

Many doctors, appalled by the size of the annual subscription to their defence body, may yearn for the past when, as in 1885, the annual payment was only ten shillings. But—and here is the rub—this only covered advice and defence; it merely provided lawyers and paid their fees. Also the value of ten shillings has risen considerably since then (Figure 8) but the annual subscription has increased far more, partly due to the provision of full coverage and partly due to rocketing of the amounts awarded to plaintiffs.

Thus, during the first twenty-five years the privileges of membership were limited. The question of payment by the MDU of any costs or damages awarded against a member unsuccessfully defended had been raised several times but, supported by their solicitor's opinion, no obligation to make such payments was considered necessary. The matter again came up in 1907 as a proposal from an insurance broker to negotiate insurance for medical practitioners against liabilities in actions for negligence and malpractice with underwriters at Lloyd's. One reason put forward was the 'greatly increased danger of fictitious claims being made owing to the spirit fostered by the Workman's Compensation Act of 1906 among the wage-earning classes'. But again the Council decided that it was undesirable as it might encourage careless medical practice; also the premium to cover all risks (including adverse verdicts), the cost of the 'other side', and damages, would be high, and that the courts were unlikely to favour such a scheme. Moreover, the proportion of cases lost by the MDU was so small that costly further insurance seemed unnecessary. Another argument was stated in the annual report of 1907: that it was wholly immoral to cover medical members against damages and costs of the other side and that 'surgeons might be even more reckless'. However, this policy was soon changed and the MPS led the way.

The London and Counties Medical Protection Society wrote to the MDU in 1908 proposing a conference to discuss further insurance but this was declined. The idea was, however, pursued and an arrangement was concluded with an insurance company which undertook to indemnify, to the extent of £2,000 in any one year and for a premium of ten shillings, any member who wished to take out such an insurance; indemnity insurances for qualified assistants or dispensers could be effected for the extra premiums of five shillings and two shillings and sixpence respectively. The MDU thereupon changed its mind, reporting that indemnity insurance was neither illegal nor unethical, and arranged with the Yorkshire Insurance Company for members to insure themselves for up to £2,000 in any one action for an annual premium of only seven shillings and sixpence, or £2,500 for a premium of nine shillings; in

33

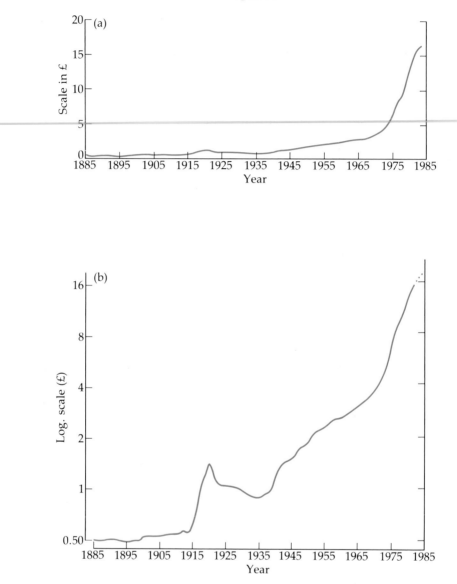

FIGURE 8. The change in the value of ten shillings (50 p) from 1885 to 1985, according to the Retail Price Index (RPI). (a) Arithmetic scale (calculated by Lloyds Bank Group Economics Department); (b) logarithmic scale to show relative (percentage) changes (calculated by the Economic Study Association). The graphs are a guide rather than an accurate record because of alterations in the definition of the RPI over this period, and the sharp fall in the general price level during the interwar years.

1917 the 'Yorkshire' reduced the annual premium to a single amount, namely seven shillings and sixpence for an indemnity up to £2,500.

The medical world in 1924 was startled by the notorious case of *Harnett* v. *Bond and Adams* when damages amounting to £25,000 were awarded against two doctors jointly for wrongly certifying and detaining a man under the Lunacy Acts (p. 59). Although the judgement was reversed on appeal, the possibility of a repetition of such an astonishing verdict had to be reckoned with, and a maximum indemnity of £3,000 was hardly adequate. This case resulted in members being indemnified against all costs of defence and partially against excessive adverse costs and damages, and benefits were extended so that members could receive complete and unlimited indemnity against all possible financial loss, subject to the Articles of Association [28]. The MDU achieved this policy partly by self-financing and partly through brokers at Lloyd's. This unlimited indemnity, with a subscription unaffected in the year following a claim, was then recognized 'as a godsend'. Since 1924, this has rarely been refused to any member and then only for a good reason and after careful consideration.

SUBSCRIPTIONS

The two London-based defence bodies, MDU and MPS, now have an annual subscription of £288 (1985) while that of the Scottish Union (MDDUS) is £258. These amounts are minimal compared with those paid by American doctors, while lawyers in the UK have to pay at least £1,500 a year. Financially, the defence bodies must be strong in order to cover the following: inflation, enormous awards (an amount of quarter of a million pounds is not uncommon), increasing legal and court expenses, and the need to build reserves to cover 'the tail' which results from the long duration of cases with an unknown quantity accumulating at the end. Some members, concerned by the rate at which subscriptions are rising, have attempted to forecast the likely figure for the year 2003; this is more likely to be £814 [29] than the £36,989 annually suggested by the computer of another member. An independent analysis of the causes for the ever-increasing subscription rates is provided in an article entitled 'The medical negligence crisis' by Professor W. A. Harland and R. S. Jandoo [30].

Members understandably get paranoid about payment of subscriptions; for example, whether low risk groups are subsidizing high risk ones or GPs subsidizing hospital doctors. Members working overseas, such as those in parts of Africa, wonder whether they are subsidizing the large awards current in the UK, since the risk of a medico-legal action is lower amongst the Whites abroad and almost non-existent from the Blacks, but subscription rates are adjusted with this in mind and are less than those in the UK.

Differential subscription rates are also arranged for newly qualified doctors and for members who do not need indemnity and the idea of extending them on the basis of risk rating to all doctors has been discussed by the defence bodies for several years. This is the practice in the USA (see Chapter 9). If organized in the UK, an anaesthetist might pay £500 per annum and a general practitioner (GP) £150 but this might be reversed a year later if, for example, two or three cases of malaria are missed by GPs (see Chapter 4). But obviously some fields of medical practice are more likely than others to lead to costly awards and this difference, relatively insignificant in early years, has become more relevant recently because of the escalation in the size of awards. The medical defence bodies have special problems partly because of the type of practice here compared with the USA and because of their world-wide membership (Figure 9): it is difficult to classify doctors where the distinction between specialist and generalist is obscure and, even in the UK, there is the example of the GP who is also an anaesthetist or performs minor surgery like vasectomy—and others may have two specialities; this is even more marked in less-developed countries where so many doctors have to be generalists. GPs have their subscriptions fully reimbursed in the expenses element of their pay and also draw heaviest on the advisory service; one inquiry alone, especially if legal opinions are needed, may cost several times a member's subscription. Risk rating can more easily be done with the present computerized records but to organize it anywhere will cost the defence bodies more.

The types of membership are shown in Appendix I. Retired members no longer pay a fee, yet they are covered against actions arising from former patients; a safeguard that was started in 1965. The estates of doctors who have died are also protected. Payment by instalment was begun in 1983.

Failure to pay the subscription can be disastrous. A surgeon received a letter from solicitors claiming damages on behalf of a patient after vasectomy. The patient's wife had conceived and sperm tests had shown that he was still fertile. The surgeon told the MDU 'before giving details of this problem, I must explain that I have been very worried as to whether I can claim your help. I have discovered to my dismay that I have not paid my subscription. I was under the impression that it was paid by banker's order but I was mistaken'. The MDU is precluded by its Articles of Association from assisting doctors who have allowed their membership to lapse. Variable direct debit is the method of choice for paying subscriptions to the MDU. If a member fails to pay his subscription, two reminder notices are sent out and there is a period of grace of four months before his name is removed from the list of members.

Membership of the defence bodies extends throughout the world, except for the USA where members are not defended; dentists as well as doctors are

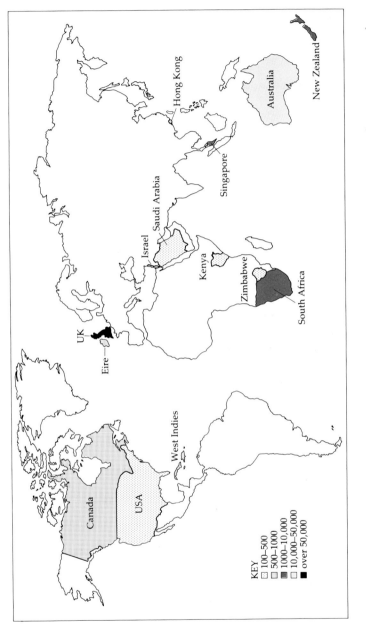

FIGURE 9. The Medical Defence Union has members in most countries of the world. The map indicates countries with the greatest membership. (See Key for details.)

covered and each defence body has its own lawyers who virtually specialize in medical problems. The benefits of membership of the MDU today are listed in Appendix II.

Medical defence bodies help any doctor who is a member at the time, though there is no contract whereby they have to pay if certain conditions are not fulfilled; in practice refusal to indemnify a member is very rare and then only for a good reason and after careful consideration. However, some doctors, notably juniors, were unconvinced and pointed out that they would not insure their homes or cars on this basis; they also objected to the defence bodies seeming to raise their subscriptions in unison. So the MDU decided to resolve the question as to whether the medical defence bodies fell within the provisions of the various acts of parliament that regulate activities of insurance companies by a judicial decision [31]. Any previous lack of enthusiasm was hardly surprising for the Insurance Companies Act in 1974 created a system of control of insurance companies: fiscal and procedural requirements were imposed on them and the Secretary of State was granted extensive powers to intervene in their affairs.

Fortunately the case *The Medical Defence Union Ltd* v. *The Department of Trade* (1979) was decided in favour of the MDU [32] for various reasons, one of which, 'the entitlement of the person insured', included benefits such as the wide-ranging advisory and educational services.

Members have wondered whether their subscriptions might be reduced if the MDU had become an insurance company. If the case had been lost, the defence bodies would have been obliged, in fact, to raise members' subscriptions to comply with the Act's requirements.

Protection by insurance is still used by doctors in the USA, Europe, Asia and elsewhere. The differences between a mutual non-profit-making defence association and commercial insurance are as follows:

* Insurance companies can load a doctor's premium if he makes a claim, whereas a member of a medical defence body is only required to pay the appropriate annual subscription—however many claims he makes.
* Renewal of membership could be refused by an insurance company because of a high level of claim or claims (when the policy is renewed).
* An insurance company will sometimes settle out of court if there is a pecuniary advantage irrespective of the merits of the case or wishes of the doctor.
* Additional insurance cover would be necessary for retired members or for the estates of those who had died.

WHY NOT BE PROTECTED THROUGH AN INSURANCE COMPANY?

Some doctors suggest that it would be a simple matter to arrange for an insurance company to provide medical defence but this overlooks two important factors:

1 The defence bodies have built, over nearly a hundred years, a skill in preventing the 90 per cent of unjustified or misinformed claims being pursued and in settling justified ones. It is doubtful whether any insurance company or its lawyers possess these skills in medical cases. The handling of medical claims is not akin to handling car or other accident claims. Inefficient and unskilled handling of these matters and expediency settlements could lead to more claims and higher premiums.

2 The personal advisory service given by trained doctors and dentists.

It would be ironic if the medical defence bodies, now the envy of the world and currently being developed in the USA, were to be weakened by competition from insurance companies. Subscriptions are now kept to a minimum as members normally stay for a lifetime. If doctors started to 'shop around' for lower premiums, they might be satisfied in the short term because of loss leaders, whereby low premiums are advertised to tempt them, but in the longer term they could have to pay more as in the USA. The system of defence by professional mutual funds is the most economical method of providing a service because there is no profit to shareholders, and no profit is required for the holding company.

The chairman of the Education Committee of the American College of Legal Medicine gave his own opinion when he wrote 'it is incomprehensible to me that British physicians should, at this critical time, seriously consider purchasing professional liability from a commercial underwriter who has virtually no experience in the field of medical malpractice and risk management, rather than continuing to rely on the experience and expertise of the societies which have served them so well for many, many decades. Such a move will surely bring to British physicians the same disastrous results that their American colleagues are now trying so desperately to overcome' [33].

Evolution of the defence bodies

The annual reports, published since 1888, provide a valuable record for any medical or social historian; they also illustrate how the work of the defence bodies has evolved over the years. Unfortunately the early reports, written by the MDU's solicitor, often lack information—especially of clinical details. However, since the Second World War, they have been comprehensive and as

39

well as providing information on the Council's work, lists of officers, objects and work of the MDU and advice to members, they have sections on the following: actions fought and won, claims resisted, indefensible claims, dental problems, finance and membership and special articles on such topics as drugs and the law, ethical problems, and certification and warnings. Brief case histories, selected by the secretariat, are described, their purpose being to illustrate problems which doctors meet rather than to provide a statistical record of the year's work.

The lay press receives copies of the annual reports and may comment; the stories which attract the lay journalist are sometimes either the least important and more bizarre ones (therefore unrepresentative), or those with a little humour. Inappropriate publicity is occasionally inevitable and publishing case summaries could encourage litigation against doctors and hospitals or raise unwarranted anxiety about the relatively small risks of modern procedures; but this has to be balanced against the duty to give the membership examples of cases that have gone wrong in the current year, in the hope that such damage to patients may be avoided in the future. Members often feel that they need a sedative before reading these reports and appreciate why the telegraphic address of the MDU is 'Damocles' (he sat at a sumptuous banquet but a sword was suspended above him by a hair so that he was afraid to stir and the banquet was a tantalizing torment). The sword of Damocles symbolizes the medico-legal risk which confronts every doctor in his professional life; it may fall on the first day in practice or on the last, after retirement or not at all. Each year about 10 per cent of members consult the MDU on a new matter.

CHANGING ATTITUDE TOWARD LITIGIOUS PATIENTS

Anyone who studies these reports over the century will notice the striking change in attitude towards litigious patients. Early ones allude to the obstinacy and stupidity of the plaintiffs and the worthlessness of the allegations; this authoritative and paternalistic approach was general for at least half of the century, an approach that, coupled with a more docile public, led to medico-legal successes undreamed of today, with statements such as 'early and vigorous opposition to threatened claims against doctors discouraged many claims which would have proceeded much further if the frightened doctors had to depend on their own resources' and 'our member received a letter from the patient demanding compensation and threatening in the alternative, an action at law. The letter was replied to by the secretary of the Union, stating that the solicitors were prepared to accept service on behalf of the attacked member. This led to the collapse of the case' [34]. Almost every case seemed to collapse and the solicitors reported in 1904 that 'it stands out as a signal fact of which the Union may feel justly and deservedly proud that of the 383 cases undertaken within the last nine years on behalf of its members to vindicate and protect their professional honour and reputation, in only three have there been adverse verdicts against them' [35].

It was often considered impertinent for a patient to take his doctor to court and this attitude was accepted uncritically by Forbes in his *Sixty Years of Medical Defence* [13] when describing the two Dulwich practitioners, Dr Bower and Dr Keates, who failed to diagnose a case of diphtheria (see Chapter 1): he wrote of the indignation of the profession and how the *British Medical Journal* had described the law suit as 'very little on the hither side of vexatious litigation' and the remark of the magistrate that 'if he allowed the enquiry to proceed further, he would not only be sanctioning a prosecution, but a persecution as well, and that it would be next to wickedness on his part to commit, as he could not see one tittle of evidence to support the allegations set forth in the indictment'. Many situations giving rise to complaints and claims have changed very little over the years; it is the outcome that is strikingly different.

A change was noticed in the annual report of 1947/8:

> 'it is becoming easier for a claimant in an action for negligence
> against a medical practitioner to prove his case to the satisfaction of
> a court. A study . . . of the decisions of the courts over the years . . .
> reveals . . . a definite trend of judicial opinion . . . there is an increas-
> ing tendency for plaintiffs to be successful in all those classes of
> actions which arise out of insurable risks, the most obvious exam-
> ples of which are road traffic cases and workmen's compensation
> claims. Therefore, the tipping of the scales in favour of plaintiffs in
> cases in which the Union is involved is only a part of a larger
> whole . . . for whatever reason, it is inescapable that the courts have
> felt justified in accepting as proof of negligence evidence which
> would not have satisfied them, say, before the War. It is probable
> that this leniency to plaintiffs is only temporary and that its origin
> lies in the belief that plaintiffs have hitherto been required to go
> further than was reasonable in proving negligence. If this be right,
> one may expect in the future to see a reversal of the trend and a
> recognition by judges that the pendulum has swung too far' [36].

Some doctors might think it regrettable that this prophecy has not come true; others believe that it is preferable for patient–doctor confrontation to be on a more equal footing.

Ideas are still changing and the *Hatcher* v. *Black* (1954) case illustrated this [37, 38]. The plaintiff, a young woman who had done freelance broadcasting from time to time, developed a toxic goitre. Her GP sent her to see a consultant physician at a London teaching hospital; he discussed with her the possible alternatives of a partial thyroidectomy or medical treatment and advised that operation was the better course. The operation was performed by a consultant surgeon to the hospital. When Mrs Hatcher asked him on the night before the operation whether there was any risk to the voice, he told her that there was none.

Unfortunately her voice was weak after the operation due to paralysis of the left vocal cord from damage to the recurrent laryngeal nerve which passes behind the thyroid gland. Her complaint against the physician was that, according to her, he had negligently advised her that operation involved no risk to her voice, and that had she known that there was any risk she would have chosen medical treatment, not operation. Her complaint against the surgeon was that he had performed the operation negligently. In his summing-up Lord Justice Denning said that it would be wrong, and bad law, to say that simply because a mishap occurred the hospital and doctors were liable, and it would be disastrous for the community. It would mean that a doctor examining a patient or a surgeon operating at the table, instead of getting on with his work, would be for ever looking over his shoulder to see if someone were coming up with a dagger. An action for negligence against the doctor was like a dagger which could wound his reputation as severely as it could his body. A doctor was only negligent when he had fallen short of the standard of reasonable medical care, when he deserves censure. An illustration was the first question raised in the action: what should the doctor tell the patient? The doctor had told the plaintiff that there was no risk to her voice, although he knew there was some slight risk. This he had done for her own good because of the vital importance to her that in her condition she should not worry; he had told a lie which in the circumstances was justifiable. It was a matter which in law was left to the conscience of the doctor himself. The jury returned a verdict in favour of the defendants, and judgement was duly entered from them with costs.

The annual report of the MDU referred to this case as 'an illustration of the way in which . . . members of the public will institute proceedings against medical men on any pretext or none . . .'. However when two experienced members of the staff of the MDU were asked in 1984 to give their views, they thought that she should have been told of this risk.

ACTING TO DEFEND DOCTORS

Negligence only became a major issue about thirty years after the birth of the

MDU—until then many doctors did not consider the risk great enough to join in spite of exhortations to become members. The surgeon, Marmaduke Shield, in 1900 advised 'never attend a fracture unless you have joined the MDU' and Dr Savage in a lecture at Guy's Hospital in 1904 advised students 'when you go into practice one of the first things you should do is to invest 10 shillings in the Medical Defence Union'; as an example he told how he had been called in to see rather an odd lady who kept about forty dogs in her house. Although one or two of them had died, she proposed to keep them still in her room but later thought that about two dozen of the dogs needed a change of air, so she took them on a first class express train from the Midlands to Folkestone at the cost of about £150. . . . The Commissioners in Lunacy decided that she should not be considered a lunatic but she stayed as a voluntary boarder in an asylum for a time and then left—after leaving she brought an action against Dr Savage who stated that 'all I did was to refer her to the Medical Defence Union'.

In 1899 a Dr Woodley Stocker wrote to the *Lancet* about an action for £50 damages brought against him for improper treatment of a damaged hand. He thought that the woman would not have brought this had it not been for the new Employers' Liability Act which provided her with her full week's earnings for some months, and he wrote 'was this insurance money used in order to bring a trumpery action against her medical adviser? If this is the case it adds another terror to medical practice and is another strong argument in favour of every medical man joining one or both of our excellent defence societies. I should like here publicly to acknowledge my indebtedness to the London and Counties Medical Protection Society which took up my case and so ably carried it to a successful issue . . .' [39].

There were only five cases of alleged negligence amongst a hundred others in 1894 and twenty-five from 150 in the following year but in 1927 the President of the MDU stated that these undoubtedly made up the greater proportion of cases in any year.

DOCTORS SUBJECT TO SLANDER AND LIBEL

Cases of defamation—both slander and libel—occupied most of the early reports, malpractice being second. The annual report of 1910 stated that

> Perhaps the highest tribute which can be paid to the work of the
> Union lies in the fact that within the past 15 years 697 cases have
> been either instituted or defended on behalf of Members for Libel and
> Slander and only 3 of these have been lost . . . Of the 697 cases, fully
> three fourths have concerned the prosecution, as distinct from the
> defence, of Libel and Slander actions on behalf of Members . . . In no

single instance however has an action been lost in which proceedings have been instituted on behalf of a Member in vindication of his professional honour and reputation . . . Regard being had to the idiosyncrasies of Juries and the present attitude of the Bench towards Libel and Slander actions this may I think be claimed as constituting a record not to be equalled and certainly not surpassed . . . [40].

Mention was then made of the difficulty in recovering costs: in two cases the plaintiff was a nurse employed at a small salary; others were a working carpenter, a groom, an agricultural labourer, a charwoman, and the wife of a police constable—'members may be left to judge as to the likelihood of recovering costs from persons moving in these financial circles', the solicitor reported. The frequency of these cases was curious: perhaps people were less charitable and more outspoken, or patients grumbled about their doctors because there were no official channels of complaint.

An early case of slander was a reference to a doctor by a clergyman in the words 'he is not qualified. His greatest advertisement is his carriage and pair and his consummate cheek.' The annual report stated that 'the reverend gentleman very properly apologised and paid 10 guineas towards the expenses'.

Language was sometimes more colourful, and in another libel case, a nurse had written to a patient to say that the doctor was a 'contemptible cur', and the annual report of 1890 mentioned that

Your Council took energetic steps to trace and bring to justice the social reptiles who annoyed two members by writing filthy letters to them and about them . . . in one, letters were posted accusing the doctor of immoral relations with his servants and the same kind of letters were addressed to his wife . . . and in the other the predecessor of the complaining member was driven to sell his practice by the same pestilential annoyance, the *modus operandi* being to send a vile letter to any lady whom our member attended professionally, accusing her of improper relations with the surgeon; by the same post the lady's husband, if she were married, was so informed by the same means; and simultaneously the surgeon received a letter telling him that these letters had been sent and promising to continue these attentions to every patient until he was driven from the town! A man may well feel the comfort of an alliance to give him moral and material support under such hideous circumstances. These letters arrived daily, sometimes twice a day!

A detective was sent and spent ten days in the town but failed to find the culprit but in this case as well as the first, the annoyance ceased soon after the visit of the detective.

The case of Dr Cameron Kidd was reported in the *Lancet.* He was Medical Officer of Health of the district around Bromsgrove and Droitwich and an article in a local newspaper alleged neglect, malpractice, and mismanagement of his hospital practice, stating that 'a patient was in the hospital one week and three days and never saw the doctor once, and all the six weeks and three days she was there she never had one drop of medicine' [41]. Other accusations about the poor treatment of patients were made but Dr Kidd's character was completely vindicated.

The press, whether local or national, can ruin a doctor's reputation. Medicine is a popular topic and, whereas there is joy in heaven for the sinner that repenteth, there seems undoubtedly to be joy in Fleet Street for the doctor that sins: his alleged mishap or malpractice is likely to be printed in large letters on the front page but any later news that he is judged to be innocent is likely to be written in small print on the back page. Cases of libel have continued to need the support of the defence bodies throughout the century. The annual report for 1892 stated 'advice has frequently been given to members not to be too sensitive to public newspaper criticism. Especially is this advice applicable where the complainant holds public appointments' and apparently it would be apt for this paragraph under 'Hypersensitive' to be republished today. There was probably more substance in the allegations of defamation in early years but it is still an emotive topic and many doctors would even feel upset by being referred to as 'not a good doctor'.

ON THE OFFENSIVE AGAINST UNQUALIFIED PRACTITIONERS

One of the reasons that the MDU was founded was to protect the profession against quacks, who brought the profession into disgrace, threatened the livelihood of qualified doctors, and could be a danger to patients. A leader in *The Times* in 1896 reported the case of *Regina* v. *Priestley* [42] at the Leeds assizes. Lavinia Sawdon was a servant girl in the service of a Mrs Sykes, neighbour of the prisoner who described himself as a 'herbalist' and 'maker of imitation teeth'. The girl had a toothache and was taken to this man who gave her chloroform (although she had just eaten a hearty meal of potatoes, pudding and beer), and extracted the tooth himself; as time went on Mrs Sykes became alarmed and on going into the room found the girl dead. She was sitting upright in an armchair with her dress fastened, apart from two or three buttons, and her stays were not loosened. Dental surgeons from Bradford Infirmary, called in at the inquest, said that it was their rule always to call in a medical man to give the anaesthetic. In summing up, the judge regretted that the law allowed an unqualified person to give anaesthetics and operate, and called attention to the dangerous results 'that might arise from allowing ignorant persons to use and practise a skilled profession and the ease with which statutes may be evaded. Cunning is not the quality in which the most dangerous and most flourishing orders of quacks can afford to be deficient, and they have no difficulty in breaking through the puerile obstacles to their proceedings contained in such statutes as the Medical Acts and Dentists' Acts. In fashionable quarters, the sham doctor simply puts up a brass plate on his door with Mr Jones or Dr Brown on it. He does not infringe the acts. Nobody can touch him.' Priestley was prosecuted for manslaughter.

The 'Indian oculists' were described in the first annual report of the MPS in 1892. They extracted large sums of money from many hopelessly blind persons, who, 'with the infatuation that leads drowning persons to catch at straws, have begged and borrowed money for the purpose of consulting these quacks'. They were prosecuted by the MPS at Marylebone Police Court as they called themselves doctor on their handbills, but the magistrate dismissed the case thinking that they were simple-minded foreigners who knew no better— and they promised not to do it again. However, they increased in numbers and boldness and pretended that they could cure optic atrophy about which they claimed the Moorfields' doctors were mistaken. So the MPS decided 'it is intended to prefer more serious charges against these oculists very shortly, if they continue to "cure" the blind in this country. Members are asked for information as to the whereabouts of these men.'

The *British Medical Journal* wrote in 1889, 'We believe that the real complaint now should be, not of the inefficiency of the law, but of the apathy of some of the bodies which ought to enforce it'. They were referring to the General Medical Council and paid a flattering compliment to the MDU which 'seems disposed to act for the benefit of the profession, and deserves the support of its members'. Two years later an editorial in the *Lancet* stated 'the annual report of the MDU is a document which has interest for our readers. Our profession is a very undefended profession . . . the General Medical Council and examining bodies prescribed terms of admission and had disciplinary powers over their members but then leave their diplomates to take care of themselves . . . the MDU is in the meantime doing some of the work that the medical authorities ought to do in the way of instigating prosecutions of those who disgrace the profession by irregular methods of practice and by association with quacks.'

The minutes of the early Council and general meetings of the MDU make interesting reading: the story of Harness, the electropathic quack, and of Mr Valentine Simpson 'FRCS' who finally entered the workhouse at Doncaster as a tramp and on his death bed there confessed that his medical antecedents would not bear investigation; also 'Dr' Boy, the venereal quack of Marylebone Road (1890). Remarkable cases of impersonation occurred: a country GP, Dr R. H. Barber, was drowned while attempting to cross a river on horseback to reach a sick patient; a verdict of accidental drowning was made at the inquest but no official notice of the death was sent to the General Medical Council and so the entry in the register remained with the last notified address. In 1907, a letter was received by the registrar of the GMC purporting to be sent by Dr R. H. Barber, requesting that his address be changed to one in Liverpool. This new Dr Barber was Harry Virtue, an unqualified veterinary surgeon, who proceeded to do locum GP appointments throughout the country. The efforts of the MDU to track him down read like a detective novel: once, when nearing London, he escaped from the custody of the police and threw himself out of the train after a struggle, and when arrested again he pretended to be mad, was pronounced insane and certified in an asylum. The Secretary of the MDU was convinced that he was shamming and arranged for his mental condition to be tested by an expert; then he was discharged from the asylum. When brought to Bow Street Police Station later he refused to speak and shammed complete indifference to his surroundings. He was eventually found guilty of forgery and sentenced to nine months imprisonment. The case was unique in the annals of the GMC, and the MDU thanked the public prosecutor and other people such as the chief detective inspector who had dealt with the case [43].

Abuse of the title of Doctor has caused trouble over the century. The use of the prefix is not controlled in the UK by the Medical Act or by any other legislation. But the description MD is another matter: section 31 of the Medical Act, 1956, while not forbidding practice by the unqualified, was intended to enable the public to distinguish between qualified and unqualified practitioners; it prescribed penalties for the unlawful use of certain well-recognized titles including 'Doctor of Medicine' or any description implying that the user is registered under the Medical Act, but the word doctor is not so included. Hence a Doctor of Philosophy (PhD) is able to legally practise hypnotism and deal with medical problems.

In 1923, the solicitors of the MDU reported that since 1898 no less than 284 actions had been taken against unqualified practitioners, although tabulations in the annual reports then indicated that the MDU was dealing with fewer and fewer cases because the law was so vague and a conviction was seldom possible. So 'to suppress or prosecute unqualified practitioners' was omitted from the objects of the defence bodies. If notified about them, the matter would be put to the GMC; this happened about 1964 when a doctor, who was the self-appointed director of a Cancer Detection Centre, advertised and operated an electrical machine called a 'bioelectrometer' for diagnosing cancer. Not all charlatans are unqualified; Bernard Shaw observed this, when Sir Ralph Bloomfield Bonnington in *The Doctor's Dilemma* remarked 'I daresay I am a quack, a quack with a qualification'. Today, the public has channels such as their GP who advises qualified specialists through the NHS, whereas in 1885 there was no medical organization: the doctor or quack had to be paid a fee, and anyone could easily be misled. Now the incidence of medical treatment by the unqualified is increasing and sometimes it has been raised in status by the term 'alternative medicine'.

'Covering' was the term used when doctors employed unqualified assistants and the MDU took active measures to expose them. E. S. Turner in his book, *Call the Doctor* [44], writes

> In the last decade of the century the General Medical Council began to tackle a notable abuse: the employment by doctors of unqualified assistants. There were some ten thousands of them, ranging from striplings to old men. The stripling, as a rule, intended to go on to medical school; it was a side-door to medicine through which many doctors and surgeons passed. In theory the youngster, like the old-time apprentice, confined his activities to his master's premises, spending much of his time mixing routine medicines; but every now and then, in his master's absence, he would go out with a black bag and bring a baby into the world, a daunting assignment, it would now seem, for a youth in his middle teens. The best that could be said for such a practice was that it bred self-reliance in the assistant, even if it bred consternation in the patient . . . all through the 1890s coroners in industrial areas raised their voices against this unethical practice. So did county court judges, who struck out of doctors' bills those charges which represented the work of assistants. The whole system, they said, was a swindle on the poor; if a person paid for a doctor he was entitled to be treated by one.

ADVICE ABOUT ETHICAL MATTERS

The jibe that doctors create medical ethics to protect their own interests rather than those of the patients is surely unfair. For it has been accepted from time immemorial that practitioners of medicine could and should conform to a general code of behaviour which would ensure that the position of advantage held by the trained physician over the sick should not be abused [45]. In fact, medicine is the only branch of science which has had a unified ethic for thousands of years: from the Hippocratic oath and declaration of Geneva (see Appendices V and VI) to professional conduct and discipline issued by the

General Medical Council [46]. Professor Robert Saundby, a founder member of the MDU, aptly described the three principles which may be regarded as the corner stones of medical ethics.

> In the relation of a medical practitioner towards his colleagues, he should obey the golden rule, which teaches that, 'Whatsoever ye would that men should do to you, do ye even so to them' (St Matthew vii, 12); in his relations to his patients, their interests should be his highest consideration—'Aegroti salus suprema lex'; in his relation to the State, to the laws of his country, and his civic duties, there is no better guiding principle than the words of the Gospel, 'Render, therefore, unto Caesar the things that be Caesar's' (St Luke xx, 25); in other words, obey all lawful authority [14].

This makes somewhat turgid reading these days when neither the scriptures nor classical languages are commonly taught. If the English translation does not come instantly to mind for the reader, the Latin means 'the welfare of the sick is the supreme law'.

The subject of ethics, described as the collective conscience of the profession, is an even greater problem today with the advances of medicine, and there is no ethical check-list—nor easy solutions to the moral dilemmas facing doctors. Ethical anxiety is one of the commonest causes of members consulting the defence bodies who are often able, from their experience, to obviate an attendance before the General Medical or Dental Council. Matters range from sending articles to be read before being submitted to medical journals to avoid the risk of libel, to ethical issues in prenatal diagnosis, to doctors holding shares in drug companies, to submitting letters for vetting where there may be an element of advertising, and to new issues concerning artificial reproduction.

Advertising. Hundreds of members write or telephone each year seeking advice on their professional position regarding advertising. Their attention is drawn to guidance given by the General Medical and Dental Councils and the Central Ethical Committee of the BMA and the British Dental Association. If this is followed to the letter, problems do not arise but it is always easy to be wise after the event. In 1978 two experienced consultants were called to account by the GMC after a television broadcast in one case and a newspaper interview in the other. In neither was there a public hearing because explanations advanced on behalf of the doctors by the MDU were accepted by the Penal Cases Committee. Both doctors experienced considerable anxiety and the annual report stated 'it is hoped other members will spare themselves by looking before they leap' [47].

Methods of medical advertising are diverse and sometimes are founded on those pioneered by Robert Sawyer, Esquire (formerly of Guy's Hospital in the

Borough) as described by Charles Dickens in *The Pickwick Papers.* When he qualified, he settled as a GP in Bristol. He put up a splendid name-plate with the words 'Sawyer, late Nockemorf' which caught the eye of passers-by; he put on a black suit of clothes and pair of spectacles, and hired a boy to take impressive bottles of medicine to important houses in the area—the label with his name would be read and returned to his surgery believing it to have been delivered to the wrong address by mistake. He also arranged to be paged when in church so that the whole congregation would remember his name when he rushed off to see the mythical urgent case. Canvassing for patients remains an occasional problem, although more so for doctors coming to the UK from other countries where the customs and ethics of practice may be different.

The code concerning advertising was strict at the start of the century and Saundby wrote in *Medical Ethics* in 1902 that 'the only advertisement to the public now permissible is the door-plate which should be of modest size, and should preferably contain nothing but the practitioner's name, though it is not uncommon to see the words "physician and surgeon" on it' [14]. The Dentists' Register in 1985 also gave advice about lettering and stated 'neither the plate itself nor the lettering should be unnecessarily large or brightly coloured'. The position of doctors advertising today is complex and unclear. It is a far cry from 1906 when Sir William Osler, a founder of modern clinical medicine, wrote:

> In the life of every successful physician there comes the temptation to toy with the Delilah of the press—daily and otherwise. There are times when she may be courted with satisfaction but beware! Sooner or later she is sure to play the harlot and has left many a man shorn of his strength, viz, the confidence of his professional brethren [48].

Now there is radio, television and video tape; all may produce problems for the doctor. Dr Michael O'Donnell described the remarkable situation which has developed in the USA: the medical public relations business which doctors can contact so that they are promoted in newspapers, magazines, or television comments—and apparently some doctors retain press agents. 'In general,' he writes, 'doctors' official attitude to personal publicity is much the same there as it is here and at the moment we seem to tolerate it so long as it is subtle—Americans might say inefficient' [49]. But few would wish this situation to develop here and anonymity of doctors was called for at the annual representatives meeting of the BMA in 1984. A certain amount of hypocrisy enshrouds self-publicity, and it can be irritating yet no-one does anything about it or complains to the GMC; perhaps this is because of the method of complaining, for the identity of the person must be known to the victim and, as both may often work in the same specialty or area, or be in financial rivalry, the person does not want to be seen to be complaining. Unfortunately, there is a tendency to announce new discoveries directly to the public before their assessment in scientific journals so that 'celebrities' are then created by the news media.

The remarkable growth of enquiries, tribunals and appeals has greatly altered and increased the work of the defence bodies; these include hospital and other enquiries, industrial tribunals and disciplinary committees. The considerable experience of the defence bodies assists doctors and dentists who face these worrying and time-consuming procedures. Members' cases are prepared, solicitors are briefed if necessary, and someone from the defence body will attend the committee. Support is given for those who have to appear before the General Medical or General Dental Council if accused of the following: disregard of personal responsibilities to patients, breach of professional confidence, personal relationships of any emotional or sexual nature with a patient, and alleged advertising or canvassing.

All through the annual reports, certainly from 1887 to 1948, there are repeated examples of disputes between doctors which went to arbitration and commonly concerned partnership agreements and restraints on practice if an assistant to a GP set up another practice within too close a radius of his principal's practice; the object of arbitration then was to avoid publicity. This sort of dispute has become less common since boundaries were defined after the setting up of the National Health Service in 1948.

Supersession can cause friction between doctors. The word means 'the act of treating a patient who is already under the care of another doctor'; it was clearly a common problem at the beginning of the century since Saundby spent some time lecturing on it to medical students: for example the importance of the patient going through the GP to a consultant and bringing a letter of introduction giving details of the case together with the GP's diagnosis and treatment so that 'the consultant may not unwittingly raise doubts in the patient's mind as to the propriety of any of these. The consultant should in turn write to the practitioner, giving his opinion of the case, and describing the treatment and regimen he recommends, and enclose the prescription. It is usual to hand this letter to the patient.' The importance of the consultant not intruding on the work of the GP was emphasized. The last such case in the reports was in 1977 from South Africa when a member was represented by the MDU's legal advisers: a complaint was made to the Medical Council that a works' doctor had accused him of supersession because he had treated an industrial finger injury sustained by a man who lived near his surgery; the patient had first been seen by the works' doctor but as the factory was fifteen miles from his home, the man preferred to attend the member [50].

Professional disloyalty, when a doctor criticizes a colleague in front of the patient, may start an entirely unjustified complaint by the patient.

The matter of disputed accounts repeatedly came before the Council although the fact that 'it was no business of the MDU to act as a debt collecting agency' was stated in 1920—unless payment of accounts was refused on the ground of improper or negligent treatment when the member would be supported to achieve full payment. The counterclaim for negligence was a common sequel to a summons for refusal to pay fees and occasionally still is—both for doctors and dentists. Generally financial problems disappeared within five or six years after the introduction of the National Health Service although they no doubt still concern those in private practice. These problems have, however, been replaced by others, like disputes with the NHS as paymaster.

> *The Medical Defence Union has two functions equally important: one is to protect the doctor, the other to compensate the patient.*
>
> **Dr S. Cochrane Shanks, former President**

MEDICO-SOCIAL MATTERS

Acts of Parliament and legislation have always provided hurdles for doctors who are more concerned with clinical matters. The Health Insurance Act of 1912 was, in the words of the historian G. M. Trevelyan in 1947, 'a contribution scheme to ensure the whole working population against sickness, which has since proved a blessing to the working-classes, and no ill friend to doctors, who at first looked at it with natural misgivings, sharpened by political prejudice' [51]. The BMA then drew up a list of demands that included: free choice of doctor by the patient; doctors to be answerable, not to friendly societies, but to insurance committees on which the profession was represented; an income limit of two pounds per insured person, and a capitation fee of eight shillings and sixpence exclusive of drugs. Led by Sir Victor Horsley, the BMA generally achieved these concessions.

The advent of the National Health Service in 1948, which resulted in a reasonable degree of equality of medicine throughout the UK, caused similar fears and initial hostility like those before 1912; many concessions for doctors were again achieved and fears later seemed to be unfounded. It did, however, result in a considerable section of the profession being brought, for the first time, into contact with rules and regulations of which they had little or no previous knowledge and indeed, in the first year, 382 doctors appeared before medical service committees: 13 were removed from the service, 110 fined, 69 warned, but against 190 no action was taken. E. S. Turner in reporting this wrote 'whatever they thought about the workings of the disciplinary committees, doctors could not complain that their lapses were blazened to the world. It has been a matter for comment that doctors guilty of the most startling indiscretions and derelictions have had their identities concealed as 'Dr A' and 'Dr X' [44].

The defence bodies played an active role in guiding doctors about the interpretation and observation of regulations in the NHS, as happened with the National Insurance Act of 1912. Regarding medico-legal cases, an agreement relating to the hospital service between the Department of Health and the defence bodies ensured that, irrespective of which party might be cited, proportionate liability would reflect the degree of involvement of each party in those aspects of the care of the patient relevant to the case; but if a patient by his own negligence increased the harm he suffered, then the court would deduct from the damages appropriate to full liability a proportion consistent with the harm resulting from the plaintiff's own negligence.

Evidence has, over the years, been given to government departments and to commissions. Negotiation has also taken place, for example, to support a doctor's prescription of a substance which he considers a drug although it has been labelled as a food. Liaison has also taken place with other bodies in producing reports. The MDU has played a role in the interpretation of the law, for example by taking counsel's opinion on the legality of sterilization and by issuing a memorandum concerning the Abortion Act of 1967 [52]. In 1967 a book called *Sans Everything—A Case to Answer* appeared (see Chapter 11) which contained serious allegations against unnamed hospitals and unnamed members of their staffs [53]. This caused a sensation and various committees were set up by the government to make findings and recommendations for the care of the elderly in certain hospitals (HMSO, 1968). The effect of this illustrated the wider activities of the defence bodies, for the various enquiries that this book initiated involved enormous time, labour and costs, both legal and otherwise—as well as the work connected with supporting the doctors against libel.

DEXTRA DARE

'Dextra dare' was the motto coined by the MDU in its early days when Latin was fashionable. Now the consensus of opinion is that it was designed to mean 'the need to give rightly—neither too much nor too little; the concept of fairness'. And no doubt all defence bodies have aimed to achieve this. A

generous approach is illustrated by the following tragic case when a doctor
died in distressing circumstances and his widow was assisted:

> A farmer in 1958 decided that his well should be cleaned and a firm
> of builders was employed to do this. The well had to be emptied and
> the builders decided to use a petrol-driven pump which caused such
> exhaust fumes that the workmen had to come back to the surface.
> Next day a workman went down to restart the engine but collapsed,
> and one of the other workmen who went to assist his companion
> was also overcome by fumes. The first of the rescuers to arrive on
> the scene was the GP who felt in honour bound to do whatever he
> could for the two men collapsed at the bottom of the well. After
> tying a rope around his waist he told some women onlookers that
> he would let them know when he should be hauled to the surface.
> When he found that both men were dead and that nothing could be
> done for them he shouted and asked the women to haul him up. By
> this time a man had arrived and he and the women began to pull on
> the rope. Unfortunately the rope became entangled around the solid
> metal pipe that ran down the inside of the well and it was impossible
> to pull the doctor to the surface. The police and fire brigade were
> summoned and eventually brought him to the surface, but he was
> unconscious and died in the ambulance on the way to the hospital.
> He left a widow and two small children; she sought assistance from
> the MDU and a claim was instituted on her behalf against the firm
> that had undertaken the job of cleaning out the well. The firm's
> insurance company repudiated liability and the matter was made
> the subject of a court action. Judgement for a substantial sum was
> awarded in favour of the widow and children; the insurance com-
> pany appealed to the Court of Appeal but there too the widow and
> the children were successful.

A later example was that of a young woman doctor doing a locum resident job
in paediatrics: when on duty, she received an urgent call from another hospital
without appropriate specialist facilities to accept a new-born infant who
needed urgent surgery. She travelled in the back of an ambulance with a police
escort at high speed but the ambulance collided with a car so that she was
thrown forward and dislocated her right patella; she reduced this herself,
continued the journey in another ambulance so that the baby was safely
transferred to her hospital and treated successfully. The next day blood was
aspirated from her knee joint and the leg was put in plaster for six weeks. At
first she was given the impression by the hospital administrators that their

solicitors would make the appropriate claim but a year later these solicitors advised her that she would not succeed in any action against the ambulance authority or driver of the other vehicle and they sent her a bill for £54; the MDU at once settled this and instructed their own solicitors to pursue the claim. An orthopaedic surgeon who assessed her injury expressed the opinion that there could be further trouble in the knee joint, possibly osteoarthritis. Writs were issued against the ambulance authority and both drivers, and two years later the MDU's solicitors were able to report that the claim had been settled by the defendants; in 1974 costs were recovered and the member received £2,250 damages [54]. No doubt the other defence bodies could provide similar examples of cases in which rules were stretched on behalf of members.

BIZARRE REQUESTS

Bizarre requests have occurred throughout the century. An entry in the 1891 report ran 'amongst varied problems about which members have been advised was the taxability of a non-resident pageboy'. In the early 1920s, members of both the MDU and MPS were approached by water companies and asked to pay an increased water rate in line with industrial water users, the water used for dispensing being considered business usage. Water formed the basis of most medicines in those days, nearly all of which were placebos; but the bottle of medicine—coloured and flavoured or foul tasting—often had a beneficial effect, due to faith or suggestion. Incidentally, the bottle of medicine was far cheaper than the expensive tablets used as placebos today. This water problem recurred but members were always defended successfully.

Doctors, like ordinary citizens, are accused of drunken driving or tax evasion but these, and such matters dealt with in the criminal rather than civil courts, are not considered by the defence bodies: in 1964, the MDU was even approached by a member who had been out in his car for a birthday celebration and asked for help with three summonses—two were for speeding and one was for poaching!

It is also said that a candidate who had failed his examination once asked for help to bring an action against his examiners; if he really thought that this was a function of the MDU, it was not surprising that he failed.

References

1 Shaw B. *The Doctor's Dilemma*. Middlesex, England: Penguin Books, 1975. p. 115.
2 Bond F.J. The Medical Defence Union (letter) *British Medical Journal* Nov 7: (1885) 895–6.
3 Rideal C.F. The Medical Defence Union (letter). *British Medical Journal* Nov 14: (1885) 936.

4 Brown G. The Medical Defence Union (letter) *British Medical Journal* Nov 7: (1885) 896.
5 Rideal C.F. The Medical Defence Union (letter). *British Medical Journal* Dec 15: (1885) 1085–6.
6 Proposed Medical Defence Union (Leader) *British Medical Journal* May 15: (1886) 943–4.
7 The Medical Defence Union. *British Medical Journal* Dec 3: (1887) 1227.
8 McKay W.J.S. *Lawson Tait: His Life and Work.* London: Bailliere Tindall & Cox, 1922.
9 Flack I.H. *Lawson Tait: 1845–1899.* London: Heinemann, 1949.
10 Shepherd J.A. *Lawson Tait 1845–1899: The Rebellious Surgeon.* Kansas: Coronado Press, 1980.
11 Tait L. *General Summary of Conclusions from One Thousand Cases of Abdominal Section.* Birmingham, England: R. Birbeck, 1884.
12 Clapesattle H. *Doctors Mayo.* Minneapolis: The University of Minnesota Press, 1941.
13 Forbes R. *Sixty Years of Medical Defence.* London: Medical Defence Union, 1948.
14 Saundby R. *Medical Ethics.* London: Charles Griffin, 1902.
15 *Denholm v. Lawson Tait. British Medical Journal.* 1 (1892): 739.
16 Reynolds E.S., Wild R.B. & Annacker E. *Denholm v. Tait* (letter). *British Medical Journal* 1 (1892): 787–8.
17 Brockbank E.M. (1947) quoted by Flack I.H. in *Lawson Tait,* 1949. p. 65.
18 Paget S. *Sir Victor Horsley.* London: Constable and Company Ltd, 1919.
19 Woods H. The Medical Defence Union (letter) *British Medical Journal* 1 (1892): 93–4.
20 Editorial. *Lancet* July 25 (1896): 251.
21 Obituary. Sir Jonathan Hutchinson. *Lancet.* 1 (1913): 1832–5.
22 Resolution adopted by the East Anglian branch of the BMA. *British Medical Journal* 1 (1886): 323.
23 The question of medical defence (annotation). *Lancet.* April 4 (1896): 937.
24 Proposed professional indemnity insurance scheme for BMA members. Statement by BMA. *British Medical Journal* 1 (1977): 1297–9.
25 Proposed professional indemnity insurance scheme for BMA members. Statements by MDU, MPS and MDDUS. *Ibid.* 1: 1300.
26 Medical defence (editorial) *Ibid.* 1: 1615–6.
27 British Medical Association. Annual Report of Council 1976–7. *Ibid.* 1: 1093(10.4).
28 *Annual Report.* London: Medical Protection Society, 1924.
29 Jandoo R. Medical indemnity. *British Medical Journal* 11 (1984): 1984.
30 Harland W.A. & Jandoo, R.S. The medical negligence crisis. *Medical Science and Law.* 24 (1984): 123–9.
31 *The Medical Defence Union Limited* v. *The Department of Trade. All England Law Reports* 2 (1979): 421–432.
32 MDU wins test case (annotation). *British Medical Journal* 1 (1979): 68.
33 Reed E.A. Professional indemnity (letter). *British Medical Journal* 2 (1977): 185–6.
34 *Annual Report.* London: Medical Defence Union, 1894. p. 9–19.
35 *Ibid.* 1904.
36 *Ibid.* 1948, 17–18.
37 *Hatcher v. Black. Current Law Year Book,* 1954. p. 2289.
38 *Hatcher v. Black. British Medical Journal* ii (1954): 106.
39 Stocker W.W. A trumpery action for malpraxi, the value of a defence association (letter). *Lancet* 2 (1899): 52.
40 *Annual Report.* London: Medical Defence Union, 1910.
41 Kidd Cameron. Unfounded charges of professional misconduct: an appreciation of the Medical Defence Union (letter). *Lancet* 2 (1899): 430.
42 *Regina v. Priestley. Times* May 28 (1896) 9.
43 *Annual Report.* London: Medical Defence Union, 1912.
44 Turner E.S. *Call the Doctor: A Social History of Medical Men.* London: Michael Joseph, 1958.
45 Hadfield S.J. *Law and Ethics for Doctors.* London: Eyre & Spottiswoode, 1958.
46 *Professional Conduct and Discipline: Fitness to Practice.* General Medical Council, 1985.
47 *Annual Report.* London Medical Defence Union, 1979. p. 11.

48 Osler W. *Internal Medicine as a Vocation in Aequanimitas, with other Addresses to Medical Students, Nurses and Practitioners of Medicine*. London: H. K. Lewis, 1906, p. 144.
49 O'Donnell M. One man's burden. *British Medical Journal* 287 (1983): 1889.
50 *Annual Report*. London: Medical Defence Union, 1977, p. 46.
51 Trevelyan G.M. *History of England*. London: Longman, Green & Co, 1947.
52 The Abortion Act 1967—memorandum from the Medical Defence Union. *British Medical Journal* 1 (1968): 759–62.
53 Robb B. *Sans Everything—A Case to Answer*. Presented on behalf of AEGIS. London: Nelson, 1967.
54 *Annual Report*. London: Medical Defence Union, 1975, p. 18.

3

Protection, advice and education

'The Medical Defence Union is a shield but the arbiter is the law.'
ANON.

A medical defence body acts as a buffer between the doctor and the law, providing advice and handling all matters which might lead to a claim. The work includes interviewing members, dealing with letters and telephone calls, obtaining experts' reports, arranging and attending interviews with the solicitors, joining conferences with counsel and attending courts. Just as advice is given by a doctor specializing in medico-legal matters, the solicitors employed devote their time predominantly to medical and dental problems.

How legal proceedings are conducted on behalf of members

THE COMPLAINTS PROCEDURE

Any request is immediately referred to a member of the secretariat: a doctor or dentist, but not to a lawyer as in the USA. The problem may need the immediate attention of a lawyer if a member has been served with a writ or is likely to be served, and when a court case has already been instituted, but 99 per cent continue to be dealt with by a member of the secretariat—in either case it will be referred to a medical or dental committee for a decision to settle or defend. All three defence bodies are controlled by a council, whereas day-to-day matters are in the hands of the professional secretariat. Appointments to the staff are not made solely on the basis of specialist knowledge, for adaptability and a capacity to keep abreast of developments throughout medicine and dentistry are considered most important. The full Council meets monthly throughout the year and considers major claims and important matters of policy. For a major claim, the Council may have before it a number of specialists' reports prepared by both Council members and outside experts. In a typical quarter during 1983 there were no fewer than 118 expert reports commissioned by the secretariat, and, in addition, a substantial number were commissioned by the solicitors. Various committees of the Council meet during the month to consider other cases presented by the solicitors or members of the secretariat.

Some cases dealt with throughout the century

Negligence cases were scarce in the early years of the MDU as many complaints were withdrawn immediately following a letter from the defence body; but the case histories that follow are of particular interest for the principles they raise.

> *Wrong diagnosis.* In 1894 a claim for damages was made in the county court by a patient for alleged negligence, as his doctor had certified that he was suffering from scarlet fever 'when such was not the case'. The Council of the MDU directed the defence of this member, and Mr Horace Brown, Barrister, instructed by Mr Hempson, acting as solicitor for the Union, appeared on his behalf. 'After an attempt was made by the solicitor appearing for the plaintiff to gain suffrages of the jury by stating that his client was fighting a rich association of 25,000 members, and putting the plaintiff in the box, the case utterly collapsed; and the judge, after stating that in his opinion no negligence had been proved, and the jury agreeing, nonsuited the plaintiff with costs against him' [1]. Costs could not be recovered because the plaintiff was practically penniless.

> *Alleged wrongful certification of lunatic. Harnett v. Bond and Adams* (1924) [2]. A medical owner of a private asylum in 1912 allowed a patient out on leave of absence; the order for leave reserved power to the doctor to recover the patient should his medical condition require it. Within two days the doctor was informed over the telephone by one of the Commissioners in Lunacy that the patient was at the office and in the Commissioner's opinion was not fit to be at large. So the doctor sent the car with two attendants to retake the patient and bring him back to the asylum. He was then examined by the doctor who considered that he should be detained and about two months later he was taken to another institution.
> Nothing further was heard of the matter until 1922 when a writ was issued by the patient against the doctor and the Commissioner, claiming damages; the doctors were accused of conspiracy, assault and false imprisonment. It was alleged that the doctor had no power to retake the patient during the leave of absence and that, even if he had, he should not have exercised it without going to see the patient

59

himself and forming his own opinion before retaking him, and that 'acting as he did on the telephone information he had acted negligently and without reasonable and proper care and that because of this he was liable in damages not only for the actual retaking but for the whole subsequent period of the patient's detention, which in this case was between eight and nine years'.

Dr Bond was represented throughout his tribulations and supported by the Commissioners of Lunacy, and Dr Adams was a member of the MPS. This trial, which lasted twelve days on the first occasion, is described in detail by Sir Patrick Hastings, Attorney General. Mr Harnett, a well-to-do Kentish farmer, 'conducted his own defence and for hours cross-examined witnesses for the prosecution and conducted legal arguments in a matter so reasoned and restrained that he satisfied every person in the court that he was as sane as they were; and then suddenly a point arose of no significance which seemed to incense him without reason. He burst into a tirade of abuse, particularly against the Royal Family, so violent and absurd that within two minutes the same people were satisfied beyond all question not only that he was mad, but probably a homicidal maniac—without that outburst the jury could quite possibly have been induced to make a grave mistake'.

Yet the trial in the King's Bench Division, which had lasted eighteen days, resulted in a verdict against the member and his co-defendant with an award in damages of £25,000. This startled the medical profession and caused a rapid increase in membership of both defence bodies. However, when the appeal, which lasted five days, came up later, the judgement was reversed and given in favour of the doctor. This result was also upheld in a decision by the House of Lords. The publicity of the trial stimulated other cases for wrongful certification.

Practice boundary dispute. Routh and Wilson v. Jones (1946) [3]. This case was important because both doctors, Routh and Wilson, were members of the MDU. It concerned the problem of an assistantship agreement which prohibited a former assistant from setting up in practice in the immediate vicinity of his former principal's practice. At that time the case raised an issue of such importance to every general practitioner that the MDU collaborated with the BMA in paying the costs of both parties to enable the matter to be taken to the Court of Appeal. The ruling upset many pre-existing ideas by stating that it was not possible in law to restrain altogether an assistant from competing with his former principal to obtain patients. As a result of this decision it became necessary to formulate a new clause which could be safely used in assistantship agreements to prevent practice within a reasonable radius or from attending any of the principal's patients even outside that radius.

However, in recent years, the MDU seldom had the problem of restrictive covenants and other partnership disputes on its hands. Since the advent of the National Health Service, practice areas have been outlined by Executive Councils (later the Family Practioner Committees) often with the support of the Medical Practices Committees; gradually practice areas and the position of surgery premises, including branch surgeries, have been clarified by the NHS authorities.

> *Alleged assault by senior surgeon because house surgeon operated for him. Michael v. Molesworth* (1950) [4]. A senior surgeon at the Royal Victoria Hospital, Folkestone, advised a man—an antique dealer—to have an operation for a hernia and he was admitted to the public ward. The senior surgeon could not attend the hospital on the day fixed for the operation and he asked the house surgeon to operate. The patient brought an action against the senior surgeon asserting that the house surgeon had operated without leave or licence. Although the operation was successful, the patient won his case and was awarded nominal damages of £1 against the senior surgeon.

This case resulted in an extra clause being put in the consent form to state that no assurance could be given that the operation would be performed by a particular surgeon (deleted for a private patient who expects his surgeon to operate); in practice, the surgeon whom the patient sees in a hospital out-patient department will usually be the person who operates but the clause is necessary in order to protect an alternative surgeon who performs the operation. In the NHS a patient is entitled to choose his own general practitioner but not to choose his surgeon; he may, however, select the hospital which he attends for treatment.

The following account of a doctor accused of murder is the most important criminal trial ever undertaken by the MDU and was full of drama. Apart from the legal literature, the journalist Sybille Bedford published a book *The Best We Can Do* shortly after the trial. Another publication was *Two Men Were Acquitted* by Percy Hoskins (1984) who was crime reporter of the *Daily Express*, closely associated with the case, and convinced from the start of the defendant's innocence—in contrast to accusations of guilt from the rest of the Press. But of particular interest is the book *Easing the Passing* by Lord Devlin (1984) as this is the first full-length account by a judge of a trial over which he presided.

A Doctor Accused of Murder. Regina v. Bodkin Adams (1957) [5]. Dr John Bodkin Adams was a respectable general practitioner in the fashionable town of Eastbourne where many wealthy people retired. He was a caring doctor, a good clinician and active in the local BMA, but he received remarkable legacies and gifts (e.g. a Rolls Royce car) from his elderly patients who died. This caused much rumour and gossip and resulted in a press campaign which came near to prejudicing his trial; this was precipitated in July 1956 when a Mrs Gertrude Hullett died from an alleged overdose of barbiturate drugs prescribed by him. At the inquest evidence was given that shortly before her death Mrs Hullett had made out a cheque for £1,000 in Dr Adams' favour. Although the coroner returned a verdict of suicide, 'tongues began to wag' and as a result Superintendent H. Hannan of Scotland Yard was sent to Eastbourne to investigate the rumours. After four months, he had collected sufficient evidence to charge Dr Adams with falsification of certain cremation certificates and offences under the Dangerous Drugs Act. Further investigations revealed that in November 1950 a Mrs Edith Morrell, an 81-year-old widow, had died and that during the last few days of her life approximately 40 gr. (grains) (2·6 g) of heroin and 40 gr. (2·6 g) of morphine had been prescribed for her by Dr Adams.

The Attorney General, Sir Reginald Manningham-Buller QC, MP, Mr Melford Stevenson QC, and Mr Malcolm Morris, instructed by the Director of Public Prosecutions, appeared on behalf of the Crown. Mr Geoffrey Lawrence QC and Mr Edward Clarke and Mr John Heritage, instructed by Messrs Hempsons, the solicitors of the MDU, appeared on behalf of the accused. In opening the case for the prosecution the Attorney General said, 'this is a very unusual case. It is not often that a charge of murder is brought against a doctor . . . Mrs Morrell was an old woman . . . a widow, a wealthy widow . . . she left £157,000'. He submitted that Dr Adams had killed Mrs Morrell by administering drugs and that these were given to her with the intention of killing. She had previously suffered a stroke which left her paralysed. One of the many problems was whether it was reasonable to give these drugs to a patient after a stroke to calm an anxious agitated and disturbed mental state; another was whether the dosage was therapeutic or intended to kill.

The most incriminating evidence was given by nurses who looked after the patient and who stated what they remembered about Dr Adams' instructions. Dr Adams had retained several books of nursing records after Mrs Morrell's death but did not know where they were. Remarkably, the solicitors apparently searched his house and found them at the back of a drawer. This provided a dramatic moment for Geoffrey Lawrence when, apparently without the slightest change in his voice, he said to Nurse Stronach: 'I want you to have a look at that book please'. He glanced at one of the solicitors who began to open the envelope and produce an insignificant-looking notebook which was handed to the nurse in the witness box. The notebooks, believed long since lost, contained the nurses' day-to-day and, indeed, hour-to-hour record of the treatment of their elderly woman patient; all the visits from Dr Adams; all the details of her condition and behaviour; and these notebooks showed that the nurse's recollected evidence bore little or no resemblance at all to what she and her colleagues had noted at the time.

Various expert witnesses were called and the chief medical witness for the Crown was Dr A. H. Douthwaite, Senior Consultant Physician at Guy's Hospital and editor of a book on therapeutics. He was dogmatic in his assertion that morphine and heroin were never indicated for any patient after a stroke and that the amounts prescribed were sufficient to cause death—in other words that Dr Adams was guilty of murder. Cross-examination by Mr Lawrence revealed that Mrs Morrell had first been treated at a cottage hospital in Cheshire by two doctors, one of whom was a consultant, and that during the last eight days of her stay she had been given a nightly injection of morphine to overcome her distress and complaints of pain; her agitation and distress had been great and numerous other sedatives had been tried before the resort to morphine. Dr Douthwaite also raised the question of addiction but withdrew this later as being irrelevant in a crippled invalid of eighty years.

On the thirteenth day of the trial Mr Lawrence, opening the defence, said: 'My first witness will be Dr John Bishop Harman MD FRCP FRCS, and I think I should tell your lordship that the defence has decided in the circumstances of the case not to call the accused'. The decision not to call the accused created a great commotion and reporters rushed out to telephone their respective newspapers; for it had been generally believed that the Attorney General would cross-examine the accused at length and would hint obliquely at all the evil rumours that had been going on—and the Press, of course, had been looking forward to this. Dr Harman, a distinguished physician and an authority on drugs, was not prepared to condemn the use of morphine if the patient was suffering from pain and was restless and he could not agree that she had died a 'morphine death' where coma and respiratory paralysis are typical. He saw no necessity to link the patient's death with the dose of morphine and heroin although a link was possible; there was no reason why heroin should not be given to elderly people and nothing astonishing in the direction to the nurses to give morphine and heroin when necess-ary—he frequently did it himself, leaving it to the nurses' discretion. After he had dealt with numerous other questions put to him by Mr Lawrence, the judge asked Dr Harman some questions about the instructions that the patient should be 'kept under'; he replied that during the last few days of her life she would have remained excited, distressed and uncontrollable if she had not been kept under the influence of drugs.

In summing up the judge told the jury that Counsel for the defence had said that the treatment given was designed to promote comfort and if it was the right and proper treatment the fact that it shortened life did not convict him of murder. And, amongst many other points, he referred to the evidence of the doctors by stating that 'men of science cannot always give precise, clear and unquali-fied answers, particularly if they are dealing with an illness which occurred years ago at which they were not present. Dr Douthwaite's evidence was quite clear and uncompromising—he regarded the dose of drugs as causing the death . . . what Dr Harman said in effect was that when you get an old lady of over eighty and one who is suffering from cerebral thrombosis she may die of anything at any time and no one can say beyond reasonable doubt what it was that she actually died of'. The jury reached their verdict of 'not guilty' in forty-four minutes on the seventeenth day of the longest murder trial recorded in Britain up to that time.

An aftermath was that in July 1957 fines totalling £2,400 and the costs of the prosecution were imposed on Dr Adams at Lewes Assizes: he pleaded guilty to fourteen of sixteen charges of alleged offences under the Forgery, Larceny, Cremation and Dangerous Drugs Acts. The charges involved NHS prescriptions, making false statements on cremation certificates, failing to keep a register of dangerous drugs, obstructing a police officer and attempting to conceal two phials of morphine. In the November he appeared before the General Medical Council and was erased from the register, his name only being restored in 1960.

Doctors who are accused of criminal charges are not normally supported by the defence bodies as this would be a misuse of members' subscriptions. However there are no clauses in small print (as may occur with insurance policies) and each case is decided on its merits. Here, when the Council of the MDU considered Dr Adams' request for assistance in respect of the murder charge, some members of the Council were opposed to affording him assistance. Other members felt that it was only proper that he should be assisted because the charge arose out of his treatment of a patient. The legal costs amounted to £23,000 and Dr Adams subsequently made a generous present to the MDU. After his acquittal, a handful of members wrote and expressed their dissatisfaction at the decision to assist him and four resigned because of this. The case also refutes an accusation that there is difficulty in obtaining expert medical witnesses to act for the prosecution against a doctor: Dr Douthwaite, a vice-president of the MDU, did so and Dr Harman (later the President of the MDU) testified for the defence.

> *Dentist's libel action against the BMA. Drummond-Jackson v. British Medical Association (as publishers of the British Medical Journal) and others* [6]. In 1968 four members of the Department of Anaesthetics of Birmingham University and a dental surgeon carried out a detailed investigation of the physiological responses of thirty patients to intermittent methohexitone as an anaesthetic for conservative dentistry. Their results were published in the *British Medical Journal.* Shortly afterwards a dental surgeon with wide experience of this drug alleged that the article was gravely defamatory of him and he started proceedings for libel. The defendants contended that the article was true in substance and, in fact, that it had been their duty to publish their findings and in so doing they were protected by qualified privilege and that the conclusions drawn constituted fair comment on a matter of public interest.
>
> The plaintiff countered the claim of privilege by alleging that the writers had been actuated by malice towards him and he alleged dishonesty on their part. An expert witness called by him testified that the writers had carried out a dishonest investigation designed to discredit the plaintiff and the technique which he had practised and advocated. The trial before a jury started in June 1972 and, when discontinued in October, the plaintiff's case had not been completed although he had called nine witnesses and a vast quantity of

documents had been produced; it was then expected to last another three months by which time the financial burden upon all the parties would have been enormous. So, on the thirty-eighth day of the trial—after pointed advice by the judge—the plaintiff disconti- nued his action. The terms were that the parties should bear their own costs and that a statement as follows should be made: 'The defendants all recognise and acknowledge that the plaintiff is a man of the highest integrity and skill and of outstanding ability as a dentist. The plaintiff, for his part, withdraws any allegation against the defendants or any of them of dishonesty or impropriety. Further, he recognises and acknowledges that the *British Medical Journal* has a right and duty to its members and to the medical profession generally to print articles such as that submitted to them by the individual defendants and to comment on them.'

Afterwards, an editorial in the *British Medical Journal* entitled 'Freedom of the Medical Press' stated:

One of the features common to all professions is the search for truth, which is as inherent in the doctor/patient relationship as in the confrontation between advocate and witness in cross-examinations . . . an argument among fellow workers is the fermentation that leads to truth, and truly effective argument needs communication which should be fettered only by the demands of good faith. Editors of scientific and medical journals must hold the ring. In so doing they must test articles by criteria of originality, scientific reliability, and professional ethics. They submit them to scrutiny by experts on whose integrity they rely. Before publication they negotiate with authors over important changes needed, and after publication allow free argument in the journal's correspondence columns.

All this is a heavy burden but the traditionally good tempered hurly-burly of medical and scientific argument testifies that this approach does result in freedom and responsibility. Fortunately, it is rare for anyone to challenge it—and certainly in a court of law. Although the libel case did not come up for judgement, it is to be hoped that the result will remind those contemplating such an action of Milton's argument against censorship, written over 300 years ago: 'where there is much desire to learn, there of necessity will be much arguing, much writing, many opinions; for opinion in good men is but knowledge in the making' [7].

This case, a long and most expensive medico-legal libel case, illustrated the incongruous situation of a scientific argument being fought out in a court of law instead of through the correspondence columns of a medical journal. A possible factor, and one that may arise in the future, is the ease with which doctors present their results to newspapers, the radio or television even before the medical world has had a chance to read them in a journal. This converts the matter into a public issue at the start.

HOW A MODERN DEFENCE BODY FUNCTIONS

The functions of the defence bodies have evolved over the century to fit the needs of doctors and dentists as the medical and social scenes have changed, and so their organizations have increased in size and complexity. Details of the staffing of the defence bodies, including that of the solicitors, are given in each annual report together with the account of the Annual General Meeting of that year.

The number of vice-presidents arose in 1890 when, by a resolution of the Council, the President and honorary secretaries of all branches throughout the UK were made ex-officio vice-presidents; since 1893 the MDU has been

FIGURE 10. The computer. Terminals are fed into it from the information room and from the offices of various members of the secretariat.

centralized in London but an office was opened in Manchester in 1970 and one in Sydney, Australia, in 1979.

Matters today are fed into a computer (Figure 10)—a far cry from the days when the honorary secretary of the MDU had to write the minutes of meetings and requested a typewriter—and this will enable statistical and other information to be passed on to members. Both information and membership data are recorded. The former retains the following details: the 120 Acts of Parliament in the UK which may concern members, and details of all problems and cases as well as advice requested by doctors and how all these were dealt with. (The thesaurus of the computer lists 15,000 words structured to allow searches for cases of a similar nature.) Membership data provides immediate information about members: payment, whether by direct debit, standing order or instalments; special group schemes; changes in type of membership, erased, deceased, retired, etc.; and facts about those who may be in or out of membership such as women doctors or dentists with children and those on the

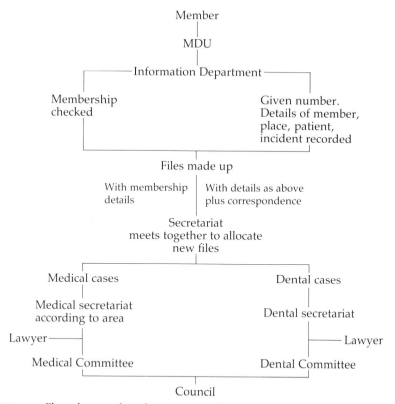

FIGURE 11. Flow chart to show how a request from a member is dealt with by the Medical Defence Union.

Protection, advice and education

TABLE I. A selection of requests received by the MDU during one week in 1983 illustrates the great variety of subjects with which it has to deal.

Responsibility of member for pregnant woman who insists on having her baby at home against member's advice.

Press report on House of Lords ruling that local councillors should have access to confidential files in adoption cases.

MDU cover for member going abroad with choir.

Consent: gastric lavage following overdose.

Delay in diagnosis of hepatitis—death.

Death following operation to separate adhesions.

Damage to ear following syringing.

Piece of tubing left in bronchus following road traffic accident (RTA).

Industrial injury claim: wrong diagnosis resulted in failure of patient's claim.

FPC complaint: delay in referral to hospital—death from cerebrovascular accident and congestive cardiac failure.

Ancillary staff problems in operating theatre.

Consent: blood sample for alcohol level taken against patient's wishes.

Alleged negligent treatment of child's jaw following tonsillectomy.

FPC complaint: failure to diagnose pregnancy.

HSC (Ombudsman) complaint: disabled patient discharged to uninhabitable flat—death.

Death from congenital heart disease of baby born at home against medical advice.

Complaint to MP: failure to visit epileptic patient.

Delay in diagnosis of congenital dislocation of left hip.

Inadequate treatment of eye injury following fall aboard ship.

Release of records to solicitors: death of psychiatric patient from fall from train.

Failure to diagnose diabetes.

Cardiac arrest and pulmonary embolism following emergency caesarean section for fetal distress—death.

Child born with spina bifida—alleged negligent antenatal care.

Release of records—claim for damages for personal injuries sustained in RTA.

Claim for damages for personal injury—accident with scalpel blade while assisting member at operation.

Arthritis of right knee diagnosed in error for deep vein thrombosis.

Testamentary capacity of now deceased elderly patient.

Retained foreign body—failure to X-ray laceration on sole of left foot.

FPC complaint: refusal to visit.

Patient attended with pain in left shoulder, upper arm and abdomen—alleged assault by police.

Complaint about treatment during twin delivery—second baby brain-damaged.

Clinical responsibility when prescribing drugs for patient undergoing chemotherapy for secondary cancer.

Burns following laser removal of tattoos.

Slanderous remarks about member's management of patient made by patient's husband.

Adverse reaction to penicillin prescribed for syphilis.

Member summoned to appear as prosecution witness: nurse accused of ill-treating patient.

Private patient dissatisfied with result of bilateral augmentation mammoplasty (refashioning of breasts).

Haemorrhage following dental clearance and denture fitting.

Complaint by daughter of elderly patient about slanderous remarks made to patient about her.

Alleged libel by nursing officer criticizing member's handling of case of psychotic patient.

FPC complaint: refusal to give antenatal care to pregnant patient who could not speak English.

Delay in diagnosis of growth behind ear: operation performed in USA—demand for return of expenses.

Delay in diagnosis of critical state of abdomen.

FPC complaint: failure to visit patient with extensive bleeding from eye.

Release of records: patient with asbestosis claiming damages.

Refusal of patient to pay examination fee.

FPC complaint: unethical behaviour by member during consultation with patient.

Death from multiple injuries sustained when psychiatric patient jumped from hospital window.

Failure to diagnose fracture of scaphoid sustained when patient fell from bicycle.

Demand for return of cost of additional dental treatment caused by leaving cotton wool on tooth after filling.

retainer scheme (Department of Health and Social Security circulars PM(79)3 and HC(79)11). Junior doctors move from post to post, but the computer cannot keep up with them unless the new address is provided by the doctor himself.

When a member writes or telephones a request, his membership is checked by the Information Department and details of the incident entered on the computer. A file is then made up and the secretariat meets to allocate this either to the medical or dental groups (Figure 11). Cases where claims are involved are dealt with according to the quantum (the likely cost): the Secretariat Committee, the Cases & General Purposes Committee or President's Committee. The last also deals with some claims in which settlement of the claim or action has been authorized by the Council or Cases & General Purposes Committee and the only decision required is on the quantum of damages to be offered or paid to the claimant. Prompt and fair compensation for patients who have been badly treated is a principle with all defence bodies. However, most cases are averted before reaching the courts.

Protection, advice and education

Most of the time and activity of the defence bodies is occupied with giving advice and help on matters unconnected with litigation or indemnity—and this fact is not generally appreciated. A personal answering service receives calls twenty-four hours a day every single day of the year and there is always an expert doctor available on call. One defence body alone may receive 12,000 telephone calls a year and open 10,000 or more new files as well as receive thousands of letters on existing files. This is provided not only for medical and dental members in the UK but also from the London offices of the MDU for members abroad and from the Sydney office for members in Australia, New Zealand, and the Far East.

Many of the queries coming from doctors are dilemmas but answers can usually be given because of the accumulated knowledge of handling such matters; these may vary from the trivial to, for example, a threatened claim about incontinence following hysterectomy or an urgent telephone call on a Sunday afternoon concerning a Jehovah's witness who fell off his bicycle injuring himself and needing a blood transfusion which was refused on religious grounds. The variety of requests is so interesting that a selection from the many received by the MDU during one week in 1983 is shown in Table 1.

EDUCATION AND PREVENTION

Prevention of mishap and malpractice is the constant aim of doctors and it is true, if trite, to state that the doctor's and patient's interests are entwined. The aim is to educate and prevent—not to tell the doctor or dentist how to treat. Many of the staff of the defence bodies lecture at under- and postgraduate level throughout the world; they also address symposia arranged by the Royal Colleges, the Law Society and BMA joint meetings. Student essay competitions were started in 1969, one for medical and one for dental students, and ran for some years. The subjects covered both ethical matters and practical problems. Elective bursary competitions provide financial sponsorship for students' elective periods and the bursaries are awarded after success in doing a multiple choice paper of thirty questions on medico-legal topics so as to increase awareness of the legal and ethical dimensions of medical practice. In 1984, £500 was awarded to the candidate who achieved the highest marks and thirty-eight bursaries each of £225 for others who had reached a satisfactory standard.

Advances in medical technology may carry hazards and, throughout the century, warnings have been given to members through the annual reports. These almost trace the history of medicine: for example, the need to X-ray fractures, written information for the patient concerning over-tight plasters, the risk of X-ray burns and the avoidance of anaesthetic deaths because of wrongful coupling of gas cylinders. Colouring of gas cylinders was achieved by co-operation with the Association of Anaesthetists and British manufacturers of anaesthetic equipment and the British Standards Institution in 1943. Agreement on the numbering of fingers to avoid the wrong one being operated upon was brought about in 1955. A booklet entitled *Theatre Safeguards* outlines the sources of error in operating theatres and recommends precautions; it was published in co-operation with the other defence organizations, the Royal College of Nursing and the National Association of Theatre Nurses. All such booklets and the educational films available are listed in Appendix III: the former are free of charge to all members and the films (16mm colour and optical sound) and video casettes can be loaned.

References

1 *Annual Report.* London: Medical Defence Union, 1894, p. 9–19.
2 *Harnett* v. *Bond and Adams. British Medical Journal* 1 (1924): 939–43; 1 (1925): 533–5; 974–5; 989–93; 1 (1927): 1084–5.
3 *Annual Report.* London: Medical Defence Union, 1946/7, 16.
4 *Michael* v. *Molesworth. British Medical Journal.* 2 (1950): 171–2.
5 *Regina* v. *Bodkin Adams. British Medical Journal.* 1 (1957): 712–3; 771–2; 828–34; 889–94; 954–5.
6 Dentist's Libel Action against British Medical Association and British Medical Journal. *British Medical Journal* 1 (1972): 774–5; 4:254 and 313–4.
7 Freedom of the Medical Press. *British Medical Journal* 2 (1972): 313–4.

4

Hazards for doctors and dentists the world over

'New developments in medicine bring litigation in their wake.'
ANON.

'But for the Grace of God, there goes John Bradford', was Bradford's own thought when watching criminals being taken to execution, and many readers no doubt substitute themselves when reading the annual reports of the medical defence bodies. These recount some of the medico-legal problems of the previous year and make worrying reading as dramatic subtitles lure the reader on: Venesection Disaster; Amorous Allegation; Retained Glass; No Notes—No Defence; Unexpected Pregnancy; Fracture Missed—GP Misled; Vas Recanalized; Must I Tell the Police?; Exam Fraud; Bad Writing Cost £55,000; Careful What You Sign; Genetic Counselling Problems; Careless Prescriptions Cost Lives.

Their object is to warn and prevent such happenings by illustrating potential pitfalls. Risks vary each year; anaesthetists and orthopaedic surgeons may top the list one year only to be replaced on another occasion by general practitioners because of the great expense incurred, for example, when two cases of malaria have been missed. Generally speaking, the training grades are most at risk partly from inexperience and partly from being in the front line as in accident departments, and each specialty produces its own crop of problems.

Hazards for all doctors

FAILURE OF COMMUNICATION

Defective communication is common in all walks of life, from marital disharmony to industrial disputes. Medicine is no exception: in a hundred consecutive problems analysed by the Medical Protection Society, no fewer than twenty-six were due mainly to failure of communication between a doctor and his patient or between two doctors, or between a doctor and a nurse [1]. Disaster can, for example, follow failure to inform a woman that her smear test for cervical cancer was positive. Diagnosis and treatment over the telephone is also fraught with possible errors.

73

Failure of doctor–doctor communication is almost a weekly matter for the defence bodies. In hospital, failures may occur between the clinician and his colleagues in the departments of radiology or pathology—or between him and the sister in charge of the ward. Discharge summaries from hospitals have a reputation for arriving late or not at all and sometimes only a discharge letter giving the bare facts is sent. Every aspect of this problem was studied and suggestions for improvement made by a Nuffield Working Party on Communication in a booklet *Doctor to doctor: Writing and Talking about Patients.* [2].

Immediate communication is essential in accident departments and the letter can be given to the patient. The following legal case, *Chapman v. Rix* (1959) illustrates the need for this:

> In 1955 Mr Chapman, a butcher, nicked his abdomen when boning a rump of beef. A doctor happened to be at Brentwood District Hospital (a cottage hospital with no resident staff) when a telephone call was received there about the accident; at once he went to the butcher's shop and saw a small wound which was not bleeding. Next he examined him more thoroughly at the hospital and concluded that, though the deep fascia had been cut, the wound had not penetrated the peritoneum; so the wound was stitched and dressed and the butcher sent home—with instructions to see his general practitioner that evening. His GP did not appreciate that the doctor was not a casualty officer and accepted the patient's statement that the wound was superficial—and diagnosed a digestive disorder.
>
> The butcher died and post-mortem showed that the knife had penetrated the small intestine. In an action by the widow, the judge found that the doctor had been negligent in failing to communicate directly with the man's GP after he had dealt with him. This judgement was, however, reversed by the Court of Appeal; the plaintiff's further appeal to the House of Lords on whether the failure of the defendant to communicate was negligent was also dismissed. [3]

Information sent from general practitioner to hospital can also be poor: for example, antibiotics or drug allergies are not mentioned and may delay successful treatment or endanger life as not all patients are able to tell of their sensitivities, for language reasons if for no other. Whilst most letters today are informative and typed, this has not always been so: once a man in diabetic coma arrived in the accident department and the only communication from the general practitioner was a visiting card pinned to his pyjamas 'this is to introduce . . .'.

Communication within the hospital reaches a peak of importance at the 'hand-over'. Covering arrangements between doctors on different wards and units have become more complex than ever because of improved off-duty arrangements for junior medical staff. Case records and progress notes should be complete so that the deputizing doctor has the appropriate data to help him deal with a patient not normally under his care. The best plan is for the covering doctor to be taken to see the patients, especially the very ill ones, and to be given oral as well as written details. Similar communication is needed to bring him up to date with the night's or weekend's events on his return. The weekend can be a risky time for patients in hospital partly from failure in communication and partly due to unfamiliar and sometimes inexperienced staff; the danger applies especially to post-operative and accident cases.

AMOROUS ACCUSATIONS

Accusations of improper conduct (Figure 12) by a doctor are easy to make and

FIGURE 12. Every doctor should show real interest in the patient as a person but must beware of the risk of amorous accusations.

sometimes difficult to refute. 'For each occasion on which a doctor really behaves improperly towards a patient—and they are rare indeed—there is a host of false accusations and this should be fully appreciated, especially by new graduates', wrote Dr Phillip Addison (1971), former Secretary of the MDU, when emphasizing the importance of a chaperone. He continued, 'allegations of unprofessional conduct occur not once in a decade, as some appear to think, but several times each year. Quite often practitioners who have to appear in a Magistrate's Court, or before the Disciplinary Committee of the General Medical Council, to answer a charge of sexual assault are unable to call any supporting evidence because there was no one else present at the time of the examination' [4].

Allegations can vary from breast-fondling during routine examination of the chest to assault when a cervical smear was taken or rape when a doctor was fitting an IUCD (intra-uterine contraceptive device):

> An experienced GP fitted an IUCD and as the patient was nervous he gave her an intravenous anaesthetic, a member of the surgery staff being present. That evening the police phoned the surgery to inform him that the patient had accused him of rape. He was later charged and committed for trial at a Crown Court. The MDU mounted a formidable defence led by Senior Counsel and supported by expert witnesses. The member was acquitted by unanimous vote of the jury. The MDU's costs of £9,157 were reimbursed by the State [5].

> A rural GP in New South Wales was invited to appear before the Investigating Committee of his State Medical Board which had received an explicit six-page complaint from a thirty-year-old patient. The shy retiring woman had been seeing the doctor with increasing frequency over a six-month period, when she was openly expressing her love for him and was often seen lingering in the street outside his house. He then received a call from her husband who said that she had confessed to having a three-month affair with the doctor, and that for a sum of $A5,000 the matter might be forgotten. The allegations were denied and payment refused. The MDU's solicitors examined the doctor's personal diary with particular reference to the dates and places of alleged dalliance, and her claims clearly could not be substantiated. She failed to attend the Investigating Committee Hearing and on examination of the documents the Committee found no evidence to support the complaint of misconduct. The doctor, however, had no redress for the inconvenience, embarrassment, and months of distress [6].

The employment of chaperones is advised by the defence bodies, one function being to vouch for the doctor's conduct when his behaviour is attacked. In practice, this is often impractical (particularly for GPs) and many patients prefer to be seen alone but, when thought necessary, the doctor's receptionist or a relative could act. In court it can tell against the doctor if it is shown that he could have had a chaperone but did not avail himself of one.

It is distressing for a doctor to receive a completely unwarranted declaration of love from a patient. Once the MDU was able to relieve a member's anxiety by establishing from a previous file that the same patient, three years earlier, had declared equally undying love for a neighbouring practitioner. On the former occasion she had started her letter 'Dear A, I think this is the most difficult letter that I have ever written . . .'; to her second chosen one she wrote 'Dear B, This is without doubt the most difficult letter that I have ever written . . .'.

ACCIDENTAL INJURIES TO PATIENTS

The hazards of everyday life may befall patients on the doctor's premises: tripping over carpets or slipping on stairs—and damage to clothing may be caused by medicaments. Falling off the doctor's couch, the radiologist's table or from the operating theatre table has caused the MDU to be involved in various ways although most injuries are not covered and need an appropriate insurance to cover 'third party' accidents.

Suicides of patients in hospital are likely to increase due to shortage of nurses on psychiatric wards, and these are the responsibility of the hospital authorities, providing that the doctor has taken reasonable care to avoid it happening.

ASSAULTS ON DOCTORS BY PATIENTS

Doctors frequently consult defence bodies because of abuse and assault by patients but the following is an extreme case where nuisance turned into real damage:

> A GP in 1979 in the Home Counties was gravely harassed by a former patient who had been removed from his list and also from that of four other doctors because of her wild behaviour. She had made abusive telephone calls to his home, broken his windows, and when drunk assaulted him at the surgery. In desperation he consulted the MDU and legal advice was sought on obtaining a High Court injunction and on suing her for damages. She then appeared to have ceased her activities and the matter was left in abeyance

since she had already been charged with criminal damage arising out of two incidents and had been bound over to keep the peace. Notwithstanding this she climbed over a fence specially erected to keep her out of the surgery premises and smashed four windows—a doctor and a patient narrowly escaping injury. Again she was bound over to keep the peace.

Later while the doctor was abroad, she walked into a partner's consulting room in a violent and abusive state; the police were called and this time she was remanded in custody. She was charged with threatening behaviour likely to occasion a breach of the peace and sentenced to one month's imprisonment plus a further six months for breach of the previous orders.

Counsel advised that it would be inappropriate to seek an injunction whilst she was in prison as this might provoke her to further violence on release and it was hoped that the prison sentence would act as a deterrent. However, soon after her release she caused further trouble, was prosecuted and sent to jail for three months [7].

Revenge was taken on a GP by an aggrieved spouse who imagined that the doctor had been responsible for his wife's death because he did not send her to hospital when she had a heart attack: he shot and killed the doctor. Psychiatric patients present the greatest problem and psychiatrists are the most likely among practitioners to suffer physical injury. A doctor has written as follows:

I am employed as a hospital practitioner at a mental hospital. On the morning of 19 April I entered one of the wards which I customarily visit and observed a young schizophrenic patient in the act of striking two nurses. Since they were the only two nurses on the ward at that moment and there were several elderly patients present, I was afraid he would strike one of them; consequently I caught hold of his arms. He then struck me in the face and there was a short struggle which ended in the two of us lying on the floor where I pinioned his arms until help arrived. Ten minutes later my right knee became extremely swollen and painful. I visited an orthopaedic surgeon and in his opinion I have sustained a tear of the internal cartilage. This has not so far completely disabled me, but it is no better and I fear that it may need operative treatment, in which case of course I would be completely unable to work for a time.

The solicitors were instructed on the member's behalf. He was examined by another specialist and an application was made to the Criminal Injuries Compensation Board. He later received £704 in compensation. A board member commented that 'if surgical intervention in this knee has to be undertaken in the future and if such surgery is then proved to be attributable to this incident, this application may be reconsidered' [8].

THE GOOD SAMARITAN

Some doctors express concern about helping someone who has had a car accident or has collapsed in an aircraft—in case of possible litigation later from alleged incompetence. This fear is a myth: no case has ever come to court and a law protects the doctor in many states in the USA.

Hazards for special groups of doctor

GENERAL PRACTITIONERS

General practitioners are the biggest users of any defence body. Most problems can be discussed and resolved over the telephone but only after lengthy and often time-consuming discussions. Many concern complaints to Family Practitioner Committees (FPC) and sometimes local medical committees; an analysis of a hundred consecutive complaints to FPCs dealt with by one member of the MDU secretariat in 1982 is shown in Table 2; the number is not surprising, for the GP is a generalist dealing with the greatest variety of problems and having to prescribe the greatest number of different drugs— besides which, he is usually first on the scene.

Some remarks made in letters to Family Practitioner Committees are not only highly derogatory of the family doctor but also malicious; however, complaints addressed to FPCs are covered by absolute privilege and cannot be made the subject of a successful action for defamation. The two commonest complaints are failure to visit and failure to diagnose.

FAILURE TO VISIT

Failure to visit has reached over 50 per cent of the total complaints and reflects the trend in general practice as shown by Dr John Fry in *Present State and Future Needs in General Practice*: the frequency of home visits has come down by 41 per cent and all face-to-face consultations by 4·5 per cent [9]. The decision whether or not to visit is a difficult one, as shown by the following case:

> A woman visited her doctor's surgery to collect a letter to support
> her application for rehousing. While speaking to the doctor she
> requested a visit for her husband who was at home with lumbago.

TABLE 2. One hundred consecutive complaints to Family Practitioner Committees dealt with by one member of the secretariat of the Medical Defence Union in 1982.

Complaint	Informal procedure	Formal procedure			Total
		Decided on correspondence —no further action	Hearing		
			Not in breach	In breach	
Failure to visit	4	6	7	10	27
Failure to diagnose	4	14	7	—	25
Failure to admit/refer to hospital	2	15	—	1	18
Failure to treat	1	5	—	1	7
Failure to keep adequate records	—	—	—	2	2
Manner and attitude (inc. receptionists')	3	2	—	—	5
Failure to issue certificates	—	3	—	—	3
Miscellaneous	3	6	1	3	13
Total	17	51	15	17	100

In breach—penalties imposed:

Reprimand	1
Caution	4
Warned to comply	8
Withholdings from remuneration (£200, £250, £300, £300)	4

The doctor took a careful history from her, decided that a visit was not necessary and gave appropriate advice about management, supplementing it with a prescription for an analgesic. The wife appeared satisfied with the advice and left the surgery. The following evening a deputizing doctor was called to the patient's home, found the man's backache was worse and arranged his admission to an orthopaedic ward. Subsequently he was transferred to a surgical ward for an exploratory laparotomy, but no abnormality was found.

The doctor's failure to visit the patient was the subject of an informal inquiry by the FPC, but the patient's wife remained dissatisfied and demanded that her complaint be treated formally. The doctor was requested to provide an explanation within the statutory four weeks. A suitable reply was prepared, emphasizing that the doctor's decision not to visit was made after she exercised her clinical judgement, having listened to a description of the patient's symptoms. The doctor heard no more about the matter for nine months but when she enquired, the FPC informed her that the complaint had been dismissed without a hearing [10].

TELEPHONE ADVICE

The telephone is indispensable for a doctor but it can be a snare.

> A 29-year-old woman telephoned her GP because of a headache. He advised her to take Panadol and attend the surgery the next day. She came and as her vision was affected, the doctor diagnosed migraine. The following day her husband telephoned to say that she was still ill with headache, giddiness and double vision. A further prescription was given. Next day the doctor was told by telephone that the headache was better but that she was drowsy. On the sixth day he was told over the telephone that she was agitated and uncontrollable; he did not visit but prescribed Largactil. Later that day she was admitted to hospital unconscious and died from pyogenic meningitis. The claim from the widower was indefensible and was settled for £26,000 including costs [11].

FAILURE TO DIAGNOSE

Accuracy in diagnosis is limited, as symptoms often do not fit the expected pattern of a disease and two and two may therefore not make four. Compared with the hospital doctor, the GP frequently makes no more than a tentative diagnosis as he seldom has facilities such as X-rays and laboratory services to confirm his opinion.

Malaria can easily be missed because it is not suspected.

> In 1973 a GP was found by a court to have been negligent in failing to diagnose malaria in a man aged thirty-seven complaining of vague ill health, lassitude, loss of appetite and 'aches and pains'. The patient said that he had returned from Malawi two weeks previously but had not taken malarial prophylatics as they were not considered necessary during the winter months. The GP entered on the record card 'flu? malaria?' and decided that he would treat him for

81

influenza with codeine and rest in bed—with instructions to contact him if the temperature rose. There was little change in the man's condition over the next two days but since he had not improved, the doctor prescribed antimalarial tablets, four days after the first consultation. After another two days the patient suddenly lapsed into coma and was urgently admitted into hospital where he died the same day from cerebral malaria. Necropsy showed the cause of death to be renal failure due to malaria.

In deciding whether the claim could be resisted, the Council was advised that in 1968 the Ministry of Health had circulated to all general practitioners a booklet entitled *Communicable Diseases Contracted Outside Great Britain*, emphasizing the need to obtain specialist advice at once if there was any possibility of malaria and in March 1975 the Department of Health and the Welsh Office circulated a map, showing the countries where malaria is prevalent.

At the conclusion of the High Court trial in 1975, judgement was given for the plaintiff's widow, who had small children, for £81,797; the MDU also had to pay the costs of both parties which amounted to £3,397. After careful consideration of Counsel's opinion, the Council reluctantly decided that an appeal would not be justified.

In a similar case where damages of £15,093 were awarded to a widow whose husband had died from malaria, the judge said that in these days of fast travel, general knowledge and medical literature had for some time alerted doctors to the dangers of illnesses acquired abroad. Malaria was not a disease which normally came in the way of the ordinary general practitioner but if a general practitioner knew that a patient whom he thought had influenza had just come back from the tropics and was not getting better, it should have entered his head that it might be a tropical disease of some kind. He might not be capable of diagnosing malaria but he should be alert to the possibility [12].

A total of 1,471 cases of malaria were imported to Britain in 1982 and the most severe form of malaria, *Plasmodium falciparum*, increased. Travellers returning from sub-Saharan Africa contributed the greatest number of malignant cases, whereas those returning from India imported most of the benign tertian malaria [13]. A false sense of security is given when the patient is emphatic about having been taking antimalarial drugs throughout his visit, as parasites are becoming increasingly resistant to drugs such as chloroquine.

Mosquitoes may be transported by aircraft coming from endemic areas and survive around airports in the UK causing 'airport malaria' [14].

Meningitis is uncommon so that the threshold of suspicion of the doctor is low, since he may only see about one case each year. There were twenty-two allegations of missed meningitis in 1982. When in 1985 over £250,000 may be payable in a single case of brain damage, the significance of these figures becomes obvious.

Diabetes is easily missed unless the urine is tested. During an eighteen-month period, sixty cases relating to diabetes were reported to the MDU. Of these, fourteen were FPC complaints of failure to diagnose diabetes, or to treat it adequately. Several cases led to inquests and members received assistance. The commonest complaint was failure in the initial diagnosis.

> A typical case concerned a general practitioner who was consulted by a boy of sixteen complaining of lethargy and weight loss. He found the tongue bright red and the breath sweet, the result, he thought, of drinking a large quantity of cherryade. He took blood for various tests but failed to test the urine, and was horrified to hear forty-eight hours later that the patient had been found dead. It was subsequently reported that the blood glucose was 50·8 mmol/l [15]. A claim followed which was settled.

Clinical lapses are not uncommon, such as failure to take the blood pressure.

> Damages were paid to a woman who at the age of forty-four suffered a cerebrovascular accident resulting in paralysis of the right side of the body. In a pregnancy fourteen years earlier, her blood pressure had been raised. In the last six years she had been treated by the general practitioner and his partner with hormone pills, but there was no record of the blood pressure being taken that time. When admitted to hospital with hemiplegia her blood pressure was found to be 300/170 mmHg. As there was no evidence of the blood pressure having been taken the claim for damages was indefensible [16].

Confirming death can be surprisingly difficult:

> A GP was asked by a woman to certify the death of her 84-year-old mother. He found the patient sitting motionless upright on her sofa: she had a pale wax-like appearance, breathing had ceased and no pulse could be felt; the pupils did not react to light and no heart or breath sounds could be heard through a stethoscope. Examination

was conducted in an unhurried manner in the presence of the daughter and another relative. He had no doubt that the patient was dead and issued a certificate. A few hours after the body had been removed to the undertakers, snoring could be heard. The body was rushed to hospital where it was found that she was alive though unconscious. She regained consciousness, made a remarkable recovery and was discharged within a few weeks [17].

COMPLAINTS AND THEIR RESOLUTION

No complaint should be regarded lightly. Although few in the National Health Service result in a penalty being imposed on a doctor, individual 'fines' or 'withholdings from remuneration' may amount to several thousands of pounds; and, more significantly, a breach of the terms of service may be reported to the General Medical Council. So, if a FPC requests comments on a complaint the GP should contact his defence body.

Many, although not all, FPCs try to resolve complaints by an informal procedure: the GP, the complainant and a lay member of the Medical Service Committee, assisted by a doctor, discuss the complaint together and try to resolve it. This, however, is not always possible and the complainant may insist on a formal procedure. Then the GP will be sent a copy of the complaint and asked to reply within four weeks; this reply is most important and should be carefully drafted, for a doctor's case may be spoilt by a poorly worded or inadequate reply. Apparently few complaints result in penalties; more often a warning to comply more closely with the terms of service follows. In the eyes of service committees the most heinous crime is that of refusing to visit a patient when requested; few other complaints result in adverse findings.

DENTAL SURGEONS

Dental surgeons are subject to the hazards that may affect any doctor but in addition may extract the wrong tooth or allow foreign bodies to be inhaled (Figure 13) or swallowed (Figure 14). Teeth are set so closely together in such a confined space that it is easy to remove the wrong one, and the junction of the larynx and pharynx makes it easy for foreign bodies to be inhaled rather than harmlessly swallowed—a pity that the Creator did not separate these channels. Dentures too, however perfect, may not satisfy the fastidious client and are thus a common cause of trouble.

Lord Nathan in 1957 wrote about the importance of making sure that the patient consents to the treatment proposed and that no medical or dental

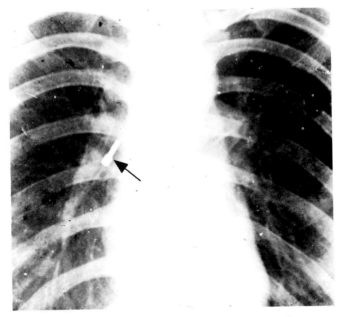

FIGURE 13. An inhaled foreign body—dental post holder in bronchus.

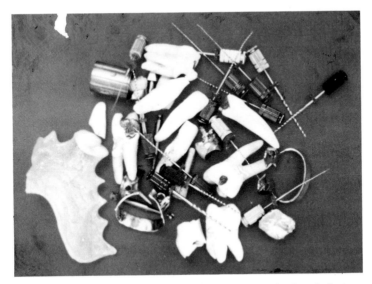

FIGURE 14. Items that have been swallowed or inhaled: teeth, dental plate, reamers, rubber dam clamp, copper ring, matrix band, burr, and post crown—preparatory to fitting. These have no statistical significance.

person should in general be permitted 'to adopt the attitude that it is the patient's own funeral if he fails to make his wishes understood' [18]. He quoted a Canadian case *Boase* v. *Paul*: in 1931, a dentist failed to find out the exact extent of the work the patient wished to have done and, relying upon an X-ray plate, extracted twelve teeth instead of the one the patient wished to have extracted: he was held liable for an assault [19].

Another example might be when two patients of the same name arrive at the same session: one needs three teeth extracted and the other a clearance; the wrong card is handed to the dentist who sees a mouth full of teeth with extensive periodontal disease and extracts all the teeth from a patient who had contracted for only two or three at a time—again, difficult to defend. Both of these are obvious cases and minor mistakes are probably more common; the teeth to be extracted can be ringed on the chart on the dental consent form sometimes used in hospital practice.

An inhaled foreign body can be disastrous and the missing tooth, crown, reamer (minute drill) or throat pack provide the commonest objects. If not recognized immediately, a lung abscess and other complications can follow and if retrieval by bronchoscopy is impossible, thoracotomy will be necessary which will leave a scar on the chest that can be expensive in terms of damages.

> A 37-year-old man was undergoing treatment for a dental abscess and the root canal was being opened. No safety precautions had been taken to avoid inhalation or ingestion of foreign bodies. He coughed and sat up and the reamer disappeared; the dental surgeon thought that the patient had swallowed it but it was removed from the lower lobe bronchus four days later at operation. The resulting claim had to be settled and four and a half years after the mishap a payment of £5,001 was made to the plaintiff by the MDU [20].

Swallowing an item used by a dental surgeon should cause no trouble and the patient may usually be reassured that it will pass through uneventfully. Serial X-rays of the abdomen will generally show that this has happened. If, by chance, it did remain in the stomach, it could be extracted by endoscopy (an instrument is passed through the gullet into the stomach); only rarely is laparotomy (operation on abdomen) required. The manoeuvre 'going through the motions', as happened in the following case, would be unnecessary unless something valuable like a gold crown needed to be retrieved.

> A newly qualified practitioner accidentally dropped onto the floor of the mouth a crown which she was about to cement, whereupon the patient swallowed it. The patient was advised that he should exa-

mine his stools in the WC to ensure that the crown had passed and so that he could retrieve it.

This was followed by a note to the effect that if he had not found the crown he should ask his doctor to arrange for an X-ray of the abdomen to locate it. The next development was a letter of claim by the patient who was a lawyer. He wittily wrote:

> Quite apart from all the worry—very considerable indeed—the toothlessness is also a factor—I have had personally to perform the disgusting job 20 times of 'searching' for the missing tooth. No court would assess that at less than £5 a time and allowing for nine days' worry and shortage of teeth I reckon that the minimum proper damages are not less than £218. However, because the lady was so charming—and because she comes from a part of England which I know and love—I shall make what is in the circumstances the most moderate claim I can think of, namely £44 but not a penny less. We will make a mutually convenient appointment with Miss . . . for her to refit the tooth after sterilisation [21].

Patients should always be told when anything is missing and reassured, for even a sharp instrument like a reamer is extremely unlikely to penetrate a viscus and should cause no symptoms as it passes through the gut.

Foreign bodies may be inhaled or swallowed because of the following:
* The tilting backwards of the dental chair.
* The use of local or general anaesthesia which may depress the swallowing reflex.
* The lack of any rubber dam, throat pack, 'parachute' safety device or even a length of dental floss silk tied to the hand-held reamer and to the patient's bib.
* Failure to count teeth.

A broken jaw (Figure 15) sounds like carelessness or a consequence of undue force, yet this accident has happened even to the most eminent members of the profession. It usually complicates a difficult extraction:

> A woman of fifty-one was found to need extraction of $\underline{1}/$, $\overline{5/}$, $/\overline{8}$; a radiograph was taken and an appointment made for extractions under general anaesthesia. A consultant anaesthetist gave the anaesthetic and the dental surgeon proceeded but the crown of 8 fractured and the surgeon attempted to extract the roots but with difficulty as they were complete and had grown into the bone. While the distal root was being removed it fractured once more, and some

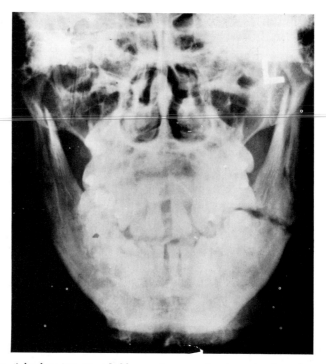

FIGURE 15. A broken jaw sounds like carelessness due to undue force but is not necessarily so. This is a fractured mandible sustained during a dental extraction.

bone was removed with it and also with the mesial root. The patient was put on antibiotics and asked to call again two days later, with the intention of taking a further radiograph to see what parts of the roots remained. She then complained of pain in the swollen left side of her face, tingling of the lower left lip, and a click when closing her mouth due to a fractured jaw. She was referred to a maxillo-facial surgeon and admitted for removal of the remaining root of /8, which was in the line of the fracture of the mandible, requiring the jaw to be immobilized with eyelet wiring and inter-maxillary fixations.

Expert advice was taken on the technique adopted, the taking of radiographs, and the use of elevators and other instruments together with the brittleness of the mandible at the age of fifty-one compared with that in youth and the inherent weakness in the jaw in the region of the third molars. Although the member was not considered to have been negligent, it was thought that the claim might be difficult to conduct successfully before a jury so it was settled for £1,000 plus costs of £314 [22].

Needles used sometimes to break (Figure 16) and could not be retrieved. This was because the surgeon, anxious to minimize the discomfort of a frightened patient, used a short small needle which had to be inserted to the hilt instead of a longer one which would not have fractured at the site of the hub; this accident is almost unknown since the advent of disposable needles which are longer and less likely to break. Jaundice, due to hepatitis B which has an incubation period from four weeks to six months, is conveyed by needles or any sharp instruments; disposable needles are safe if only used once. The dental surgeon is especially at risk and should take all possible protective steps; the virus of hepatitis is also transmitted by infected blood and possibly saliva so that an air-turbine drill may disseminate these by its aerosol effect. If a dental surgeon suspects that he may have acquired the infection he should tell his general practitioner, possibly receive an injection of high titre immunoglobulin and have his blood checked for the hepatitis B antigen (HbsAg) at three-monthly intervals afterwards.

Assaults on children, even minor ones (such as a slap on the face) can cause

FIGURE 16. Broken needle in gum. The accident is almost unknown since the advent of disposable needles.

medico-legal trouble. The defence of 'treating hysteria' is unlikely to succeed these days; dental surgeons are best advised on no account to hit children.

> A mother brought her three-year-old son to the surgery. The mother put him in the chair but he struggled and the dental surgeon held him as he seemed likely to fall. When he tried to examine him, the child resisted and slid down in the chair. The member slapped the top of his head and repositioned him. The boy stopped struggling but while his teeth were being examined he bit the member's finger. The dentist shouted at him to open his mouth and then completed his examination. Next day the mother wrote a letter of complaint about the incident to the General Dental Council (GDC) in which she admitted that her son misbehaved but said she deplored the dentist's method of dealing with him. The GDC sent the letter to him and asked for his observations. Though not a matter within its formal disciplinary jurisdiction it felt that 'any allegation of discourtesy on the part of a dentist to a patient or a patient's parent must be of concern to the Council as reflecting adversely on the profession as a whole'. The MDU's lawyers helped the member with his reply and no further action was taken [23].

ENDODONTICS, PERIODONTICS, ORTHODONTICS, AND PROSTHETICS

Endodontics, the practice of preserving a tooth by root canal therapy rather than extracting it, can be a source of mishap: breakage of instruments in the canal (Figure 17), over-filling or under-filling it, using toxic filling materials (some of which are neurotoxic), and perforation of the side of the root canal during instrumentation.

The whole dental team may be involved in the prevention and treatment of periodontal disease and this may mean prolonged treatment of the gums, so defence bodies advise that all should be protected against claims resulting from allegations of professional negligence; hygienists are welcomed as members. Prosthetics provides problems: patients may complain that dentures do not fit and repudiate fees and sue for substantial damages for pain and suffering. 'Who is to say', wrote Sir Ernest Rock Carling in 1960 when he was President of the Medical Protection Society, 'whether the article supplied complies with the guarantee of satisfaction: that it fits, articulates correctly, gives the requisite appearance and is comfortable! No matter how many adjustments, how many remakings there have been, no matter how much devoted attention and trouble, the result may be unacceptable and a fee, if a private patient, refused' [24].

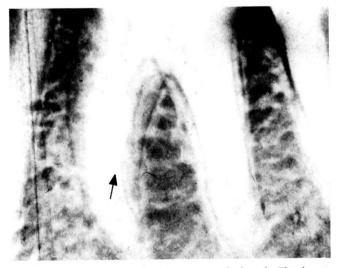

FIGURE 17. Broken reamer (minute drill) in root canal of tooth. This happened during an attempt to preserve the tooth.

COMMON PROBLEMS

The variety of cases discussed at one typical meeting of the Dental Committee of the MDU is shown in Table 3. Other common difficulties can concern over-treatment, mixing private and NHS treatment, and dishonest claims for work done; the last is an especial temptation because improved dentition due to fluoride has resulted in too many dentists chasing too few cavities. Complaints should be dealt with by dentists as described under *How the doctor reacts to a complaint* (page 161).

Allegations of advertising can occur unexpectedly as shown in the following example of unwanted publicity:

> A dental surgeon decided to interest children in preventive dentistry and to capture their imagination he redesigned his preventive unit as a space ship in which they could be instructed in the care of their teeth during a 'journey into space'. Unwisely a circular letter about the scheme was sent to headmasters in the area, asking for pupils to help in preparing art-work for it. A local newspaper heard of the innovation, reports and photographs in local and national news-papers appeared and the surgery address was given. Television producers were soon on the scene, wanting to make a film about the project. The dental surgeon was distressed and worried by all this publicity but it proved difficult to stop.

TABLE 3. The variety of cases discussed at one meeting of the Dental Committee.

County court claim; alleged unsatisfactory dentures.

High court action; wrong teeth extracted from ten-year-old boy.

Out-of-time court proceedings; return of fees for alleged unsatisfactory crown and bridge work. Patient used several aliases when attending different dentists and has been committed for trial on charges of deception.

Claim; infective endocarditis following failure to provide antibiotic cover during restorative work on patient who had had major heart surgery.

Court proceedings by husband who is dissatisfied with appearance of wife's dentures. Arbitration.

Claim; numbness of arm following attempted intravenous injection of Valium.

Claim; extraction of wrong teeth from twelve-year-old girl during orthodontic treatment. Reimbursement of parents' fees for specialist opinion.

Threatened claim for loss of income while undergoing treatment for removal of retained root in antrum.

Claim; perforation of distal wall of $\underline{3/}$ during reaming.

County court proceedings. In 1978 unerupted teeth found under bridge fitted in 1971.

Unsuccessful appeal to Privy Council against erasure of member from Register following caution by dental service committee for covering unregistered practice by dental surgery assistant.

Settlement of overseas claim in which patient suffered cardiac arrest in chair while anaesthetized for treatment.

Claim; mandible fractured during extraction of wisdom tooth.

Claim; inhaled reamer removed by thoracotomy, 37-year-old man.

The GDC asked for his observations on the circular letter and the press publicity, and the MDU's lawyers prepared a letter of explanation for the Council. He was then summoned to appear before the disciplinary committee on a charge of infamous or disgraceful conduct in a professional respect. His novel approach to children's dentistry was supported at the hearing by expert evidence and he was found not guilty of unprofessional conduct. That was not the end of the story for, as a result of the GDC inquiry, interest by the press and television increased still further but the member referred all journalists to the MDU and refused to make any comment himself [25].

In any dealings with the media about the practice of medicine or dentistry members need to be extremely careful and discreet if they are to avoid criticism from jealous or outraged colleagues for advertising or canvassing. The dental secretaries of the defence bodies are always ready to help with prophylactic advice.

DENTAL ANAESTHESIA

An anaesthetic administered for dental treatment in a surgery is very different from general anaesthesia performed within a hospital. Patients are ambulatory, often un-premedicated, anxious and nervous, and they expect to be incapacitated for a short time only. The operation is carried out in the oral cavity, a part of the vital airway itself, where blood and saliva, operative debris and throat packs are potential hazards to the patency of the airway. Death in the dental chair is particularly tragic and often affects a fit person, usually young, and having a minor operation.

> In 1976 a young woman in Israel, frightened of treatment, attended for fillings and extractions. She requested general anaesthesia which was given by an anaesthetist. As treatment started she had a cardiac arrest. Despite resuscitation she remained unconscious in hospital until her death at the end of 1979. In 1977 her parents claimed against the dentist and anaesthetist; the latter only had limited insurance cover and was not a member of a defence body. The principal allegations of negligence were delayed diagnosis of cardiac arrest and lack of proper resuscitation. On experts' advice the Council of the MDU decided to defend the member and the action was tried in the District Court in 1978. The judge ruled that the maxim of *res ipsa loquitur*—the fact speaks for itself—applied and awarded damages of £95,000 against the member and anaesthetist, both jointly and severally. He said that a qualified nurse should have been present in the surgery as well as the dentist and the anaesthetist, and based the amount of damages on an estimated life expectancy of ten years. The solicitor's agents advised the MDU to appeal both on liability and on quantum, but before this could be done the whole of the damages of £95,000 had to be paid into court. In November 1979 the appeal was dismissed with costs. The plaintiff died a month later.

It was the anaesthetist at fault, if anyone, and the dentist had no part in the alleged negligence, but the Israeli law required the whole payment to be made; so the dentist who was a member of the MDU had to be supported in paying the amount for the anaesthetist who was inadequately covered. Those who work with colleagues anywhere should see that they are adequately covered [26].

Deaths associated with general anaesthesia for dentistry were investigated in a study of those occurring in the UK during the ten-year period 1970–9. There were altogether a hundred—in ten years; but just over one-third were in hospital patients especially admitted because of their poor medical condition. It was reported that doctors and second dentists (non-operating) were safer than a dentist acting as operator/anaesthetist: the last had an unfavourable record but his safety, when using sedation and analgesia—the patient just being drowsy—was of a high order [27]. The practice of a dentist acting both as an operator and an anaesthetist has officially been frowned upon for twenty years and should now be obsolete, for the General Dental Council acted to stop it in 1983. Also an incentive not to be both operator and anaesthetist was given by the chief dental officer of the Department of Health and Social Security when he announced that no fees would be paid for an operator who administered general anaesthesia for dentistry after 1 April 1983.

The GDC issued guidelines for general anaesthesia and sedative techniques and these are listed in the booklet *Guide for Dental Students and Practitioners* issued by the Medical Defence Union in 1984.

The Wylie Report on Training in Dental Anaesthesia suggested recommendations for making general anaesthesia safer. Simple sedation was also defined, this being as follows: 'A technique in which the use of a drug or drugs produces a state of depression of the central nervous system enabling treatment to be carried out, but during which verbal contact with the patient is maintained throughout the period of sedation. The drugs and techniques used should carry a margin of safety wide enough to render unintended loss of consciousness unlikely' [28]. The Seward Report, formed to consider the implementation of the Wylie Report, stated that for sedation—whether intravenous or inhalational—the dentist can assume entire responsibility provided that a second appropriate person (e.g. dental surgery assistant) is present throughout to monitor the clinical condition and to assist the dentist if an emergency occurs [29].

SURGEONS

Heroic operations like transplantation which force forward the frontiers of knowledge do not generate problems of litigation for surgeons in spite of their high risk to patients; it is often the small routine operations—the so-called 'minor ops'—that provide hazards; perhaps the word minor is a misnomer.

Classical Surgical Pitfalls

Damage to:
  Recurrent laryngeal nerve when operating upon the
  thyroid gland
  Facial nerve during operations on the parotid gland
  The bile duct
  The ureter

Mistaking the femoral artery for the vein at operations to
  cure varicose veins

VARICOSE VEINS

Varicose veins can be treated either by injecting an irritant substance to cause thrombosis and obliteration, or by stripping the long saphenous vein and destroying the principal superficial venous channels: disasters may occur in both operations when the artery is mistaken for the vein.

A shop manager aged forty-one was the fourth on an operating list. The surgeon performed the first three operations assisted by a GP who was a clinical assistant. The GP started the fourth operation at the request of the surgeon who had been called to the out-patient department; he had assisted at many operations for varicose veins and had performed several without supervision. A vein-stripper was inserted into a small vein over the inner side of the ankle and passed up without difficulty to a point in the groin. An incision was made over the upper end of the stripper and the vein in which it was lying was identified. During blunt dissection a non-pulsating vessel passing upwards along the middle of the femoral triangle began to bleed and, thinking that this was an abnormal branch of the vein, he clamped this and another vein-stripper was introduced into it and passed towards the ankle but this stripper did not enter the long saphenous vein. There was suddenly a brisk haemorrhage from the wound in the groin. The surgeon returning to the theatre, identified the bleeding vessel as the femoral artery and immediate arrangements were made for grafting to re-establish the arterial circulation; in spite of being transferred to the care of a specialist in vascular surgery, an arteriogram several months later showed a poor circulation and the patient suffered severe disability though he just avoided amputation of the limb. There was no defence and a final settlement was agreed at £10,000, which included the plaintiff's legal costs [30].

Several cases of intra-arterial injection have arisen as the result of Fegan's compression sclerotherapy.

A 43-year-old man attended an outpatient clinic because of varicose veins. The surgical registrar injected 0·5 ml of Thrombovar into what he thought was a varicose vein at the left ankle. The patient complained of pain at the site of the injection but as this was not intense he was allowed to leave the clinic. Five minutes later he returned with severe pain in his foot; when the bandages were removed the toes were found to be pale and cold. The registrar realized that he had injected the posterior tibial artery and immediately injected papaverine 1·0 ml and Priscol 1·0 ml into the femoral artery, and admitted the patient to the ward where an intravenous infusion of Rheomacrodex was set up. This was continued and also heparin, antibiotics and analgesics. Three weeks later left lumbar sympathectomy was performed. In spite of this, the lateral four toes and part of the forefoot had to be amputated because of gangrene. The case was settled in 1971 for £2,500 plus the patient's legal costs [31].

VASECTOMY

In 1982 there were thirteen allegations of failed vasectomy and forty-two files were opened on vasectomy-related problems, though not amounting to allegations of failure. However carefully the operation is done there is a failure rate, sometimes later because the vas becomes recanalized. This should be mentioned on the consent form to the operation, or told to the man and recorded in the case notes.

An experienced GP performed a vasectomy under local anaesthesia; all went well and the patient was given the usual instructions about the need for two negative sperm counts. He submitted two samples as directed and both were positive but despite this a nurse at the clinic signed and despatched an 'all clear' form to the patient; within weeks his wife was pregnant and subsequently had a termination. A further sperm test was positive and a negligence claim was made against the member. The solicitor of the MDU opened negotiations with the managers of the clinic and with the patient's lawyer: liability was admitted and apportioned equally between the member and the clinic as the nurse's employer. It is not usual to equate failed vasectomy with negligence, but the facts of this unusual case made defence impossible. The problem was the failure of communication from clinic to patient [32].

Vasectomies are undertaken on out-patients, in nursing homes, or in surgery premises—and if complications occur patients are referred to hospital. Counselling is important: consent should be obtained from the patient and agreement by the partner is advisable. An unusual problem arose when a young medical officer at a remote base in Antarctic conditions sent an enthusiastic message to his senior colleague at home and mentioned his intention of undertaking a vasectomy programme amongst the ice-bound company faced with a long winter there. The senior doctor, perturbed, contacted the MDU and subsequently sent a radio message dissuading his colleague from proceeding.

CIRCUMCISION

A knowledge of the anatomy is important. A case was reported in a newspaper of an accident occurring at a Moslem religious rite: at the height of the ceremony the doctor wielding the knife removed part of the penis instead of merely the foreskin—the child was rushed to hospital and the part sewn back. The case came to court when the boy was in his teens and an award made to the child for loss of sensation and to the parents for the shock and worry caused by the error. In a different case:

> A general practitioner/obstetrician in Australia agreed to a mother's request to circumcise her son when he was five days old but asked a paediatrician to see him because of a possible bleeding tendency; but through other commitments the latter could not see him and circumcision went ahead. Bleeding was difficult to stop and two hours later he was taken back to the theatre for suture with cat-gut and a compression bandage. He was then transferred to the care of the paediatrician. Next day the baby was unable to pass urine and the bandage was loosened but not removed, relieving the obstruc-tion; bleeding had stopped, the penis appeared normal and he was allowed to go home. A week after discharge the mother brought him back, and the penile shaft was gangrenous. The case could not be

97

successfully defended and the claim was settled in 1975 for a total of $A35,000 (£21,960) to which the MDU contributed 25 per cent on behalf of the paediatrician plus costs equivalent to £5,503 [33].

ORTHOPAEDIC AND PLASTIC SURGERY

Orthopaedic surgeons, responsible for accident departments and treating fractures, are a high-risk group. Operations upon the cervical vertebrae, whether performed by an orthopaedic or neurosurgeon, carry the hazard of paraplegia from damage to the spinal cord; this risk, which can amount to 3 per cent, is—rightly or wrongly—on occasions concealed from the patient even though the operation may be one of choice and not of necessity, so an accusation of lack of consent occurs. Damages are naturally great, an example being one case that was settled in 1974 for £35,000.

Cosmetic plastic surgery is a medico-legal mine-field and only suitably trained and experienced doctors should undertake such work. Hair transplants, removal of scars by lasers, face-lifting operations, breast lifting and breast reducing all have resulted in alleged negligence, a precipitating factor sometimes being the odd type of person who requests such treatment.

> A plastic surgeon in an antipodean city was consulted by a young man on account of an enlargement of his breasts because he was proposing to remarry and wished the surgeon to reduce them. At operation the wounds were closed with suction drains and the patient, embarrassed, left hospital as soon as possible; four days later a haematoma on the left side was evacuated and this was repeated on two other occasions. A low-grade inflammation developed and antibiotics were given causing the inflammation to subside, but the patient then complained of perianal itching for which he was referred to his GP. Six months later the surgeon received a letter from him stating that the pruritus ani had become worse, had needed specialist treatment, and had spoilt his honeymoon; it had extended causing 'ulcerous sores' on his leg and arm which were only just beginning to subside. He asserted that this was due to an overdose of antibiotics and claimed that it was the surgeon's fault and that he had 'been through almost six months of sheer hell, embarrassment, discomfort, colossal medical, surgical and chemist bills and that it had interfered with his marital relations at a most critical time.' His claim was repudiated and was not pressed. Shortly before reducing the size of this man's breasts the surgeon had augmented those of the patient's future wife [34].

98

BURNS

Burns have been a continuous source of litigation throughout most of the last one hundred years. Paralysed or unconscious patients are always at risk from hot water bottles. Sometimes these problems are a joint responsibility, though more often this lies with the nursing staff and is dealt with through the lawyer of the health authority or nursing home. Similarly burns from heating machines used by physiotherapists may be no concern of the medical defence bodies.

Short-wave surgical diathermy, now used in about 90 per cent of operations, unfortunately provides a supply of burns. It is used either to stop bleeding or for treatment: coagulation of the Fallopian tubes during laparoscopic sterilization, transurethral resection of bladder tumours, snaring of benign tumours in the alimentary tract, and for brain surgery. Diathermy accidents are increasing though, probably because this equipment is being used more as more operations are being carried out.

Dangers are as follows:

Ignition of inflammable solutions

The surgeon is sometimes inadvertently given an inflammable solution to cleanse the skin but occasions occur when the doctor himself is ignorant of the fire risk.

> A young girl underwent a minor gynaecological operation in the lithotomy position. The surgeon, a junior doctor, was liberal with his use of an alcohol-based skin preparation, which formed a pool under the patient's buttocks and soaked into the surrounding towels. Use of diathermy caused a fire and she was burned. Despite immediate action, there was a 4–5 per cent superficial burn with some deep areas. Her claim had to be settled [35].

Thermoelectrical burns

The commonest cause is that the indifferent electrode is applied to the skin incorrectly and the patient is surprised when he finds that he has a burn on the thigh after an operation elsewhere on the body; the whole electrode must make even contact with the skin. Burns have also arisen because someone has trodden accidently on the foot switch or even because this has slid beneath the table and become turned on; nowadays a buzzer clearly audible above the noise of the theatre indicates that the machine is being operated.

Explosion of inflammable gases

The bowel, mainly the colon, contains hydrogen and methane and either gas can be ignited when diathermy is used; this is a hazard during colonoscopy when a polyp in the colon is being removed.

OBSTETRICIANS AND GYNAECOLOGISTS

The hazards of routine practice in this specialty—obstetric disasters, failure of contraception and sterilization—have been augmented by advances in reproductive medicine. In fact, scientists have opened a Pandora's box of potential problems.

STERILIZATION

If contraceptives are unacceptable, the choice is whether the man or woman should undergo an operation for sterilization. Vasectomy has an advantage over the female operation because, while neither can be reasonably regarded as reversible, vasectomy repair is easier and safer than tubal reanastomosis. Male sterilization has the disadvantage, a wit has said, of the social limitation of not preventing pregnancy when the female partner indulges in extra-marital relations.

In 1982, eighty-eight allegations of failed female sterilization reached the MDU. Two examples from the Law Courts are as follows:

> *Chaunt v. Hertfordshire Area Health Authority (1982)*. Mrs Chaunt, a married woman aged forty-four, had a complicated history of gynae-cological difficulties. After having had one pregnancy terminated, she underwent laparoscopic sterilization but this failed and she became pregnant again. She had another termination and then a second sterilization which was successful. Afterwards, she suffered considerable pain and a vaginal hysterectomy was performed for fibroids; complications set in and she developed septicaemia, perito-nitis, bronchopneumonia and pleurisy. After a period in intensive care, she was discharged but only to be readmitted four months later with a pelvic infection. Surprisingly, she had the strength after this ordeal to sue the authority and recovered £2,000 for negligent sterilization and the unwanted pregnancy and £5,000 for the negli-gent aftercare which followed the hysterectomy and led to septi-caemia and pelvic infection. Since no child was born, no difficult questions of law arose [36].

UNWANTED BABY

Udale v. Bloomsbury Area Health Authority (1983). Mrs Udale, mother of four daughters, underwent laparoscopic sterilization in October 1977. It failed and she discovered that she was pregnant but too late for an abortion which she would have had if she had known earlier. In November 1978 she gave birth to a healthy boy who was much loved by her and her family. The defendant authority admitted liability for the surgeon's negligent performance of the operation as he had placed the right-hand clip on a nearby ligament instead of on the Fallopian tube. Mrs Udale had a second operation for sterilization just after the birth and a third nearly five years later to remove a clip left *in situ* during the original operation.

She claimed damages under four main headings: her pain and discomfort, and especially the fears and anxieties caused by the unsuccessful operation (she had been taking antibiotics and pain-killers for several months before she knew that she was pregnant and this worried her greatly for fear that she had damaged the unborn child); her loss of a year's earnings covering the pregnancy, birth, and early rearing of the baby; the cost of enlarging the family home to accommodate the baby; and the cost of its upbringing from birth to sixteen years. The defendant authority did not dispute that she was entitled to damages under the first two headings, but argued that she could not recover the cost of extending her house or bringing up the child; as a matter of public policy, the argument ran, damages should not be awarded for birth of a normal, happy and well-loved child.

This submission was accepted by the judge, Mr Justice Jupp. He decided that 'on grounds of public policy her claims should not be allowed in so far as they were based on negligence which allowed her boy to come into the world alive: firstly, [he felt] that it was highly undesirable that a child should learn that a court had publicly declared his life or birth to be a mistake, and that he or she was unwanted; secondly, a plaintiff like Mrs Udale who loved her child would get little or no damages whereas a bitter mother who resented the baby would obtain a large reward—virtue would go unrewarded and vice versa; thirdly, doctors would be placed under subconscious pressure to encourage abortion in order to avoid claims for medical negligence if the child were born' (a point made in the Law Commissions 1974 Report on Injuries to Unborn Children); lastly the judge observed, 'it has been the assumption of our culture from time immemorial that a child coming into the world even if, as some say, the world is a vale of tears, is a blessing and an occasion for rejoicing'. (A nice idea but no longer good law.)

However, the judge did not guillotine the damages at the point of birth: he regarded it as legitimate to have some regard to the disturbance of family finances caused by the pregnancy—the cost of equipment needed for a new-born child and of larger accommodation, which, for instance, could be considered by the court without regarding the child as unwanted. Accordingly he increased the award of general damages for pain, suffering, inconvenience and anxiety to take that disturbance into account. That figure was £8,000 [37].

In another case (*Emeh* v. *Kensington & Chelsea Area Health Authority*), a mother who already had three healthy children gave birth to a child with congenital deformities after she had been sterilized; she had refused an abortion for fear of its risks. The trial judge awarded £1,500 damages but the Court of Appeal in 1984 disagreed and replaced this by an award of £26,040 plus interest; this sum included damages for the upkeep of the child, the plaintiff's future loss of earnings, the pain and suffering of normal birth and subsequent sterilization, the layette, and an amount to cover the pain, suffering, and loss of amenities because of the need to care for the child.

The Court in 1984 disagreed with the judge's decision that the mother had acted unreasonably to refuse an abortion and Lord Justice Slade stressed that when the pregnancy was discovered, the fetus had grown considerably and an operation would have required three days in hospital and would not have been free from risk; this point leaves open the question whether a refusal by a mother to have an abortion could ever be declared to be unreasonable.

The decision in this case means that if a woman wishes to be sterilized there is no reason why she should not recover damages for the negligent failure to perform the necessary operation whether or not the child to which she gives birth thereafter is healthy. Here there was no claim made on behalf of the deformed child; it was not alleged that the child's deformity was caused by anyone's negligence and accordingly in the British fault-based system of compensation the child could not have been awarded compensation for the deformity nor could the child claim damages either against the hospital authority or against the mother for allowing the child to be born at all [38].

It is comforting to learn that not all patients seek financial recompense. After contemplating legal action when seven months pregnant a mother changed her mind after her confinement. She wrote to the doctor 'I am now the proud mother of a son . . . we are so delighted now at our little mistake we would not change a thing. I would willingly go through it all again for him.' This was a case of failure of tubal ligation and once bitten, twice shy! She continued 'to be on the safe side in future, hubby is going to have a vasectomy. Fingers crossed that it will be 100%' [39].

LAPAROSCOPIC STERILIZATION

This should be a straightforward and safe method but reports of mishaps are regularly received by defence bodies. A common factor is the relative inexperience of the operator, irrespective of his seniority in the profession. Incidents following laparoscopy reported during the period 1969–79 are shown in Table 4.

Nevertheless, the risks of sterilization are less than those of uncontrolled fertility and this is also true if the woman has a complicating disease as well. Members are urged never to regard laparoscopic sterlization as a minor procedure suitable for delegation to an inexperienced operator.

> A woman aged thirty suffered diathermy burns of the right ureter during laparoscopy through an incision in the right iliac fossa. Despite reconstructive surgery there was permanent impairment of the right kidney function. The patient's claim was settled for £3,000 in 1972 [40].

TABLE 4. Incidents following laparoscopy reported to the Medical Defence Union, 1969–1979.

	No.
Death	12
Pregnancy (failed sterilization)	40
Bowel damage (mechanical trauma and burns)	22
Haemorrhage (vessels include aorta, common iliac artery and vena cava)	6
Retained part of instrument	5
Skin burns	5
Anaesthetic disasters (brain damage)	3
Wound infection	2
Ureter damage	1
Stomach perforated	1
Uterus perforated	1
Total	98

Until 1984 few consent forms stated that the operation may fail; this risk is greater than with an open operation on the Fallopian tubes, is more likely in the first year, and pregnancy not sterilization (as the patient might think) may stop the periods—so that abortion may be left too late, and, furthermore, an ectopic gestation is then more likely.

TERMINATION OF PREGNANCY

Problems concerned with damages and the 'unwanted child' are illustrated by the following:

> *Sciuriaga v. Powell* (1979). An unmarried woman sued her doctor for breach of contract in failing to terminate her pregnancy by dilatation and curettage—as a result of which she gave birth to a healthy child. Counsel for the doctor argued that the failure to terminate was not the cause of the birth since the plaintiff preferred to give birth to her child rather than have another attempt at termination. This argument did not impress the judge who saw nothing to criticize in the plaintiff's conduct, holding that the sole effective cause of birth was the defendant's breach of contract. Counsel tried another novel argument that it was contrary to public policy to award damages for breach of contract arising out of a failed operation for termination of pregnancy. The judge disagreed, seeing no public policy reason why she should not recover damages. 'Surely', he said 'no one in these days would argue to the contrary if the child subsequently born was deformed or diseased. The fact that the child born is healthy cannot give rise, I think, to a different conclusion save as to the measure of damages. So I hold that the plaintiff is entitled to recover such damages as have by the evidence been proved to flow from the defendant's breach of contract'. The plaintiff was awarded a total of £18,750: £7,000 for loss of earnings to the date of trial, £7,500 for her future loss of earning capacity, £3,500 for impairment of her marriage prospects, and £750 for the pain and distress suffered in having to undergo the pregnancy and birth by caesarean section. On appeal, the judge reduced the damages to £14,000 as only the size of the award was challenged [41].

> *McKay v. Essex Area Health Authority* (1982). The argument for wrongful life was based on the allegation that doctors had been negligent in allowing the child plaintiff to be born alive after being

deformed *in utero* by her mother's rubella and that they were under a duty to the fetus to terminate its life. This concerned the more general thesis that it may be better not to be born at all than to be born deformed. The Court of Appeal declined to entertain this proposition, holding that doctors were under no legal obligation to the fetus to end its existence, that the claim was contrary to public policy as a violation of the sanctity of human life, and that it could not in any case be recognized or enforced because the court was not able to evaluate the relative merits of existence and non-existence. Later came the passing of the Congenital Disabilities (Civil Liability) Act 1976, one effect of which, supported now by the judgement of the Court of Appeal, was that no child has a cause of action based on the loss of a chance to die [42].

Consent is important in any case of abortion as there is a small risk of complications and of infertility afterwards. The twenty-eight-week limit for termination is probably no longer morally defensible as, in the modern premature unit, the baby has a 50 per cent chance of survival at this stage: the time may be reduced to twenty-four weeks. More and more children are becoming pregnant and the common law does not exclude a child under sixteen consenting to medical treatment so the consent of a child to abortion may be sufficient even in the face of parental objection (Chapter 6).

New discoveries need new ethics and points of view.

ASSISTED REPRODUCTION

The quest to solve the handicap of infertility in women has resulted in a new era of techniques: artificial insemination by donor (AID), *in vitro* fertilization (IVF), babies from frozen embryos, and surrogate mothers. The 'test tube baby' (IVF) is developed when ova taken from the woman are fertilized with the husband's semen and a fertilized ovum is re-implanted into the mother's womb. Several ova are used to make sure of success and this leaves one or more spare embryos as they are not all re-implanted. Research has developed on these for the following reasons: to improve the test-tube-baby technique itself, to study the causes of male infertility such as the behaviour of the sperm, to detect a chromosome abnormality as occurs, for example, in Down's syndrome, to diagnose and possibly correct genetic defects like sickle-cell anaemia, and to improve methods of contraception. The problem is how to define a baby or fetus: is this by its shape and appearance, whether it is like a tadpole or more like a mouse though less like that of a human fetus, or by some arbitrary legal definition! Also, how long is it justified to keep it alive?

The Warnock Committee report (1984) [43] gave guidelines on ethical and other issues and its conclusions correlated closely with those of various other committees. Established under Baroness Warnock, its sixteen members were chosen as representatives of professional, scientific, religious, legal and lay viewpoints. It recommended that a new statutory licensing authority should be set up to regulate infertility services, monitor new developments, and vet individual research projects; also that clinics which undertake IVF and embryo replacement should be licensed and subject to inspection by the licensing body, as should centres that provide AID. The committee was also united in recommending change in the legislation which currently brands children born by AID or IVF as illegitimate. It also approved of freezing embryos as this allows replacement to be made at the optimum time in the menstrual cycle, which increases the chance of a successful pregnancy and avoids repeat laparoscopies; the upper limit of storage of these should be ten years and then the right to use or dispose of the embryo should pass to the storage authority. The most controversial issue was that of research on embryos. The majority decision was that this should only be for fourteen days; this is the time when certain cells become differentiated instead of being an amorphous mass and the primitive streak—an area of rapid growth of specialized cells—can be seen. The Council for Science and Society (1984) had given an alternative time limit of six weeks—until the primitive nervous system had developed and pain could possibly be felt. The Warnock Committee recommended that legislation should be introduced to make it a criminal offence to set up or operate surrogate mother agencies, commercial or otherwise.

The remarkable advances in assisted reproduction which make it possible for the infertile woman to bear or receive a child may well provide a fertile area for medico-legal litigation, for example if a malformed child is born and blamed on the technique. Hence adequate counselling and informed consent by all parties is particularly necessary.

OBSTETRIC DISASTERS

These are tragic for the mother and very costly for any defence body.

> *Whitehouse v. Jordan.* In 1970, after a trial of forceps followed by caesarean section, Stuart Whitehouse was born with severe brain damage. On his behalf his mother sued the obstetrician (at the time

a senior registrar) alleging negligence and claiming damages for personal injuries.

The defendant gave evidence that the plaintiff's head had been a very tight fit; that with the first few pulls with the forceps with the contractions some progress had been made; that with the fifth pull he had realized that he was not making progress; that he had tried once more to see if he could ease the head past what might be minimal obstruction; that he then thought that delivery *per vaginam*, though possible, would be too traumatic; and that he next proceeded to caesarean section, first easing the head slightly upwards with the forceps. The report in the hospital case-notes was 'A trial of forceps was carried out . . . Descent . . . did not follow traction and in the interest of the child the head was disimpacted prior to . . . caesarean section'.

Lord Wilberforce said that brain damage did occur in normal births for no ascertainable reason. The case had been difficult, calling for great care. The defendant's negligence was said to lie in his having continued traction with the forceps after an obstruction had been encountered so that the head had become 'impacted'. The error, if error there had been, lay in the area of expert judgement. The plaintiff's mother had been unable, or had refused, to agree to vaginal examination during pregnancy, or to have a lateral X-ray taken, and accordingly the defendant had not had the advantage of accurate measurements of the pelvis or ischial spines.

After a trial lasting eleven days the judge at first instance found in favour of the infant plaintiff and ordered a payment of £100,000 damages. He decided that the obstetrician at the trial of forceps had pulled too hard and too long so that the fetus became wedged or stuck and that in getting it unwedged or unstuck he caused asphyxia which in turn caused the cerebral palsy. By a majority decision the Court of Appeal reversed the decision and held that the obstetrician had not been negligent. In the appeal the difference between negligence and error of judgement was widely canvassed and the Master of the Rolls, Lord Denning, said 'we must say, and say firmly, that in a professional man, an error of judgement is not negligence' [44]. This important statement was considered and amended to 'not necessarily' negligence when the case was reviewed on further appeal by the House of Lords, although the Court of Appeal judgement in favour of the obstetrician was upheld; this happened eleven years after the incident and this period caused immense workload and expense to the MDU as well as anguish for the obstetrician. In practice, to be certain whether brain damage is congenital or has occurred during birth is often impossible.

ANAESTHETISTS

It is a far cry from the days when general anaesthesia for major surgery depended upon the inhalation of vapours like ether and chloroform—'the rag and bottle' method. The practice of immobilizing the patient by curare and later by the synthetic neuromuscular blocking agents started in the 1950s. Balanced anaesthesia was then developed by using separate drugs to produce specific effects: intravenous thiopentone to induce sleep, followed by the blocking agent to produce muscle relaxation and nitrous oxide to maintain unconsciousness and to provide analgesia, perhaps supplemented by a strong analgesic drug like pethidine. An increase in the death rate occurred in the USA, though apparently not in the UK; this was not due to the blocking drugs but because of insufficient ventilation of the paralysed patient [45]. At first controlled ventilation, necessary because of the respiratory paralysis, was done manually but now various mechanical ventilators are used: unfortunately the failure of anaesthetists to understand the mechanics of some of these still leads to disasters.

THE WRONG DRUG

Anaesthetists run a risk of using the wrong drug or too much of the right one because they not only prescribe drugs but administer them, and many are potent. If an emergency arises during the operation or in the intensive therapy unit, the normal check on what drug the patient is having may not be possible and some drugs are prepared for anaesthetists by non-nursing ancillary staff; errors can be dangerous and sometimes cost lives.

INJURY TO TEETH

In 1977 the MDU alone dealt with twenty-three claims from patients for dental damage [46]. The anaesthetist had usually examined the patient pre-operatively and considered his dentition. Teeth or prostheses were thought to be at special risk in ten cases and particular care was exercised during the anaesthetic; in fifteen an endotracheal tube was used whereas oral airways had been used in the others. Dental damage included enamel chipping, loss of upper and lower incisors, loosening or removing of crowns, bridges and gold inlays. In one case a partial denture which had been left in the mouth was

108

broken during laryngoscopy. The risk of damage is increased if there is decay or periodontal disease, if teeth have been heavily filled, or if crowns, bridges and inlays are present; permanent and deciduous teeth are easily dislodged in children while in the elderly periodontal disease and brittle teeth increase the risk, and isolated teeth are especially vulnerable.

If damage occurs in spite of a careful routine which includes examination of the mouth beforehand, a claim should be defensible though, as always, good clinical notes are essential. If damage has occurred, formal complaints and claims for compensation may be avoided if a sympathetic explanation is given to the patient and when all reasonable steps are taken to repair the damage as soon as possible. The MPS published a useful article on the subject of *damage to teeth during the administration of general anaesthesia* [47].

HOARSENESS

This is not unusual because of the common use of transient endotracheal tubes for most operations but there is seldom any problem if this is explained to the patient.

SPINAL AND EPIDURAL ANAESTHESIA

In the case *Roe and Woolley* v. *Ministry of Health* (1954) a spinal injection of Nupercaine to two patients caused a spastic paraplegia owing to the infiltration of phenol in which the ampoule of Nupercaine was stored. The Court of Appeal held that in the state of medical knowledge in 1947 neither the anaesthetist nor any other members of the staff had been guilty of negligence as they could not reasonably then have suspected that phenol would percolate through invisible cracks in the ampoule [48]. However, since the case became known prevention of a recurrence would be expected; colouring the phenol so that infiltration into the anaesthetic would be noticed should suffice.

The wrong drug is a hazard with epidural anaesthesia especially when this is maintained continuously with a line (catheter) left in the epidural space. The doctor should give the first injection though midwives are allowed to 'top up' afterwards but 'topping up' with the wrong drug has proved disastrous in more than one case. High epidurals carry a risk of hypotension and, rarely, of neurological sequelae.

AWARENESS DURING OPERATION

The immobility of the patient prevents the anaesthetist knowing about the state of consciousness so that it is possible for a patient to know what is going on, as happens when major operations are done under local anaesthesia. For example, after an operation under general anaesthesia, a fifty-year-old woman claimed that she had been aware during the operation and could recall various statements made by staff.

> Although the anaesthetic agents given would normally ensure anaesthesia, the account given by the patient of the remarks proved awareness; so a settlement of £1,500 was made in 1980 [49].

Anaesthetists sometimes need to keep a seriously ill patient 'light' as this is safer. Warning the patient that he may be aware at some point and may feel a tube in the wind-pipe (intratracheal tube) is then advisable, together with reassurance that no pain will be felt.

Diagnostic investigations

New methods of diagnosis are often associated with new risks which are unforeseen and unrealized until a series of cases has been reported and investigated. When such risks are known to exist, they should be explained to the patient before submitting him to the new test. When in doubt, the doctor should ask himself whether he would order the investigation for his spouse or relative and whether it will ultimately benefit the patient.

INVASIVE VASCULAR PROCEDURES

Manoeuvres to insert a needle into a vein or artery have become sophisticated; they are usually done by junior doctors and carry occasional serious complications. Just taking a sample of blood is virtually free from risk except that a nervous person may faint; an explanation and ensuring the comfort of the patient are important. The injection of substances carries the hazard of the wrong drug. Plastic catheters have caused trouble: in 1964 a letter, signed by the Secretaries of the three defence organizations and published in the *British Medical Journal*, stated 'during the past year several members have reported incidents in which a piece of plastic catheter was lost in the patient's venous system during intravenous therapy. Great care must be taken when using these plastic catheters. If an attempt is made to withdraw the plastic catheter through the needle there is a real danger that the bevel will cut through the catheter, thus leaving part of the catheter inside the lumen of the vein. If there is any difficulty when the plastic tube is inserted into the vein through a needle, it is most important that both the catheter and the needle should be removed at the same time' [50]. Sliced-off portions have come to rest in the chambers of

the heart, in the periphery of the lung, and even in the amniotic space—
eventually being delivered with the placenta.

> A perforated appendix was removed from a five-year-old girl in the
> Republic of Ireland. As she was toxic and dehydrated, an intrave-
> nous infusion was set up; on introducing the needle and catheter
> and manoeuvring to find a favourable position, the paediatric SHO
> realized that the distal bit of the catheter had broken off. The
> antecubital area was explored under local anaesthesia but without
> success and a chest X-ray showed the fragment in the lung. The
> patient was transferred by helicopter to another hospital where at
> thoracotomy the piece of catheter was successfully removed from the
> pulmonary artery. She developed a pelvic abscess but otherwise
> recovered satisfactorily. The claim for damages centred on the
> disfiguring thoracotomy scar and its effect on the girl as she grew
> up. On counsel's advice £6,000 was paid into court after the failure
> to agree to a figure with the patient's legal advisers. This sum was
> eventually accepted in 1978; the MDU also paid the plaintiff's costs
> of £847 [51].

> *Spinal catheter accident.* In attempting epidural anaesthesia on a 21-
> year-old woman in labour a SHO anaesthetist twice encountered
> difficulties. The patient complained of severe pain in her right leg
> after introducing the first catheter which was then withdrawn and a
> second catheter was also unsatisfactorily introduced. When both
> were examined, three centimetres were missing from the first one
> and the tip from the second. The baby was successfully delivered.
> Nearly a month later laminectomy showed that the longer portion of
> catheter was pressing on the second lumbar root; the broken piece
> was removed. The second tip could not be found but the woman had
> no further pain. A claim, based on an unnecessary operation and
> pain and suffering was settled in 1976 for £1,379 including costs
> [52].

A central venous catheter from a peripheral vein in the arm to one of the
central veins of the thorax should be used with discretion and removed as soon
as possible because of the following complications: inflammation of the site of
the skin entry and subsequent bacterial invasion of the drip itself; septicaemia
caused by infection of the tip of the catheter; other possibilities are air embolus,
haemothorax and thrombophlebitis.

Arterial puncture is usually safe but an indwelling arterial cannula should be removed as soon as no longer required for it can cause gangrene of the tips of the fingers from ischaemia; a careful watch has to be kept to prevent the components of any monitoring system becoming detached as failure to do so can lead to severe loss of blood—indeed patients have committed suicide in this way. Injecting substances into the arterial system should never be done unless some benefit to the patient is possible.

> A 39-year-old man was referred for selective renal angiography to diagnose the cause of his hypertension. On recovery from the anaesthetic he was found to be paraplegic. He complained that the doctor had been negligent because the contrast medium was over-concentrated and in excessive dosage. The MDU's experts advised that, while the contrast medium was satisfactory for the aorto-graphy and identification of the renal arteries, it was too concen-trated for renal angiography and that this was probably unnecessary in view of the quality of the initial aortic X-ray. The paraplegia was due to chemical myelitis and the claim was settled for £125,000 plus £10,000 costs [53].

Lumbar puncture when used to obtain a sample of spinal fluid for analysis is a simple and safe procedure; meningitis due to a pseudomonas organism was a hazard when lumbar puncture needles were stored in so-called 'antiseptic' solutions, but this risk has gone now that equipment is dry-sterilized. In the UK the greatest hazards occur when the wrong solution is injected into the theca or whenever it is injected in the wrong concentration. Every doctor, therefore, must *himself* inspect the ampoule from which a solution has been drawn and check its nature and strength, whether it is an antibiotic, spinal anaesthetic, or radiological contrast medium.

RADIOLOGY

'Radiology as a specialty has now arrived as radiologists and not just physicians and surgeons are being sued', wryly commented a consultant radiologist. The usual cases, apart from missed fractures, are burns, when the apparatus is not shock proof, and injuries: the patient falling off the X-ray table or bits of equipment hitting him. Sometimes claims against the radiologist stem from the activities of an assistant:

> A radiologist was acting as a locum at a hospital where he had not previously worked and the X-ray apparatus was unfamiliar; he was examining this with the senior radiographer who was explaining the

controls of the machine, when the first patient, a woman of seventy-seven, was brought in and prepared for a barium enema examination. An unqualified nurse from the ward put her on the examination table and an unqualified male radiographer asked who was to insert the catheter and was told that this should be done by the nurse, as the patient was a woman: the nurse said that she had never done this but was told that all she had to do was to insert the catheter into the rectum. She did this and the radiologist allowed the barium to run in. As soon as she was turned into the oblique position he saw that something was seriously wrong, stopped the barium flow and discontinued the examination. The patient collapsed and died within two minutes and it was found that the catheter had been inserted into the vagina by mistake. At the inquest the pathologist gave the cause of death as 'shock due to a ruptured vagina due to the introduction of barium under pressure'. The Coroner in 1962 recorded a verdict of death by misadventure [54].

A sixty-year-old actor attended for a barium enema. The radiologist questioned him about previous investigations but received only monosyllabic replies. An experienced State Registered Nurse inserted the catheter. No undue pressure was exerted and he did not appear to suffer unusual discomfort; nor was any leak from the rectum detected on screening or on the X-ray film. Later the same day he returned to the hospital and further X-rays showed that barium had entered the pelvic tissues due to a perforation; a temporary colostomy was performed. Later, solicitors acting for the patient claimed that he had suffered extreme discomfort and that a self-retaining catheter should not have been used. The patient claimed loss of earnings as an actor and writer. Experts advised that perforation of the colon is a rare but well recognized hazard of a barium enema especially in patients with ulcerative colitis. The claim was settled in 1974 for £3,365 [55].

Invasive investigations have always been carried out by radiologists, from intravenous urography to bronchography, and these can result in medico-legal problems, but it is the more complicated methods such as arteriography that cause trouble nowadays. Also, the more X-rays that are done, the greater is the risk of radiation damage. During pregnancy only essential X-rays should be performed; the 'ten-day rule' which means that any X-rays should be done within the first ten days of the menstrual cycle avoids irradiation of a fetus in early pregnancy.

Incidentally, X-rays are the property of the hospital in the NHS and of the radiologist in private practice: the legal view is that the patient pays for an opinion and not for the celluloid.

Drugs

Litigation due to drug-induced disease is a growth area. This is not surprising in view of the increased number and variety of drugs used to influence human behaviour from the cradle to the grave. As Malcolm Muggeridge wrote, in an apt parody of the psalmist's song, 'I will lift up mine eyes unto the pills from whence cometh my help . . . for every ill a pill. Tranquillisers to overcome angst, pep pills to wake us up, life pills to ensure blissful sterility'. We are living in an age of pills, although the UK does not even come into the top ten European countries in terms of consumption—Switzerland and West Germany run about equal first. Prescribing usually correlates with wealth so that the more affluent the country the more drugs people consume [9].

In the UK, the law requires doctors to keep controlled drugs in safe custody. This means in a 'locked receptacle.' In cases decided by the courts, a medical bag has been considered satisfactory providing that it is kept locked. Doctors have been convicted for leaving unlocked bags even in the apparent safety of a locked car, since a judge has ruled that a car is not a receptacle. A member once consulted the MDU, stating that he often made visits near his home on a bicycle, and carried his medical bag in the basket. Although there had been a case where a bag was stolen from an unlocked car and the police took no action because the bag was locked, he was advised that he might not be so favourably treated with his bicycle; but it would be interesting to see the form of words devised by the police authority in charging him if the bag were stolen.

Many allegations are made against general practitioners but only a few, perhaps 5 per cent, come to court. Amongst the 15,800 inquiries reaching the secretariat of the MDU in an eighteen-month period between 1982 and 1983 there were 206 from GPs about drugs. The commonest was about addiction: problems usually concerned patients (though sometimes were about doctors themselves), or the forging of prescriptions and the occasional need to answer Drug Squad inquiries. Next came allegations about side-effects of drugs—patients not being warned or being allergic to them; then complaints about prescriptions being repeated without the patient having being seen or examined. Miscellaneous inquiries concerned death attributed to drugs, possibly wrong drugs being given, drugs and driving, the use of blank pre-signed prescription forms, drugs and pregnancy, prescribing the contraceptive pill to girls under sixteen and prescriptions wrongly dispensed by the chemist or pharmacist.

THE WRONG DRUG

Any number of examples can be selected from the files of any defence body to illustrate use of the wrong drug.

A well-known Continental professor of ophthalmology who was visiting England in 1947 was asked to demonstrate a corneal graft operation. All was made ready and the professor proposed, before starting, to instill into the eye a drop of adrenaline. This he did from a bottle clearly labelled 'adrenaline'. The results were startling and it was immediately obvious that what had been instilled was not adrenaline. Investigation showed that this bottle had, with others, been washed out in the hospital pharmacy with dilute hydrochloric acid and sent to the operating theatre without being refilled with adrenaline; the accident was wholly attributable to the mistake which had occurred in the hospital pharmacy. Fortunately no damage occurred and the plaintiff's solicitors did not pursue any claim [56]. This illustrated the common 'galley pot' disaster when fluids from a large bottle were poured into a small receptacle; pharmacists now prefer substances to be dispensed in small containers.

A general practitioner saw a man who was due to fly to Africa in six days' time. She intended to give him an injection of cholera vaccine but chose the wrong ampoule and injected 1 ml of Modecate, a powerful long-acting tranquillizer used for the maintenance treatment of psychotic disorders: the result was that he had to postpone his journey for one week. His solicitors, claiming damages, stated that at the airport, suffering from the effects of the injection, he had mislaid a number of items including a camera, a suit, a coat, a fountain pen and wrist watch, together with some important papers. The claim was settled for £200 plus £40 costs [57].

An elderly man with Eustachian catarrh was advised by his doctor to buy an inhalation from the chemist. The doctor wrote on a scrap of paper the words 'menthol and eucalyptus inhalation' and gave the scrap of paper to the patient, advising him how to use this. On the next evening the man returned to the surgery complaining of severe pain in the chest and back. The chemist, instead of dispensing menthol and eucalyptus inhalation, had given him Clinitest tablets.

115

The reason for this was that the bit of paper had the words 'Clinitest tabs' also written on it. The doctor had failed to notice this; moreover the chemist had failed to notice the prescription for the inhalation. It was surprising that the patient, having been told how to inhale, should have swallowed tablets. He had taken four tablets and following advice from the poison centre the doctor advised him just to drink milk. Swallowing became painful but symptoms disappeared during the next few days; twelve days later endoscopy revealed an area of sloughing of the oesophageal mucosa at the level of the aortic arch but he recovered and there were no legal sequelae [58].

A young woman, believing that she was pregnant, was concerned because a few days previously she had been in contact with German measles. The doctor asked his practice nurse, an employee of the health authority, to take a blood test for rubella antibodies. The nurse misunderstood his instructions and gave the patient rubella vaccine instead. The mistake was recognized immediately, and a blood test was taken. This showed that she was not rubella immune and a termination of pregnancy was arranged. Her solicitors later wrote to the doctor, saying that their client had suffered very considerable mental anguish, and that they looked to him to compensate her for this. The MDU in conjunction with the health authority's solicitors agreed that the claim was indefensible. It was settled in 1982 for £500 plus costs, of which the health authority paid 80 per cent [59].

ERRORS IN ADMINISTRATION OF DRUGS

Errors are likely to concern injections: subcutaneous instead of intramuscular (some drugs can cause permanent subcutaneous atrophy), into a nerve instead of the tissues, or into an artery instead of a vein.

A general practitioner employed a locum tenens who was not a member of a medical defence body. The locum injected Butazolidin into a patient's buttock and caused a complete sciatic nerve palsy. A day or two later the same locum injected pethidine into the left arm of another patient causing an injury to the radial nerve. The GP was liable for the negligence of his locum tenens and ensuing claims could not be defended. Safe areas for intramuscular injection are the upper outer quadrant of the buttock or the lateral aspect of the thigh [60].

A seventy-year-old man with Hodgkin's disease was treated with intravenous cytotoxic drugs by a medical registrar. The first and second courses of injections were uneventful, but soon after the third course the left hand became painful, swollen and red. Conservative treatment failed and a forearm amputation was necessary. There was little doubt that the third injection had accidentally gone into the radial artery. Three years later a report showed no evidence of recurrence of the Hodgkin's disease. The claim was settled in 1977 for £3,330 including costs [61].

The antecubital fossa is a dangerous area not only because of the radial artery lying near the vein but because an aberrant ulnar artery may run just under the median vein.

HOW DO MISTAKES OCCUR?

Drugs reach the patient through a complex industrial process: production of a pure drug in the right concentration, correct labelling and dispensing, storage, renewal, and carriage from place to place. For example, a bulk supply to the hospital pharmacy is broken into smaller packs and sent to the operating theatre; the ampoules may then be used individually, transferred to a second pack on an anaesthetic machine or even taken out, not used, and returned to one of the packs—perhaps the wrong one. Each handling carries a risk of error, and the more the handling the more the risk multiplies. Also, the number of new drugs with esoteric or euphonious names and synonyms has created a situation as confused as the Tower of Babel. Perusal of the list in 'Drug names that look or sound alike' [62] shows that two drugs can easily be muddled: for example, 'chlorpropamide', which reduces the blood sugar, and 'chlorpromazine' the tranquillizer. Verbal prescriptions especially when given over the telephone are a notorious source of error and should only be used in an emergency.

Bad handwriting is a proverbial fault of doctors although no-one seems to have done any comparison with handwriting of those in other walks of life. The following was a disastrous consequence both for the patient and the Medical Defence Union:

In 1974 a general practitioner saw a 23-year-old widow who was due to enter hospital for an abortion. She had a sore throat and respiratory infection, so he wrote a prescription for erythromycin and Mogadon. He visited her later that day because a neighbour was worried about her but he found nothing wrong except that she complained of dizziness. Two days later he was telephoned and told that she had just slept and had not eaten. He called on her but found no abnormality. He checked the Mogadon tablets, of which she had taken only two, but did not check the antibiotics. He said that he would call next day, but before he could do so the casualty department of the local hospital informed him that she had been admitted unconscious. He checked his prescription at the hospital's

FIGURE 18. Bad handwriting can cost lives. This is an example of prescriptions that the community pharmacist (formally retail chemist) may find difficult to decipher.

request: the script had been dispensed by a locum pharmacist who misread it and dispensed Euglucon (glibenclamide used for treating diabetes) for erythromycin, causing hypoglycaemia and brain damage.

The patient's solicitors started proceedings against the chemist alleging negligence in dispensing; he in turn claimed against the doctor on the ground that the prescription form was almost illegible. The view of the MDU was that the pharmacist should have checked the dosage of three tablets three times daily, which would be unusual for Euglucon. In 1981, the claim was settled by the chemist for £55,000, the MDU contributing a third under threat of third-party proceedings by the chemist [63].

Illegible prescriptions, although fortunately uncommon, provide a particular problem for the community pharmacist (formerly retail chemist) because he may find it difficult to contact the GP who may be on his rounds whereas the hospital pharmacist can phone the doctor on the ward. It is better if the prescription cannot be read at all, for then the drug is not dispensed; it is the ambiguous prescriptions that can be dangerous. The journal *Chemist and Druggist* holds a competition called Prescription Posers where the pharmacist who sends in the correct answer to the hieroglyphics (Figure 18) wins a prize. Some doctors who cannot write clearly solve the difficulty by using capital letters for the name of the drug.

A wrong dose may be caused by confusion between ml and mg:

A psychiatrist made a domicilliary visit to an eighty-year-old woman in an old peoples' home and prescribed a tranquillizer as she was suffering from dementia. She would not take tablets so the member wrote her up for 50 mg in syrup in the morning and 75 mg at night. Four days later she was admitted to hospital unconscious and the referral letter stated that millilitres had been administered instead of milligrams. She died two days later and at an inquest it was reported that the nurses had given her five times the intended dosage. The coroner reported death by misadventure and the doctor was exonerated.

When prescribing remember that

The wrong decimal point can be disastrous. If decimals are unavoidable, put a zero in front if there is no other figure

0·5 *not* ·5

But better still use milligrams if amount is less than 1 g

500 mg *not* 0·5 g

And for less than 1 mg use microgram spelt in full

100 micrograms *not* 0·1 mg

A misplaced decimal point has also cost lives. Digoxin is often a culprit, especially in infants or the elderly, when 1·25 mg instead of 0·125 mg is given (actually the present view is that digoxin is seldom indicated except for atrial fibrillation); other drugs that have caused disasters in this way are insulin, cytotoxic drugs like methotrexate and intrathecal penicillin. If a decimal point has to be used, a figure should always be put in front of it: 0·5 and not ·5. The British National Formulary states that micrograms should be written in full and not abbreviated for quantities less than 1 mg, so digoxin should be prescribed as 250 micrograms and not 0·25 mg.

IDENTICAL AMPOULES

Failure to read the label on the ampoule may cause cardiac arrest from intravenous potassium. Ampoules of the harmless sodium chloride (NaCl) are identical to those for potassium chloride (KCl)—in size, colour of solution, and type of lettering. What can happen is that a nurse replaces the ampoule into the wrong pack: then a doctor called to an urgent case during the night picks a KCl ampoule from the box labelled NaCl (Figure 19) and injects it causing, in a baby, instant death. Ampoules of ergotamine and vitamin K also look alike and will result in gangrene of fingers if the former is injected instead of the latter. It is surprising that no official action has been taken to avoid these recurring catastrophies by the colour coding of ampoules or by changing their shape. The doctor should still read the label on every ampoule but it would provide an added safeguard.*

* Since this was written, ampoules of potassium chloride have been supplied by the manufacturers (Antigen International Ltd) with a black plastic cap over the neck of the ampoule. These have replaced the previous ones in the West Midlands region and are available elsewhere.

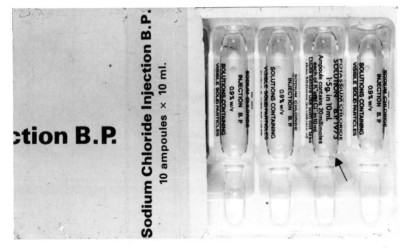

FIGURE 19. Ampoules of the harmless sodium chloride are identical to those of potassium chloride which can be fatal if injected quickly; an ampoule of this (see arrow) was put in the wrong box. The label must always be read.

ADVERSE DRUG REACTIONS

Adverse effects from drug therapy are thought to affect between 10 and 18 per cent of patients admitted to hospital and may account for one in forty consultations in general practice [64]. They are obviously an important cause of morbidity, may affect the doctor–patient relationship and deter the patient from taking drugs in the future, and can result in litigation. Some are preventable but others—the idiosyncratic reactions—come out of the blue. Of all the substances listed in the Pharmacopoeia, water (taken by mouth) is the only one free from possible side-effects.

Simple examples are an allergic rash due to penicillin or iodine sensitivity— perhaps anticipated if a detailed history had been taken. Sometimes failure to reduce the dose in someone where drug metabolism and elimination are impaired is the cause of overdosage, for example, prescribing digoxin for a patient with kidney disease. Deafness may result from streptomycin or gentamicin and can be due to inadequate follow-up, or failure to monitor blood levels, as is so necessary when using lithium for mania. No drug should ever be prescribed without its being written in the notes:

> A GP was called on a Sunday morning to see a soldier who had
> suffered a haemoptysis while staying with his fiancée. He ordered a
> chest X-ray and prescribed some tablets but made no note of these

on either a continuation sheet or temporary resident's form. Four days later he was asked to see the fiancée, who was taken to his surgery in a distressed state having swallowed 'most' of the soldier's tablets as a suicide attempt. The doctor could not remember what he had prescribed and asked the soldier to describe the tablets; told that they were glossy and chocolate-coloured, he decided that they were a vitamin preparation and assured the girl she would come to no harm. Consequently, she did not report copious black vomiting during the next two days, and sent for him only when *in extremis*. She died in hospital; the doctor had prescribed 100 tablets of an iron preparation [65].

Problems with monoamine oxidase inhibitors occurred especially when patients were not warned about avoiding an incompatible drug, or a food such as cheese, broad beans or Marmite.

A GP in 1966 prescribed Parnate 10 mg t.d.s. (thrice daily) for a married woman suffering from a depressive illness. He told her that there was 'something special' about the tablets and warned her that she must avoid eating cheese or Marmite, adding that this 'could be serious'; he tried to convey the seriousness of the warning without telling her that the combination of the two had occasionally caused death. She acknowledged the warning by saying 'all right' or words to that effect. Two days later she had a stroke and in hospital it was found that she had eaten biscuits and cheese for breakfast.

Her husband brought an action claiming damages for her loss of expectation of life and the action came to trial in 1970. The basis of the plaintiff's case was that no warning had been given or that it was inadequate, having regard to her mental condition. Great reliance at the inquest was placed upon the remarks made by the doctor when he said that on looking back he wondered whether the patient had forgotten the instruction or had not taken it in. It was claimed that he should have given written instructions. It was alleged that Parnate should not have been prescribed and that when the patient was first seen after her stroke, steps should have been taken to empty her stomach, although she was by that time almost unconscious. In the end, the only real issue concerned *the warning* and its adequacy. Judgement was in favour of the doctor with costs. The judge observed that the burden of proof which lay on the plaintiff had not been discharged but that he was not prepared to determine the case on that narrow issue but rather on the impression which the practitioner had made on him as a witness. The judge said that the doctor's clinical notes were 'quite out of the ordinary'; nobody listening to his evidence could have failed to appreciate that he was 'intelligent, knowledgeable and concerned for his patients'. He concluded by saying that the practitioner did all that could be expected of a doctor and that his patients were lucky to have him. He left the court with his reputation 'not only intact but enhanced'. The MDU was awarded costs of nearly £5,000 and insisted that the plaintiff should pay £250 by instalments, accepting that he was not in the position to pay in full [66].

Drug interactions are an increasing hazard as polypharmacy is so common (Figure 20):

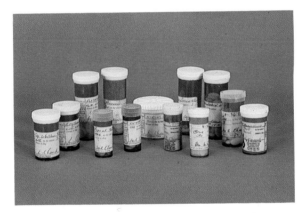

FIGURE 20. Polypharmacy increases the chance of a drug interaction. This picture shows the large number of drugs that may occasionally be prescribed for one patient.

In 1981 a 64-year-old man with rheumatic problems and a previous myocardial infarction attended his doctor who diagnosed tenosynovitis and prescribed phenylbutazone. Ten days later the patient was admitted to hospital with severe neurological abnormalities due to haemorrhage into the spinal cord. The patient had been on a long-term anticoagulant and the phenylbutazone had potentiated its effect. The notes held by the GP had the words 'on anticoagulants' written on the folder but when a new folder had been used this information had not been transferred to it. The case was settled for £44,000 [67].

FIGURE 21. The result of a failure of the contraceptive pill due to an interaction with another drug (by kind permission of Charles F. George, Professor of Clinical Pharmacology at the University of Southampton).

Professor Charles F. George of the Department of Clinical Pharmacology in the University of Southampton showed me the photograph of a small boy playing on a beach 'born as the result of a drug interaction' (Figure 21). His mother was on the contraceptive pill but was also taking phenytoin as she was an epileptic. Certain drugs—antibiotics, and anticonvulsants—may reduce the effect of the Pill. Although the risk of contraceptive failure is small, additional contraceptive cover might seem wise [68].

A patient may need to know about the possible effects of a drug on his performance: in driving or making decisions, and whether there are any interactions with alcohol or other drugs. Many do not receive all this information and there is seldom any warning on the medicine bottle about this; also few of those who are given it understand it or remember it well enough to use it fully, so written hand-outs are often essential and some are provided by the drug firms. This is particularly important with drugs that may affect driving—one woman who had been prescribed Ativan unexpectedly found herself sitting in her car in a field! In another case a GP in Canada diagnosed bronchitis and prescribed aspirin and ampicillin. Unfortunately, he dispensed a barbiturate in error for ampicillin. The next day the patient fell asleep at the wheel of his car and drove it into a telegraph pole but was uninjured. The MDU met the cost of treatment for the telegraph pole and the car.

Certain drugs are withdrawn by the Committee on Safety of Medicines because of serious side-effects but doctors have the right to prescribe what they regard as being in the best interest of their patient—and some patients may wish to continue the drug if it helps and is apparently safe for them to do so. If so, the prescription should be hand-written and signed by the doctor, perhaps with some positive endorsement by the prescriber, such as 'special order' or a signature against the product. The pharmacist would contact the prescriber as usual if the item was not absolutely clear.

AVOIDANCE OF DRUG DISASTERS

Since there are so many similar drugs on the market, it is safer if doctors restrict themselves to using a few known drugs. The data sheet issued by the manufacturer should always be studied and the instructions followed, for example, routine blood tests such as checking the white blood cells in the case of gold therapy. The pharmacist is an invaluable ally of the doctor and should diplomatically refer a prescription back to him whenever he is in doubt. Junior doctors carry a copy of the British National Formulary (BNF) in a pocket of their white coats and consult it when unsure about the dose. Prescriptions should be written as indicated in the BNF (pp. 3 & 4). In the future, computerized prescribing may be an advantage, for bad handwriting would be avoided and a tear-off slip would provide information for the patient.

TELLING THE PATIENT

Pharmacologists and lay pressure groups both criticize the lack of information given by many doctors to patients. Table 5 shows a possible check-list of what to tell the patient [69]. The community pharmacist plays an important role in informing the patient when he dispenses the GP's prescription. The author has used record cards with tablets fixed to them by Sellotape which are given to the patient on discharge from hospital; beside each tablet is its name and synonym and what it is supposed to do (Figure 22)—junior staff perform this and at the same time learn about the size and shape of tablets. Those cards are carried by

TABLE 5. What to tell the patient about the medicine [69].

---

1 Name of medicine.*

2 Whether it is meant to treat the disease or to relieve symptoms, and therefore how important it is to take it.

3 How to tell if it is working, and what to do if it appears not to be working.

4 When and how to take it, before or after meals.*†

5 What to do if a dose is missed.†

6 How long to take it.

7 Side-effects that are important for the patient, and what to do about them.

8 Possible effects on driving, on work, etc. and what precautions to take.*†

9 Interactions with alcohol and other drugs.*†

(Storage and disposal of the medicine are best mentioned by the pharmacist)

---

*=label will usually help

†=item which the pharmacist can reinforce

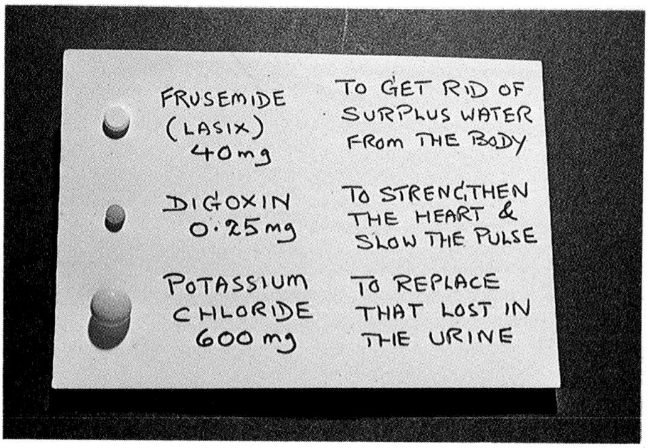

FIGURE 22. A tablet of each drug is fixed to a record card and its name and purpose written beside it. This is given to the patient and can be shown to any new doctor in an emergency. (Digoxin 250 micrograms is better—see page 120.)

the patient and, if necessary, shown to a new doctor who may not have the case notes.

A problem arises in court cases as to how soon after publication a doctor should know of the risks of a drug, for example thalidomide. Keeping up to date with drugs is a herculean task for any doctor though this is, fortunately, helped by publications such as *Drug and Therapeutics Bulletin* and *Prescribers Journal*.

Hazards for doctors and dentists the world over

Soon there may be a 'Drug Information on-Line' through Prestel where doctors can be updated monthly. A check-list of some questions worth asking [70] about what we prescribe is given in Table 6.

TABLE 6. Some questions worth asking about what we prescribe [70].

1 *Need*	Is the drug really needed? What is likely to happen if it is not used?	
2 *Class*	To what class does the drug belong? (e.g. a potassium-sparing diuretic; a phenothiazine)	
3 *Aim*	What aim is to be achieved with the drug? What disorder of function is to be corrected, or what symptom relieved? When are the treatment effects expected to begin?	
4 *Observations*	What observations should be made to judge whether the aim has been achieved? How should serious unwanted effects be watched for? When should these observations be made, and by whom?	
5 *Route and dosage*	By what route, in what dose, at what intervals and at what times is the drug to be given, and why? Up to what limit is it worth increasing dosage and/or frequency if the response is inadequate?	
6 *Alternatives*	What other drugs could be used instead of this one? Do the drugs differ notably in efficacy or safety? Do their costs differ much? (It is often advantageous in efficacy and safety to use the drug with which one is most familiar; this also saves the prescriber's neurones.)	
7 *Duration*	How long should the drug continue to be used, and how will the decision be made to stop?	
8 *Unwanted effects*	What undesirable effects may occur from the drug? Are they acceptable? What is their approximate frequency? How can they be avoided, or treated if they occur?	
9 *Elimination*	How is the drug eliminated? Will the patient's illness change the usual pattern of distribution and effects of the drug? If yes, how does this affect the dosage?	
10 *Interactions*	Are there any other drugs, foods or activities which the patient should avoid while he is receiving the drug?	
11 *Patient's ideas*	What does the patient believe about the drug? What has he been told about it and what does he remember? Does he need additional information? Will he take the drug?	

Chapter 4

References

1 Baderman H. *Communication in Medicine*. Medical Protection Society Annual Report, 1976, p. 23–7.
2 Walton J. & McLachlan G. (Eds.) *Doctor to Doctor: Writing and Talking About Patients*. A collection of essays from a Nuffield Working Party on Communication. London: The Nuffield Provincial Hospitals Trust, 1984.
3 The defence of 'usual practice' in negligence cases. British Medical Journal 2 (1959): 1190.
4 Addison P.H. Chaperones (letter). *British Medical Journal* 1 (1971): 555.
5 *Annual Report*. London: Medical Defence Union, 1980, p. 55–6.
6 *Ibid*. 1983, 55–6.
7 *Ibid*. 1980, 45–6.
8 *Ibid*. 1982, 61.
9 Fry J. *Present State and Future Needs in General Practice*. London: NTP Press for the Royal College of General Practitioners, 1983.
10 *Annual Report*. London: Medical Defence Union, 1983, p. 17.
11 *Ibid*. 1984, 43–4.
12 *Ibid*. 1976, 9–10.
13 Malaria in Britain: 1982. *British Medical Journal* 287 (1983): 1789.
14 Weir W.R.C., Hodges J.M., Wright J.F.C., Higgins A.F. & Corringham R.E.T. Atypical falciparum malaria—case report. *British Medical Journal* 289 (1984): 178.
15 *Annual Report*. London: Medical Defence Union, 1980, p. 35.
16 *Ibid*. 1979, 16.
17 *Ibid*. 1974, 96.
18 Nathan P.C. & Barrowclough A.R. *Medical Negligence*. London: Butterworth, 1957.
19 *Boase* v. *Paul. Dominion Law Reports* 1 (1931): 562.
20 *Annual Report*. London: Medical Defence Union, 1982, p. 71.
21 *Ibid*. 1981, 68–9.
22 *Ibid*. 1977, 57–8.
23 *Ibid*. 1973, 79.
24 Carling, Sir Ernest R. Current problems of medical defence organisations. *Medico-Legal Journal* 2 (1960): 60–74.
25 *Annual Report*. London: Medical Defence Union, 1982, p. 68–9.
26 *Ibid*. 1980, 67–8.
27 Deaths associated with dentistry. *British Dental Journal* 153 (1982): 351–362.
28 The Wylie Report: report of the working party on training in dental anaesthesia. *British Dental Journal*. 151 (1981): 385–8.
29 The Seward Report: of the inter-faculty working party formed to consider the implementation of the Wylie Report. *Ibid*: 389–91.
30 Annual Report. London: Medical Defence Union, 1970. p. 27–8.
31 *Ibid*. 1972, 62–3.
32 *Ibid*. 1982, 58.
33 *Ibid*. 1976, 34.
34 *Ibid*. 1972, 69–70.
35 *Ibid*. 1984, 27–8.
36 *Chaunt* v. *Hertfordshire Area Health Authority. New Law Journal* 132 (1982): 1054.
37 *Udale* v. *Bloomsbury Health Authority (1983). All England Law Reports* 2:522.
38 Medicolegal: damages and the 'unwanted child' (by our legal correspondent). *British Medical Journal* 288 (1984): 244–5 and 289: 565.
39 *Annual Report*. London: Medical Defence Union, 1982, p. 60.
40 *Ibid*. 1973, 16–17.
41 *Sciuriaga* v. *Powell. Solicitor's Journal* 123 (1979): 406.
42 *McKay* v. *Essex Area Health Authority (1982). Weekly Law Reports*. 2 (1982): 890–914.

43 *Warnock Report.* Committee of Enquiry into Human Fertilisation and Embryology (Chairman, Baroness Warnock) Report. London: HMSO, 1984.

44 *Whitehouse* v. *Jordan (1980). All England Law Reports* 650 (1981): 267–288 and *Lancet* 1 (1981): 167.

45 Beecher H.K. & Todd D.P. Deaths associated with anaesthesia and surgery, *Annals of Surgery* 140 (1954): 2–34.

46 *Annual Report.* London: Medical Defence Union, 1978, p. 11–12.

47 Wright R.B. *Damage to Teeth during the Administration of General Anaesthesia.* London: Medical Protection Society, 1973, p. 21–4.

48 *Roe and Woolley* v. *Minister of Health. Queens Bench* 2 (1954): 66.

49 *Annual Report.* London: Medical Defence Union, 1981, p. 57–8.

50 Addison P.H., Constable H. & Millar C.C. Intravenous plastic catheters (letter) *British Medical Journal* 2 (1964): 1600.

51 *Annual Report.* London: Medical Defence Union, 1979, p. 21–2.

52 *Ibid.* 1977: 40.

53 *Ibid.* 1975: 26–7.

54 *Ibid.* 1963: 38.

55 *Ibid.* 1975: 34–5.

56 *Ibid.* 1948/9: 158.

57 *Ibid.* 1974: 74.

58 *Ibid.* 1982: 27–8.

59 *Ibid.* 1983: 41.

60 *Ibid.* 1973: 57.

61 *Ibid.* 1978: 12.

62 McNulty H. & Spurr P. Drug names that look or sound alike. *British Medical Journal* 2 (1979): 836–8.

63 *Annual Report.* London: Medical Defence Union, 1982, p. 15–6.

64 Can adverse drug reactions be prevented? *Adverse Drug Reaction Bulletin.* 80 (1980): 288–90.

65 *Annual Report.* London: Medical Defence Union, 1971, p. 14.

66 *Ibid.* 1971: 47.

67 *Ibid.* 1982: 24

68 Jeffcoate S.L. The pill and antibiotics. *British Medical Journal* 289 (1984): 91.

69 Drug and Therapeutics Bulletin. What should we tell patients about their medicines? *Drug and Therapeutics Bulletin* 19 (1981): 73–4.

70 Herxheimer A. Towards parity of therapeutic clinical teaching. *Lancet* 2 (1976): 1186–7.

5

Perennial pitfalls

'All men are liable to error.'
JOHN LOCKE

'To err is human' is as true today as when Alexander Pope wrote it in the eighteenth century and, regrettably, it always will be. Mistakes in other walks of life where people are not concerned can be corrected and cause little worry, but in the medical profession the effect can be devastating to the patient and cause anguish to the doctor.

Fortunately the number of medical cases appearing in the courts in the UK is relatively small and the risk of a mishap happening to a particular patient remote, often less than the chance of an accident on the road or in the home. However no doctor is likely to be complacent and medical defence bodies are strenuous in their efforts to eliminate or at least reduce risks to a minimum, while every doctor would want a patient to receive a just award in undoubted cases.

Many cases in this chapter come under the legal term *res ipsa loquitur* ('the fact speaks for itself'), which means that an error has taken place whoever is responsible: the removal of a wrong finger or tooth, for example. Sometimes a set of circumstances increases the probability of a mistake happening: anyone who has worked in the accident department or operating theatre might consider it remarkable that mistakes do not happen more often. Some problems arise from not accepting the patient's view: one woman after an abdominal operation told the nurse doing the dressing 'The drain popped inside'; the nurse, unable to believe this, assumed that the rubber tube had come out and was in the discarded dressing—but the patient was right.

Accident and emergency (casualty) department

The accident and emergency department provides a medico-legal mine-field for the unwary or inexperienced doctor, which is well illustrated in an educational film 'Doctors' Dilemmas', released by the MDU in 1985. Most such departments are busy, for ten million people are seen each year in the UK—and the doctors there provide the first approach to the diagnosis and management for most emergency cases. Often the rapid turnover of patients forces the doctor to make quick decisions: to risk sending patients home as there would never be enough beds to admit all doubtful cases for observation.

The doctor may be dealing with two or three problems at the same time (Figure 23) and be plagued with distractions and interruptions: screaming children, the drunk and disorderly, or psychiatric cases—and a bad accident case may unexpectedly be brought in. Hence histories may be brief, and too brief a history is the greatest source of error: for example, 'hit in eye' or 'fell off chair'. Trainee doctors commonly staff these departments and, for some years, reliance has also been placed upon immigrant doctors whose knowledge of English and whose qualifications have sometimes been unsatisfactory; but this situation has virtually disappeared since the introduction of the Professional and Linguistic Assessment Board (PLAB) examination organized by the General Medical Council, and no evidence suggests that mistakes have been more common amongst immigrant than amongst other doctors.

Casualty doctors are often overworked but the excuse of overwork will not necessarily sway a judge, nor is it a defence in law. Consultants are usually available to give support to junior doctors and in many areas a consultant specializing in this work has been appointed. Shalley and Cross [1] analysed

FIGURE 23. A doctor working in a busy accident and emergency department may have to cope with several problems at the same time.

488 deaths occurring in an accident and emergency department over five years. Diagnoses were classified as medical, surgical, or traumatic. Medical causes accounted for 87 per cent of the deaths, of which 60 per cent were from cardiac conditions. Blood loss was an important factor in over half the deaths from surgical and traumatic causes. Lives, they stated, might have been saved by considering infectious disease in those with medical conditions, and by undertaking more rapid blood transfusion, earlier chest drainage, and lateral cervical spine X-rays in appropriate cases. The management of medical emergencies should be emphasized when training accident and emergency staff.

MISSED FRACTURES

Injuries range from minor sprains to severe damage in road accidents. If every apparently trivial case were X-rayed, work in the X-ray department would come to a halt, so discretion, but with a tendency to err on the safe side, is the right policy: an X-ray is arranged if in doubt, or if the patient reasonably requests it, or if a medico-legal situation is likely to arise. However, even when scrupulous care is taken, fractures can be missed (Table 7) and the reasons will include the following:

* The wrong part is X-rayed: for example injuries to the hip joint and pelvis when the main injury is in the legs; the failure to diagnose these occurs because the patient does not mention the pain in the hip so the doctor directs his attention to the legs where there may be fractures of the tibia and fibula. The proximal injury may be a fracture dislocation or fracture of the neck of the femur. These injuries are commonly seen in motor cyclists and pillion riders and cause severe disability if untreated; a claim for damages may then be indefensible. A similar mistake is missing a subluxation of the head of the radius because only the distal part of the forearm is X-rayed.

* The wrong site is requested due to a slip of the pen when writing the request form for the X-ray.

* Both sides should be X-rayed in children for comparison, as it is easy to miss minor slips of the epiphyses in the bones of the arms or legs.

* Poor quality X-rays and failure to X-ray bones and joints in two planes—a fracture or dislocation may easily be overlooked. If in doubt, the expert opinion of a radiologist should be sought.

* Some fractures, especially when impacted, do not show at the start, for example those of the scaphoid bone in the wrist and the neck of the femur; so another X-ray should be arranged later if there is any clinical suspicion of such possibilities.

* Failure of communication: the X-ray report never reaches the doctor treating the patient.

TABLE 7 Failure to diagnose fractures: an analysis of 128 cases reported in 1983 (from world-wide figures reported to the Medical Defence Union).

	No. of cases
Femur	11
Scaphoid	10
Rib	9
Wrist	9
Finger	9
Lumbar vertebra	8
Tibia	8
Fibula	7
Hip	6
Skull	5
Radius	5
Leg	5
Ankle	5
Neck	4
Humerus	4
Arm	4
Pelvis	4
Foot	4
Clavicle	3
Ulna	3
Metacarpal	3
Mandible	2

The *scaphoid fracture* provides a trap for the doctor. It may pass unnoticed on the initial X-ray and cause a painful wrist months later if ununited and when cystic changes have taken place. So precautions should be taken: damage to the scaphoid bone should be suspected in patients with a wrist injury and the anatomical snuff box (the hollow between the tendons at the base of the extended thumb from which snuff is taken) examined for tenderness; the radiologist should know that a scaphoid fracture is possible and arrange for special views to be taken; if X-rays are negative and a fracture is still suspected, the X-rays are repeated in two or three weeks. The following are illustrative cases:

A young man came into the casualty department with a painful and swollen right wrist from injury in a car accident. A senior house officer found and recorded tenderness in the anatomical snuff box, queried a fractured scaphoid, and arranged X-rays. He did not see a fracture on any of four films and a radiologist later concurred. The patient was not treated in plaster nor asked to return in ten days for a check film. Five months later his general practitioner referred him back because of continuing symptoms and X-rays showed an ununited scaphoid fracture. Review of the first films with the benefit of hindsight did reveal a probable fracture, and so the settlement of a negligence claim was inevitable [2].

A 28-year-old carpenter fell on his outstretched hand. He was tender in the anatomical snuff box and had pain on moving his wrist. No bone injury was seen on X-ray and he was discharged. Eight months later he was found to have a fractured scaphoid and had a bone graft, but the proximal pole of the scaphoid became necrotic. The fracture was initially impacted, so no fracture line was seen. He should have been reviewed and X-rayed again. The case was settled on behalf of the casualty officer who first saw the patient [3].

Another example of missing a fracture was due partly to poor communication to the radiologist and lack of any communication to the GP.

In January 1979 a disabled man of forty-seven years who was in a full-time job fell and broke his hip. He had a long-standing spastic quadriparesis from a high spinal abscess twenty years before, but he was able to drive. He was taken by ambulance to an accident department and a senior house officer wrote in the case notes:

> Fell Today on L side
> PMH quadriparesis
> o/e Tender L hip
> esp on flexion of hip
> X Ray No #
> R DF118 tonight

His request form gave the part to be X-rayed as 'pelvis' and the clinical history as '? # hip' (meaning ? fractured hip). The consultant radiologist reported 'repeat view of L hip desirable'. The GP's name had not been entered on to the card which bore only the name of the road and postal district. The man was sent home by ambulance.

The consultant in charge of the accident department endeavoured to review all the films ordered by junior doctors and when he saw this patient's film, he noted its mediocre quality but saw a crack without displacement in the trochanteric region. Reading the note about 'quadriparesis' he felt that no further action was necessary. His usual practice on discovering a previously undetected fracture was to write to the patient or the GP but in this case he did neither.

Next day the patient called in his GP because his hip was so painful that he could hardly move but the doctor relied on the story of no fracture and issued a certificate of incapacity for two weeks. No follow-up was suggested. Eleven days later he was admitted urgently to another hospital where the fracture was detected; he was gravely ill with broncho-pneumonia and a lung abscess; he needed tracheotomy and suffered respiratory arrest. He was eventually mobilized and after four months transferred to a special hospital for intensive physiotherapy and rehabilitation over a further four months.

The patient's solicitors demanded an explanation from the first hospital and were at once given the facts and later the casualty notes and films. The MDU felt that the claim which followed could not be resisted, the members agreed and liability was admitted. To estimate the damages due, the patient's solicitors then set out their 'heads of claim':

- (a) general damages for pain, suffering and loss of amenity;
- (b) loss of wages to date;
- (c) other expenses to date;
- (d) future loss of earning;
- (e) future expenses;
- (f) parental care to date;
- (g) parental and/or other future care.

They explained that their client, although disabled before the accident, had been almost completely independent and was doing a full-time job, but since the accident his condition had worsened so much that he was no longer independent, could not work and was unemployable. They said that the man's parents were both over seventy years old and could not be expected to continue to look after him for much longer, and he would then need assistance either at home or in an institution.

Examination in his home showed that he was wholly dependent upon the devoted exertions of his parents. The case was settled in 1982 for £230,000 [4].

Great care is needed in *neck injuries* and the cervico-dorsal junction must be included in X-rays if fractures of C8/T1 are not to be missed. A check X-ray should be ordered after reduction or manipulation of the fracture and—a point easily overlooked—the doctor should make sure that the area requested is actually shown on the films. If a patient refuses to have X-rays, a form should be signed stating this.

Disasters have happened from *tight plasters or bandages* which interfere with the circulation: a simple fracture of the leg can result in a lost limb. When a patient is sent home, written instructions are given to return at once if:

* The pain increases.
* The limb becomes cold, blue or swollen distal to the plaster.
* There is loss of sensation.

When in hospital, the nursing staff are asked to watch for the symptoms and signs of too tight a plaster and note this on the records, and call the doctor if the plaster has to be loosened; if so, it should be split *throughout* its length.

MISSED APPENDICITIS

Acute appendicitis is often easy to diagnose but it has got a sinister reputation because it can mimic other conditions like enteritis when the appendix hangs into the pelvis and causes diarrhoea. Lay people are apt to think that when the illness is not quickly diagnosed the doctor is always at fault. The young are at risk as symptoms may not be typical and the disease progresses rapidly, and the old may not be diagnosed because symptoms and signs can be minimal.

> On a Saturday morning a junior hospital doctor, deputizing for a GP, saw a seven-year-old boy suffering from abdominal pain, vomiting and fever: there was slight central abdominal tenderness but no guarding. He diagnosed a gastric upset, advised glucose drinks, and asked to be called if vomiting continued or the boy did not improve. He was called again the next day and the parents said that he had been somewhat disorientated though the vomiting had stopped. Abdominal distention and slight tenderness over the left abdomen were present but no guarding, and bowel sounds were audible. He reassured the parents and asked them to contact their GP on the Monday morning. They did so and he visited at 8 a.m. but the child died just before he arrived. The necropsy showed that death was due to peritonitis resulting from a gangrenous pelvic appendix. The parents' claim against the doctor was settled in 1970 for £140 [5].

HEAD INJURIES

Patients with head injuries are commonly seen in accident departments; most recover rapidly but a few develop complications, either fatal or disabling. One simple rule has been that, if a patient talks soon after injury, the brain damage has not been great and recovery is expected. However, a review by Professor Jennett [6] of 151 consecutive head injury necropsies in a Glasgow neurosurgical unit showed that one-third had talked at some stage after the injury. A lucid interval was also recorded in about a third of a series of surviving head injuries who were in a coma for at least six hours, most for several days. Analysis of the findings in the 'talk and die' series revealed that 75 per cent had an intracranial haematoma [7]. The other lesions found were brain swelling, ischaemic and hypoxic brain damage and intracranial infection. Analysis of cases of head injury coming to the notice of the MDU and MPS over five years showed that 68 per cent were patients who had talked and died; more than half had an intracranial haematoma which accounted for 81 per cent of those who talked and died [8].

An intracranial haematoma should obviously be diagnosed and removed by the surgeon rather than be discovered by the pathologist at post-mortem. The lucid interval gives a sense of false security and a hair-line fracture of the skull can be difficult to detect but may be of no significance. Some are misdiagnosed having suffered from a cerebrovascular accident but the greatest problem arises when the patient has been drinking and the head injury is overlooked; altered consciousness should not be attributed to alcohol unless the blood alcohol level is higher than 200 mg per 100 ml. If an open injury is overlooked there is a risk of meningitis or brain abscess.

The safest approach, if it were possible, would be to admit for observation all with any alteration of consciousness, however brief, to minimize the risk of complications developing unawares; however, most recover well and unfortunately not enough beds are available for this kind of observation. If the patient is sent home, a relative can be *warned* and told to report back if symptoms such as increasing headache, disturbances of vision or consciousness develop.

RETAINED FOREIGN BODIES (Table 8)

Foreign material in a wound can be overlooked unless the wound is probed or a finger inserted to feel for one, or an X-ray seen. Even with care, disasters may happen.

A footballer was admitted under the author's care suffering from tetanus. He had suffered a compound fracture of the radius and ulna

TABLE 8. Retained foreign bodies: analysis of 203 cases reported in 1983 (from world-wide figures reported to the Medical Defence Union)

	No. of cases
Instrument (including dental)	70
Swab	54
Suture	23
Glass	22
Miscellaneous (for example, metal, wood or bullet in wounds)	27
(In addition there were 7 cases of retained foreign bodies in the eye)	

when playing; a local surgeon had reduced the fractures, cleaned the wound and sutured it. As symptoms got rapidly worse and failed to respond to treatment, the wound in the forearm was reopened. A small black lump impacted in the end of the fractured radius was found to be a piece of earth and not a blood clot as the previous surgeon had thought; this was removed, the wound further cleaned and he was given antitoxin and antibiotics. He was then desperately ill with severe muscular and laryngeal spasms, and trismus (the typical lock-jaw) which prevented him from eating. In the intensive therapy unit, he lay like a physiological specimen for four weeks paralysed by curare to prevent spasms, fed by naso-gastric tube and attached through a tracheotomy to a respirator. He could neither move nor speak but could hear everything, so we talked to him daily on each ward round up to ten days explaining what had happened and reassuring him, though we were not certain whether or not he understood. After recovery, he took part in a seminar for students on doctor–patient communication and spoke about his experience as a patient. He had heard nothing of what we said and must have been delirious for about ten days; the explanation should have continued longer or have been put on tape so that it could be played to him repeatedly.

GLASS

Many injuries are caused by glass and glass can be missed unless the wound is palpated and X-rayed. The popular belief that glass is radio-opaque only when

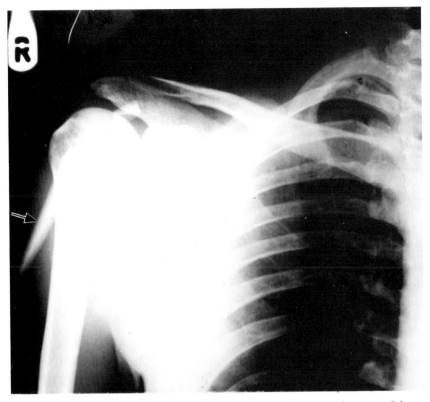

FIGURE 24. Piece of glass detected in shoulder by X-ray (see Annual Report of the Medical Defence Union, 1984, p. 31).

it contains lead was wrong, according to Dr J. D. Cameron (1970), Chief Medical Officer to Pilkington Bros, the glass manufacturer [9]. Almost all glass in common use is sufficiently radio-opaque to give a shadow when in soft tissues (Figure 24). The degree of opacity on the X-ray varies with the constituents and density of the glass: the few which may produce no shadow include some of the high soda translucent tubular lights of American pattern, some of the textiled glass fibres (borates), and occasional types of glass not likely to be met with in everyday life. Fragments of ordinary glass, even if only a millimetre or two in size, are visible in an X-ray film taken to show soft tissues and even cast recognizable shadows with sharply defined edges when superimposed on bone. Medico-legal cases caused by retained glass abound.

A girl, in 1969, fell against a glass door at school and cut her thigh. She was seen by the casualty officer at the local hospital who examined and sutured the laceration; the wound had healed when she returned a week later for removal of sutures. Sixteen months afterwards she was referred back with a note from her GP stating that she had severe pain in the thigh which must be due to a foreign body. X-rays confirmed this and a piece of glass measuring 15 mm × 20 mm was removed without difficulty. A claim for unnecessary pain and suffering for a period of sixteen months was settled out of court by a payment of £300 which included the plaintiff's costs. The casualty officer who saw her on the day of the accident had not had the thigh X-rayed because he believed that glass was not radio-opaque [10].

The duty casualty officer saw a man with multiple lacerations of his forearm, having pushed it through a pane of glass when trying to open a window; the wounds were cleaned and sutured. Six weeks later he returned to hospital complaining of difficulty in using his hand and of pain in his forearm. X-rays showed four foreign bodies. He was admitted and three pieces of glass were removed; the fourth piece could not be found and he was told that a bit of glass had been left. He instituted a claim, which was settled out of court by an inclusive payment of £115. When a doctor concerned with the original treatment was told of the claim he replied 'it must be noted that X-ray films taken of tissues containing pieces of ordinary glass, seen at the casualty department, seldom if ever show up the glass pieces when such tissues are X-rayed up to ten days from the initial embedding of the glass piece'. This is wrong, for glass is always—or nearly always—detectable on X-ray if the possibility of its presence is pointed out to the radiologist [11].

INHALED FOREIGN BODIES

Inhaled foreign bodies may cause symptoms easily misdiagnosed as due to pneumonia or other infection—especially in children. The MDU film 'Ogden v. Bell' illustrated this well: it was a fictitious story of a mother who brought her young daughter to Dr Christopher Bell with a cough, saying that it all happened at a children's party. The possibility of a marble having been inhaled was excluded when the missing marble was found in the child's clothing—she had, in fact, inhaled a peanut and this had caused pneumonia. Although Dr Bell kept excellent notes, he overlooked the repeated statements by the mother that 'it all happened at the party'. Eventually the child was sent to the hospital where a young doctor remarked tactlessly, when looking at the chest X-ray, that it was surprising that it had not been detected before. The child recovered after a chest operation to remove the peanut and an informative account of the court proceedings and outcome is given.

The character of the foreign body is important: animal and vegetable bodies—for example tooth, peanut, wool—cause more symptoms and disease than mineral ones (Figure 14) like metal rings or plastic. Children between one and three years are the commonest victims as many objects are put straight in the mouth; of those children who have inhaled a foreign body, 80 per cent give a clear history of inhalation rather than swallowing, 80 per cent choking, and up to 20 per cent becoming cyanosed [12]. The triad of cough, localized wheeze and decreased air entry can be expected in just over half of the children. A common feature on the chest X-ray is obstructive over-inflation of one or more lobes of the lungs and this is more likely than collapse. The over-inflation is best seen on an expiratory chest X-ray: an inspiratory film can be normal but an expiratory picture may show that only the normal lung is deflating because of the decrease in bronchial diameter due to the foreign body [13]. Inhaled foreign bodies can usually be removed through the bronchoscope without an open operation.

Fish or chicken bones when accidentally swallowed may stick in the throat or upper gullet and, if poorly calcified, may be very difficult to see on lateral X-rays [13]. Their radio-opacity varies and about 75 per cent should be visible on soft tissue exposures: trout and mackerel have poorly calcified bones whereas those of salmon are more opaque. The patient should be believed until the presence of a bone has been excluded; this may require the help of an ear, nose and throat surgeon since definite exclusion usually requires direct inspection through an endoscope [14, 15].

Broken needles. The cause for a retained foreign body may be iatrogenic (caused by the doctor), for example if the needle breaks when an injection is being given. Ideally the patient should be told when something goes wrong, else the doctor may be faced with an accusation of negligence for not telling. This happened when, after suturing a tear in the perineum sustained during childbirth, the doctor did not tell the patient or her husband that a piece of broken needle had been left in the tissues. However, he told the midwife and asked her to watch the patient's pulse and temperature and let him know if anything appeared to go wrong; and she understood that if the needle had not appeared in six weeks the patient was to be X-rayed and the needle removed by operation, which was, in fact, done later. In an action for negligence and breach of duty, one allegation was that the doctor had been negligent in failing to inform the patient or her husband what had happened; but he was fortunate as the judge concluded that the defendant's decision was 'not so incorrect as to afford evidence of negligence'. [16].

In another case (*Gerber* v. *Pines*, 1935) the judge stated that, as a general rule, although there might be exceptions, a patient in whose body a doctor had left some foreign substance, was entitled to be told at once, and that there had been a breach of duty and negligence in not informing the patient or her husband of the accident [17].

INTRAOCULAR FOREIGN BODIES

Foreign bodies should be suspected in all eye injuries, especially in every perforating wound of the cornea or sclera. The risk is high in certain occupations such as chiselling concrete when small particles of steel—not of concrete as the patient may think—enter the eye at very high velocity. Metals such as iron may lead to blindness from siderosis and cataract but many plastics and glass are inert and cause no trouble [18]. Stone fragments are usually septic and cause purulent endophthalmitis but iron particles are sterile owing to the heat generated by the high speed of their flight.

Foreign bodies may be seen through the ophthalmoscope or slit lamp; if not, the eye should be X-rayed or ultrascanned. Some metal foreign bodies are extracted with a magnet but glass can sometimes safely be left in place [18]. About six cases of missed intraocular foreign bodies come to the attention of the MDU each year.

> A 57-year-old yachtsman was struck in the face by a rope which smashed his spectacles. He attended a casualty department complaining of glass in his left eye. The casualty officer found conjunctivitis but did not detect a foreign body. He prescribed an antibiotic ointment and asked him to come back next morning. He returned in pain and was seen by another doctor who referred him to the eye hospital with panophthalmitis due to a fragment of glass in the globe. A claim for damages could not be defended because the casualty officer had failed to take a full history when the story of his broken glasses should have aroused suspicion of a perforating wound. Furthermore, he had not instilled fluorescein to stain damaged tissues nor tested visual acuity and had not asked for an X-ray. The claim was settled. Eye injury cases merit meticulous history taking and thorough examination [19].

> A 61-year-old man injured his left eye at work and was referred to the accident department. A clinical assistant diagnosed a corneal abrasion and prescribed antibiotic ointment without having the eye X-rayed. He did not take a full history but relied on the employer's

first aid form, which stated that the injury was due to a blow on the eyelid by a piece of pipe. Two days later a senior house officer saw the patient, noted that the abrasion was healed and that the eye was congested; he took no X-ray. Another two days passed before the patient attended the ophthalmic out-patient department and an X-ray revealed a small metallic fragment in the eye. Infection had set in and it was necessary to eviscerate the eye. The claim was settled [20].

Equipment left in the body during an operation

THE MISSING SWAB

A layman may find it difficult to understand how a swab or even a large pack can be left behind at an operation except by a most careless surgeon. Unfortunately it is only too easy, and circumstances may arise in the operating theatre which make it more likely: the patient may be very ill and the operation takes place as an emergency during the night, for example, or the site of the operation may be difficult for the surgeon. Swabs which appear so obvious before the operation (Figure 25) become screwed up and soaked with blood and, as a result, cannot be seen against a red background (Figure 26). The body is composed of various spaces and tubes, and the capacious abdomen has numerous recesses into which a swab may be manoeuvered by the peristaltic movements of the intestines.

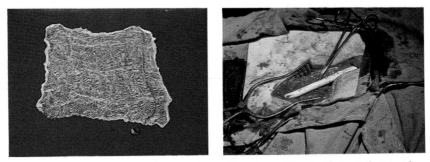

FIGURE 25 (*left*). A gauze swab contains a radio-opaque fibre so that one lost inside a patient can easily be identified by X-ray (the ring is to give an idea of size).

FIGURE 26 (*right*). A gauze swab used at an operation may be invisible when it is soaked with blood and squeezed in a ball, as shown in a wound during an operation for insertion of an arterial graft (by kind permission of Professor Frank Ashton of the Department of Surgery, University of Birmingham).

The surgeon takes a responsibility for any foreign body being left in the operating field but cases occur where he cannot take all necessary precautions to ensure that no swab or instrument has been left behind. For instance, if the patient's condition becomes grave and the operation has to be finished as quickly as possible, the surgeon may have to cut short or even dispense with his own physical check and rely entirely on a swab count by the scrub nurse.

A court will usually award damages for a retained swab or an instrument if it is causing symptoms. No one knows how often foreign bodies do cause symptoms since swabs are only discovered when they cause trouble; thus the evidence is anecdotal as no series has been studied. People walk about with bits of shrapnel from the last war inside them without knowing it, and surgeons deliberately insert foreign bodies such as artificial joints, heart valves and pacemakers. The chance of anything being left in accidentally during an operation must be remote, for over two million operations are performed each year in the UK. Unfortunately these accidents are spotlighted by the Press, and the publicity creates unnecessary alarm.

The saga of the retained swab has continued over the last hundred years and still happens in spite of every precaution. Yet this is hardly surprising in view of the vast number of operations performed and the many swabs used in each, sometimes hundreds per operation. Fortunately the insertion of a radio-opaque fibre makes a lost swab easy to detect by X-ray, though there can be errors even by this method. A swab causes trouble by setting up local infection due to the cotton disintegrating but this does not happen with inert material like forceps, though it can go rusty or undergo corrosion.

Although the abdomen is the commonest site of a missing swab, it can happen elsewhere:

> *Femoral hernia.* A discharging sinus developed in the wound after a femoral hernia had been repaired in a middle-aged woman. She was told that this was due to a stitch abscess and that a bit of suture material might come out of the wound later. A month afterwards she noticed a piece of gauze protruding from the wound. This was removed by the district nurse and handed back to the surgeon. The system for checking swabs at the hospital was defective as no confirmatory count was made after closure of the wound. Her claim was settled for a sum contributed equally by the MDU and hospital authority [21].

> *A pacemaker case.* A thoracic surgeon and radiologist were misled in a novel 'swab case'. A woman aged forty-three was admitted with

intermittent heart block for insertion of a permanent endocardial pacemaker. After the operation the heart block was well controlled but the wound discharged. Three months afterwards, despite antibiotics, the infection increased. Since this is a hazard when any foreign body (such as a pacemaker) is buried in the tissues, no particular significance was ascribed to it, but when the wound was re-explored, a gauze swab was found. A radio-opaque thread was present in the swab and could be seen on the chest X-ray taken three months earlier (Figure 27); because of the many wires in the pacemaker circuit it looked like one of the electrical filaments and so had been missed. She later had another operation for a new pacemaker. The case was reported to the MDU but nothing more was heard of the matter [22].

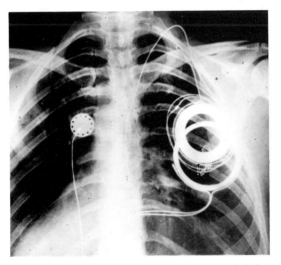

FIGURE 27. The wires in a circuit of a cardiac pacemaker misled the surgeon into thinking that the radio-opaque fibres of a missing swab were part of this.

Repair of ventricular aneurysm. A sixty-year-old man with an expectation of life of up to six months died in hospital after the resection of a ventricular aneurysm. During the swab count, a small one was reported missing; the pericardial cavity was searched but nothing was found. In an attempt to prolong the patient's life he was moved while still unconscious to the intensive therapy unit; an X-ray showed a Raytech swab at the aortic bifurcation. The man was taken back to the theatre and the swab removed during a six-hour operation but he died soon afterwards. Later investigations revealed that the missing mopping swab had no tape or attachment. The executors' claim was settled for £1,000 including costs [23].

Varicose veins operation. A surgeon in New Zealand operated on a 49-year-old man, carrying out a bilateral ligation and stripping of the saphenous veins. A swab was reported missing after the patient returned to the ward and this was confirmed by further counts. The surgeon instructed his house surgeon to have the patient X-rayed and the house surgeon reported that no swab could be seen, but unfortunately only the groins were X-rayed. A few weeks later a swab was removed at another hospital from the patient's leg. The subsequent claim, which was indefensible, was settled [24].

Episiotomy. An incision of the vulva to facilitate delivery of the baby and avoid laceration is often advisable and the small wound has to be sutured after delivery. Not uncommonly a swab is lost in the vagina, and swabs lost in the vagina after repair of an episiotomy or curettage are the subject of claims each year. This minor and simple operation is performed under difficult circumstances: the mother is in an emotional state after delivery, that area of the body is sometimes not amenable to good lighting, blood is coming from the incision together with clots and bits of tissue from the uterus; hence many swabs may be used with no theatre nurse available to count them.

A mother whose episiotomy wound was repaired after a forceps delivery claimed that eight days later her GP had removed a swab from her vagina. She had no unusual symptoms and any discomfort she suffered was obviously due to the delivery and the stitches. The obstetric registrar, a member of the MDU, the senior house officer and nurses were certain that no swabs had been left in the vagina after the episiotomy. The claim in 1973 was defended without success and the court awarded damages of £300, shared equally between the MDU and the SHO's defence society [25].

Gauze or swabs used during dental or tonsil operations can cause death by obstructing the larynx. Swabs are sometimes left in odd places such as the vagina (as already shown) or in the rectum; then the error usually has to be admitted although it is not unknown for such a claim to be fabricated and the fraud exposed. A court will generally award damages for a retained swab wherever it is found.

While the surgeon's duty is to take reasonable precautions to ensure that all swabs and instruments used during the operation are removed, the extent of his personal obligation will vary from case to case. The health authority, as employer of the nursing staff and supplier of swabs and instruments, has responsibility as well for avoiding these mishaps. Occasionally the counting technique may break down and in the USA some theatres have a nurse to act as a 'check on the checker'; also theatre drums may be filled with packs incorrectly. Many hospitals have an Operating Department Committee composed of representatives of the surgical, anaesthetic and nursing staff to keep theatre procedures under review. A memorandum entitled 'Safeguards against failure to remove swabs and instruments from patients' was prepared by the Medical Defence Union after consultations with the Royal College of Nursing. This sets out in detail potential causes of inaccurate counts and failures to remove swabs and packs, and recommends safeguards. In 1985, it was replaced by a new booklet, *Theatre Safeguards*, published by the three defence bodies and the nursing profession.

RETAINED INSTRUMENTS

Some readers may be amazed that a large instrument like a Spencer Wells forceps (Figure 28) which is used to stop bleeding from blood vessels, could inadvertently be left inside a patient. They will be even more amazed that this can produce no symptoms: for example, a man had a routine X-ray and a Spencer Wells was detected which had been left in his abdomen twenty years before. Such an instrument would be sterile and cause no irritation but its shape could cause trouble: it could penetrate a viscus such as the gut even after a long period, or infection (probably blood-borne) may be set up even if it is sterile—once, intestinal obstruction resulted from a loop of gut herniating through the ring of the forceps. Responsibility is usually easy to attribute unless the patient has had two or three operations; then the last surgeon after a successful defence may have the satisfaction of writing to a colleague 'if you are going to leave forceps in the abdomen it is just as well not to have your initials engraved upon them'—perhaps an apocryphal story, although instruments were marked by surgeons in former days.

It once happened that a sponge-holding forceps 24 cm long and 7·5 cm wide was found in the ashes after a cremation. The patient was a 76-year-old woman suffering from renal failure, known to have a non-functioning right kidney and pelvic-ureteric stenosis on the left. A pyeloplasty was carried out but she died later from renal failure and pneumonia. The renal wound

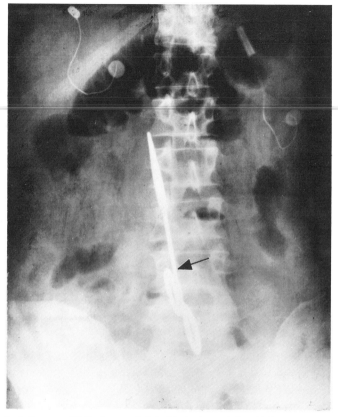

FIGURE 28. A Spencer Wells forceps left behind at an abdominal operation. It was discovered accidentally some years after, never having caused any symptoms. (The electrodes for an electrocardiogram were for a separate condition.)

measured only 17·5 cm long and 9 cm deep. The post-operative check on instruments and swabs had been signed as correct, as had a further check on the sterile supplies department. Its origin was never solved [26].

> *Olive in leg.* A surgeon ligated and stripped varicose veins on a 32-year-old woman without apparent difficulty. All went well afterwards but seven months later the general practitioner referred her to the surgeon with recurrent infection of the wound in the groin. She then drew attention to a small firm tender lump just by the scar above the ankle. The surgeon thought that this was a fibrosed clot which needed no treatment and said so to the patient on two later occasions. Sixteen months after the operation she reattended to

148

report that while having a bath she had knocked her leg, and that the scar above the ankle had burst open and revealed a piece of metal. Under local anaesthesia the surgeon removed the olive which had become detached from a flexible vein stripper; its absence had not been noted at the routine swab and instrument check. A claim which could not be resisted was settled, 50 per cent of the liability being accepted by the hospital on behalf of the theatre staff [27].

The wrong patient or/and the wrong operation

Each year the defence bodies bear the costs of several cases where the wrong patient has been operated upon or the wrong operation done, and occasionally both (Table 9). The tragedy of this is matched by the simplicity of the measures that will effectively prevent it. The Medical Defence Union in conjunction with the Royal College of Nursing produced a pamphlet on 'Safeguards against wrong operations' in 1961, revised in 1978 but now replaced by *Theatre Safeguards* (see p. 147). The Department of Health have from time to time drawn the attention of hospitals to this and hospitals have been asked to review their procedures in the light of these recommendations. The MDU also made a film 'Make No Mistake' which illustrated the principles described.

TABLE 9. Wrong operations performed: an analysis of 27 cases reported in 1983 (from world-wide figures reported to the Medical Defence Union).

	No. of cases
The wrong patient	3
The wrong operation	5
The wrong side:	
hip replacement	4
leg (not amputation)	3
fingers or toes	3
rib	1
hernia	1
knee	1
eye	1
The wrong site:	
level (laminectomy)	1
part (ankle/wrist)	2
lump (breast)	1
lymph node	1

Chapter 5

Fortunately, in spite of the ever-increasing membership together with the increasing number of operations performed, the number of wrong operations reported has declined. Rules for avoiding these mistakes include a bracelet with the name on the wrist or ankle and the marking by the surgeon or house surgeon of the part to be operated upon (if a limb) in indelible pencil or ink. The name, initials, and hospital number must be checked, because occasionally two patients on one ward may have the same name. Patients should not be sent for as 'the patient from such and such a ward' but by the name and number.

'The defence societies have given and will give advice on this when asked' stated a leading article about wrong operations in the *British Medical Journal*, 'Clearly rules in themselves even when followed to the letter are not enough, for to err is human, and human error has a way of taking us all unawares. It is the heavy burden of doctors, as of generals, that their mistakes can have tragic consequences. But are proper safeguards a part of the daily routine in every hospital?' [28].

The wrong woman. After completing the first operation on his list the surgeon asked for the second patient, a woman of twenty-three listed for excision of a fibroadenoma of the breast. The theatre sister went to fetch her and also collected the case-notes from the ward sister's office. Although she brought the right notes, she brought the wrong patient—the third patient on the list, a woman of twenty-one for appendicectomy—and did not check the identity label affixed to her wrist against the case-notes. The patient, being premedicated, did not answer the theatre sister's question about her identity sufficiently clearly to correct the mistake and she was prepared for the breast operation. The surgeon palpated the right breast but could not detect a tumour in the position indicated on the notes. He did not check the notes against the label; instead he examined the breast more closely and thought that he had detected a localized area of fibroadensosis. Thinking that his original diagnosis of fibro-adenoma had been wrong and that the swelling had been a cyst which had ruptured during preparation he made a wedge incision and removed a segment of tissue for microscopy. It was only when he was about to suture the breast that he discovered that she was supposed to be having an appendicectomy which he then carried out. Her solicitors produced photographs which showed that the 11 cm scar in the fold under the breast was a distinct blemish so she had an unanswerable claim to damages which were settled for £625 and costs, shared equally between the MDU and the hospital authority [29].

Perennial pitfalls

Wrong operation, wrong patient. A soldier's wife with irregular menstruation was admitted to a military hospital for dilatation and curettage. She was placed on the operating list of a surgeon who had not seen her previously and, for reasons never explained, she was sent to the operating theatre with the notes of a different patient who was to undergo sterilization by tubal ligation. When questioned by the theatre nurse and anaesthetist, she appeared to answer to the name of the other patient without demur; in consequence tubal ligation was performed and the mistake was discovered only after completion of the procedure when, just before the abdomen was closed, a telephone call was received in the theatre saying that the woman intended for tubal ligation was still in the ward. The incorrect identity was then verified from her wrist tag.

There could be no defence of the claim. It was agreed that the surgeon was partly responsible and the MDU agreed to contribute one-third of the damages, the balance being paid by the Ministry of Defence [30].

The wrong side. A seventeen-year-old youth was in 1976 treated as an out-patient for excision of the left toe-nail. The left foot was examined in the anaesthetic room, but despite this a nurse held up the right foot for preparation and a wedge excision was performed. On regaining consciousness he pointed out that the wrong toe had been operated on; he was anaesthetized again and the correct procedure was carried out. He was discharged on the next day. A claim was made and settled for £650 plus £138 costs [31].

The wrong end. During the annual leave of a surgeon his locum tenens saw a man complaining of difficulty with intercourse due to a tight fraenum of the penis: he was put on the waiting list for 'division of fraenum'. When the patient was admitted, the surgeon had returned from leave and came to the theatre to carry out operations decided upon by his house surgeon who had sent for the patients from the waiting list. When the case for 'division of fraenum' came to the theatre the anaesthetist discussed his 'problem with his tongue' and the patient appeared to confirm that he had trouble with his tongue. He was duly anaesthetized and his throat packed and the surgeon divided the fraenum of the tongue which appeared tight. Later in the day the surgeon noted that the entry made by his locum at out-patients had been obscured by the consent form being stuck over the relevant page. He interviewed the patient and the operation for which he had been admitted was then carried out in the ward under local anaesthetic and the patient was able to return home after the planned stay of twenty-four hours in hospital [32].

Details of all the operations included in operating lists must be sufficient to identify with certainty the part of the body which is to be operated upon.

Anaesthetic deaths

An investigation, commissioned jointly by the Association of Anaesthetists of Great Britain and Ireland and the Nuffield Provincial Hospitals Trust, was carried out in five NHS regions in the UK over one year during which over a million operations were reviewed [33]. 'This,' wrote Professor James Payne in a masterly review of the historical background and present situation concerning anaesthetic deaths, 'must be one of the largest formal inquiries into current practice ever carried out in this country and it should be compulsory reading for anaesthetists, and indeed for all those involved with the work of operating theatres and intensive therapy units' [34]. The purpose of the inquiry was to examine mortality after surgery and anaesthesia so that the clinical practice of anaesthesia might be improved. A further aim was to establish an index of contemporary standards of care within the specialty so as to provide a basis for comparison.

The main finding was that anaesthesia is remarkably safe, only one patient in 10,000 dying solely as a result of anaesthesia. Six in 1,000 died within six days of operation and there were often several factors, the anaesthetic probably being contributory. Professor Payne wrote that 'perhaps predictably the response of the press to the report was to ignore the safety aspects and to concentrate their attention on sensationalising, exaggerating, and trivialising the findings with banner headlines and ill-informed comment'. He blamed *The Times* in particular for publishing a poorly written, badly edited, leading article which sought to explain anaesthetists' mistakes on the basis of lack of professional discipline, boredom, and intellectual mediocrity. It is ironic that when doctors have been taken to task by the media and others for their unwillingness to accept criticism and for their failure to establish any form of audit or peer review, the first group of anaesthetists to do so and to provide hard data should receive so little credit for their efforts.

The causes of anaesthetic deaths can be grouped as follows:

* Mechanical or technical: these range from wrongly connected or wrongly identified cylinders to anaesthetic explosions and the failure to notice a

deficient or absent oxygen supply when cylinders become exhausted, a coupling becomes disconnected, or apparatus is misused.

∗ Misuse of drugs: more likely today because of the polypharmacy needed for modern anaesthesia.

∗ Inadequate support of respiration and circulation: responsibility may rest upon the surgeon and physician as well as the anaesthetist.

A disturbing aspect of the report was the apparent failure to learn the lessons of the past: the failure of anaesthetists to visit their patients pre-operatively, the absence of sufficient consultation between surgeon and anaesthetist in severe risk patients or in those with intercurrent disease, and the fact that too many anaesthetists in training were left unsupervised and without adequate help in dealing with emergency cases. Other lessons were the failure sometimes to keep records, and the poor facilities provided in some hospitals with lack of suitable monitoring equipment and recovery areas. The most clear-cut examples where death could have been avoided were concerned with technical failures.

The MDU was responsible, amongst other bodies, for advising the colouring of different cylinders (Chapter 3) but the next hazard concerned piped gas—gas reaching the operating theatre from a central supply—as wrong connections might occur. Now manufacturers have taken measures to make the system as foolproof as possible: connections (valves and threads) are specific for each pipe or cylinder. Certain National Health Service hospitals have also developed Quality Control departments staffed by an officer who makes regular safety inspections of the operating theatres.

References

1 Shalley M.J. & Cross A.B. Which patients are likely to die in an accident and emergency department? *British Medical Journal* 289 (1984): 419–21.
2 *Annual Report.* London: Medical Defence Union, 1982, p. 21.
3 *Ibid.* 1982, 21.
4 *Ibid.* 1983, 32–3.
5 *Ibid.* 1971, 16–17.
6 Jennett W.B. Who cares for head injuries? *British Medical Journal* 3 (1975): 267–70.
7 Reilly P.L., Graham D.L., Adams J.H. & Jennett W.B. Patients with head injury who talk and die. *Lancet* 2 (1975): 375–7.
8 Jennett W.B. Medico-legal aspects of mild head injuries. *Problems in the Accident and Emergency Department.* London: Medical Protection Society, 1976, p. 18–22.
9 Cameron J.D. Glass foreign bodies. *Annual Report.* Medical Protection Society, 1970.
10 *Annual Report.* London: Medical Defence Union, 1970, p. 25.
11 *Ibid.* 1970, 25–6.
12 Brown B.S. *et al.* Foreign bodies in the tracheobronchial tree in childhood. *Journal of the Canadian Association of Radiologists* 14 (1963): 158–71.
13 Griffiths D.M. & Freeman N.V. Expiratory chest X-ray examination in the diagnosis of inhaled foreign bodies. *British Medical Journal* 1 (1984): 1074–5.

14 Kirkham N & English Ruth. 'I have a bone stuck in my throat'. *British Medical Journal* 289 (1984): 424–5.
15 Stafford N., Youngs R. & Randall C. "I have a bone stuck in my throat" (letter). *British Medical Journal* 289 (1984): 696–7.
16 Nathan P.C. & Barrowclough A.R. *Medical Negligence*. London: Butterworth, 1957.
17 *Gerber* v. *Pines. Solicitor's Journal* 79 (1935): 13.
18 Trevor-Roper P.D. & Curran P.V. *The Eye and its Disorders*. 2nd ed. London: Blackwell Scientific Publications 1984.
19 *Annual Report*, London: Medical Defence Union, 1977, p. 39.
20 *Ibid.* 1973, 57–8.
21 *Ibid.* 1963, 19.
22 *Ibid.* 1971, 60–1.
23 *Ibid.* 1975, 27–8.
24 *Ibid.* 1973, 63.
25 *Ibid.* 1975, 27.
26 *Ibid.* 1980, 20.
27 *Ibid.* 1976, 28.
28 Wrong operations (leader). *British Medical Journal* 2 (1970): 420–1.
29 *Annual Report*. London: Medical Defence Union, 1969, p. 60.
30 *Ibid.* 1971, 55.
31 *Ibid.* 1977, 37.
32 *Ibid.* 1971, 64–5.
33 Lunn J.N. & Mushin W.W. *Mortality Associated with Anaesthesia*. London: Nuffield Provincial Hospital Trust, 1982.
34 Payne J.P. Anaesthetic deaths. *British Journal of Hospital Medicine* 30 (1983): 411–414.

6

Patient–doctor confrontation: from complaint to court

'In the emotion-charged situation of troubled patient and puzzled doctor it is small wonder that the kinds of failure of understanding which underlie so many of the cases reported by the Ombudsman in his report just published should be so common and so distressing.'
From an editorial published by
The Patients Association [1]

Mishaps and malpractice are inevitable in all human affairs; if these happen in medical practice, every patient should have the opportunity of redress and compensation. But not all claims are just, and a competent and conscientious doctor has a right to be protected against unfounded claims and suits (Figure 29).

The perfect complaints procedure should be quick and efficient, easy for the patient to understand and undertake, cause the least embarrassment to both parties, avoid anyone starting an action that can never be won, save the doctor's time, and deter the pursuit of trifling problems. But, whereas channels of complaints procedures are older and probably more readily available in the UK than anywhere else, having been developed in the National Health Service, none is perfect [2].

Most doctors have noticed a curious paradox: patients who have had a bad deal, and clearly understand that a failure has occurred, seldom take up the matter and indeed may overwhelm the doctor and his staff with gratitude. On the other hand, when someone has been looked after with the utmost devotion and efficiency, a complaint may unexpectedly be lodged—due sometimes to social or psychological reasons rather than because of a failure in medical care. Some of the underlying causes of complaints are as follows:

(a) A failure to communicate after a bad or tragic result.
(b) Resentment because the doctor seems too busy to talk.
(c) To prevent it happening to other people. 'Nothing can replace Mum, but we want to make sure that it does not happen to another mum', so it is said.

FIGURE 29. Ninety per cent of the defence bodies' funds are spent on doing 10 per cent of their work: settling claims of negligence and defending doctors in civil courts in Britain and abroad.

(d) The family cannot believe that the loved one—though in the last stages of an incurable disease—was doomed, and assuage their natural grief by supposing that the death could only have been due to the neglect or default of the doctor concerned.

(e) To obtain vengeance if mishandled, or possibly to make easy money.

(f) Bereaved relatives may have a feeling of guilt and absolve themselves by blaming the doctor. When anyone dies or is disabled, there is often someone who may feel guilt for not calling in the doctor, for not giving the medicine regularly or even for ignoring the patient's complaints. Many misleading accusations are due to this.

(g) Pressure from others, as illustrated in the following case:

> Miss G was born handicapped by cerebral palsy; she was tetraplegic, blind and unable to speak, and her hands and feet were not properly developed. Her mother who had nursed her for thirty-one years suffered mental and physical strain; on numerous occasions she was offered help and arrangements were made to place the daughter in an institution but at the last moment she cancelled them.
>
> During an epidemic of influenza Miss G became ill and comatose.

156

The doctor after a thorough examination decided that her condition was a result of cerebral palsy but prescribed an antibiotic; he told the mother that she was the best person to nurse her daughter and that no hospital treatment could alter the prognosis. The partners also formed the same opinion and agreed about the diagnosis which was plainly stated to the mother more than once, and in due course the patient died. Two hours before her death a neighbour, a qualified nurse, telephoned the practice requesting a visit because the mother could not feel her daughter's pulse and was worried, but the doctor explained that there was nothing he could do and that the mother had been well informed of the position. Next day he issued a death certificate stating that the cause of death was cerebral palsy, with spasticity and blindness as secondary features.

Five weeks later the mother wrote to the Executive Council (later changed to the FPC) complaining that the cause of her daughter's death was not shown on the death certificate, and that her daughter would not have died had she been taken to hospital and that the doctor refused to visit her when her neighbour, a nurse, asked him to do so. The doctor replied to the council giving details of the last illness, explaining how his partners had agreed with him that no hospital treatment was indicated and that Miss G's condition was the result of cerebral palsy. Having studied a copy of the doctor's comments the mother informed the clerk that much of the doctor's letter was untrue and that her daughter's life had been sacrificed through negligence. Although the mother repeated her three allegations with force, her description of the sequence of events was almost identical with the facts given by the doctor; the three allegations were all matters of opinion. The Executive Council held an oral investigation and at the end of a long, and at times bitter, hearing before the Medical Service Committee which the doctor and his partners attended, no breach of the terms of service was found. The dissatisfied mother appealed to the Secretary of State but in reply to his inquiry the doctor could only emphasize that he had correctly stated the cause of death and that the complainant could not, or would not, accept this fact. The Secretary of State decided not to allow the appeal [3].

This was an example of a meticulous and caring mother totally devoted to her child but who had become embittered through the mischievous neighbour. The GP had gone to great lengths to satisfy the mother, so the horrific attacks and accusations which were called across the committee floor were most frustrating and he had to restrain himself in replying.

Such cases are indeed often bizarre and can take up much of the secretariat's and lawyers' time. Another case, which was dismissed by the MDU and never came to court, was in 1930, when a surgeon did a cystoscopy and removed a stone: the patient complained that this was an unauthorized operation because he had agreed to cystoscopy only. Another was in 1981 when a consultant gynaecologist was amazed to receive a solicitor's letter claiming damages. It was alleged that he had left a foreign body in the patient at caesarean section six years before. Radiographs which appeared to show an ordinary domestic steel sewing pin near the gall bladder were produced. The member was emphatic that in his thirty years of practice he had never used a sewing pin in the theatre. Liability was denied and no more was heard of it [4].

> *Every year brings new types of complaints and claims, so new as well as old classic medico-legal pitfalls are ever present.*

COMPLAINTS AGAINST GENERAL PRACTITIONERS

Misunderstandings, not misdeeds, cause most problems and fortunately people, by and large, are ready to accept a reasoned explanation so that a discussion with the general practitioner can abort many problems. Some practices, in fact, have Patient Participation Groups, the aim being for patients, doctors and other staff to work together. There are discussions giving patients a chance to express their own views and suggestions; health education meetings may be organized and schemes started to supplement National Health Service provisions, for example collecting prescriptions for the housebound or long-term visiting of the elderly. If the patient is dissatisfied, the complaint can be reported to the Family Practitioner Committee (FPC) which is composed of various professional and lay people; the address is given on the patient's medical card issued as a record of registration with the NHS. The FPC has disciplinary powers over doctors, dentists, opticians and pharmacists but it cannot award damages to the patient. A complaint has to be made in writing within eight weeks but a late investigation is possible with the agreement of the FPC and the GP. *A Patient's Guide to the National Health Service* provides details of all complaints procedures and other matters. [5].

COMPLAINTS IN HOSPITAL

Some complaints need attention at once and others only come to light in the course of time. The first happens when a patient thinks, for example, that a young nurse is clumsy when giving an injection or becomes convinced that he is being expected to take drugs intended for the man in the next bed; when relatives wait anxiously outside a room where a patient has been taken after an accident for what seems like hours with no sign of a doctor, or when a patient and his family cannot get anybody to tell them what is going on, what is wrong with him, whether he is going to get better, or how long it will take— the list is endless. These cases often arise from misunderstanding or ignorance of hospital procedures and should be dealt with at once. Many hospitals have leaflets for patients or notices put up on the wall which encourage comments, and some wards have a complaints box in which written complaints can be deposited. The quickest way of getting 'action' is by talking to the sister in charge, who will deal with it or discuss it with the consultant.

Other complaints develop more slowly: for example, the patient is found to have been treated for the wrong condition or given the wrong drug. Again, it is best for this to be discussed with the doctor or ward sister who will arrange for the consultant to talk to the patient. If not satisfied, a complaint in writing can be sent to the hospital administrator and he will deal with it or take it to a higher authority when necessary. Details of the complaints procedure are fully explained in the DHSS Health Circular HC(81)5.

THE HEALTH SERVICE COMMISSIONER (HSC) OR OMBUDSMAN

This office was set up by an Act of Parliament in 1973, and it operates separately from the National Health Service. Its purpose is to investigate complaints of alleged injustice or hardship because of failure in a service or maladministration: late arrival of ambulances, delays in out-patient clinics, lack of refreshments, loss of patients' belongings, poor standard of nursing services, or allegations that an authority has made no provision for drug addicts. Complaints where clinical judgement is concerned are excluded from the ombudsman's jurisdiction although often there is no clear dividing line between clinical and administrative failure.

The yearly reports published by the Commissioner indicate that it is often small mishaps and misunderstandings which, singly or in combination, have provoked the suspicion, anger and resentment of patients and their relatives. Complaints, trivial in themselves, easily come to prey on the mind of the complainant if not dealt with fully and *promptly* by Health Authorities; for delay in dealing with these so often creates unnecessary suspicion.

Legal action

Legal action can be taken whether or not the patient has tried other complaints procedures, unless he also intends complaining to the Health Service Commissioner—this is the way to obtain financial compensation. There must be some recognizable damage which the patient associates with the treatment received. A wrong diagnosis would be negligent if a doctor failed to carry out any essential tests or examination but if he had made every effort to find out what was wrong and still had made an incorrect diagnosis, the patient would probably not win the case. Suing for negligence because of a wrong treatment is usually easier than suing for trespass to the person because of being treated without consent. Where the action is justified less than 5 per cent come to court, the rest being settled out of court; when a defence body decides to fight, about twice as many cases are won as lost.

The Pearson Commission report in 1978 provided statistical information about the outcome of medico-legal cases (Figure 30) [6]. It also illustrated the differences between medical negligence and other personal injury litigation. Thus compensation was paid, in the years considered, in many fewer medical negligence claims (39 per cent) than in other personal injury claims (86 per cent) but the average payment was eight times as much (£8,000 against

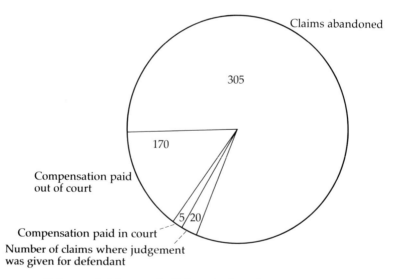

FIGURE 30. Outcome of claims on the Defence Bodies. These estimates (in round numbers) were based on data from an analysis of 500 cases (1974–5) supplied to the Pearson Commission [6]. Exact statistics are not possible as legal cases may continue for many years before being settled.

£1,000). Almost four times the number of medical actions were fought out in court, and, due to the complexity of the issues involved, the average interval between the date of injury and the disposal of the claim was five years as against three to four years for other personal injury claims.

The Legal Aid and Advice Act was passed in 1949 so that no-one is prevented from taking legal action, in personal injury cases, for example, because of poverty. All or part of the costs in most civil actions is provided to anyone whose disposable capital and income are below a specified limit. Reasonable grounds have to be shown for taking, defending or being a party to proceedings and, even if it is possible to provide these facts, an application may be refused if it seems unreasonable in the circumstances of the case; this is decided by a Legal Aid Committee. There are a quarter of a million applications yearly: 84 per cent are granted and 16 per cent refused; it usually takes about seven weeks to obtain legal aid.

Legal aid favours the plaintiff: the lawyers are quite rightly paid, the claimant or plaintiff is certain not to lose any money but the doctor could lose in prestige and reputation. The medical defence bodies bear the financial cost for the doctor, and the Health Authority when the hospital is concerned— which provides a drain on its resources—so the State subsidizes litigation and then does not pay the costs of the other side when the assisted person loses. 'But the law's become ruinously expensive', said Lord Denning in an interview with John Mortimer in 1984, 'you're all right if you're a big company, or if you've got legal aid. If you're in the middle it's impossibly expensive. I think legal aid should be extended. And I think if you're sued by a litigant with legal aid and you win the State should pay your costs. After all, it paid the man to sue you' [7]. No doubt all medical defence bodies and health authorities would agree.

HOW THE DOCTOR REACTS TO A COMPLAINT

A criticism from the doctors' side is that in many types of enquiry and investigation into their behaviour, participants do not meet as equals, so they have no way of answering back to the irresponsible complainant who never gets criticized. Outbursts may occur and the committee seems to accept or at any rate not to refute these; so the doctor feels himself at a disadvantage and may well be tempted to match abuse with abuse.

Medical defence bodies are maligned by the suggestion of a conspiracy of silence. This is due to a misunderstanding. There may be two stages in any complaint. At the outset every medical defence body would urge the doctor to be frank and to explain and apologize if anything goes wrong; many problems are solved at this stage. Cover-up, denial or prevarication is likely to worsen the situation. So the accusation that doctors are urged 'don't talk', or 'don't admit anything' is untrue. Good communication prevents trouble.

A second stage arises when there is the threat of a possible court case. The doctor may first hear of this from a telephone call, from a colleague or from the hospital administrator, or a writ of summons may be served on him; this can be by first class post rather than by personal service, and service is effective on the seventh day after posting. Members who receive a writ are advised to forward it immediately to their defence body so that an acknowledgement of service can be filed on their behalf. Writs should always be treated with respect, for failure to appear within the prescribed time limit could have serious legal consequences such as judgement by default. It is *at this stage* that doctors are warned to be careful of what they say until more is heard about the accusation. Another accusation which is considered unfair is that medical defence bodies do not co-operate when an expert medical witness is needed to appear for the plaintiff. On the contrary, the attitude has always been to advise members who have the appropriate expertise to assist a claimant's solicitors as fully as possible because considerations of natural justice must always take precedence over professional loyalty; in addition, the defence bodies would prefer to respond to litigation with the plaintiff when advised by an acknowledged expert.

WHAT THE DOCTOR SHOULD DO WHEN AN INCIDENT OCCURS

If a doctor suspects the possibility of a medico-legal matter arising (however unreasonable), he should notify the defence body immediately. This can be done by telephone but should be put in writing. All that is needed at this stage is a plain statement of the facts without any comment or expression of opinion; the patient's name and age should be given. It should all be typed, and the doctor's signature included. *This is the incident report.*

Later a *full report* may be requested by the MDU. This needs the most careful attention and trouble and the following details are included in recommendations suggested by The Medical Protection Society:

* The appointment of the member.

* The member's experience of the particular problem and, where appropriate, whether supervised and, if so, by whom.

* The names and appointments of all others (including ancillary staff) concerned in the matter.

* Copies, if possible, of the relevant case-notes with the authors of the entries identified.

The doctor should ensure that the case-notes are fully written up and not tampered with at a later date; any retrospective entries should be clearly marked so. All documents and any relevant evidence must be kept safely: X-rays, fractured needles, pieces of equipment and so on. Discussions or conversations with either the patient or other members of the staff should be recorded. Advice should be sought before replying to requests for reports from solicitors or other interested parties. Careful drafting of the initial reply may obviate a hearing.

An amicable relationship with the patient should, as far as possible, be maintained and follow-up treatment given if necessary.

DOCTORS' ATTITUDE TO LAWYERS

Doctors often avoid medico-legal problems because of the time-consuming nature of the work, the use of the subpoena, and their dislike of attending court. Everything in court, they believe, seems to be arranged for the lawyer's convenience with lack of concern about others' time, even for those called as expert witnesses. Time is wasted because of having to stay even though not wanted at the time, and methods are frequently outdated so that evidence has to be taken down in longhand without use of modern methods such as a tape recorder. Furthermore, courts often appear to the doctor to be a debating chamber where the object of a barrister is to outwit his opponent and to demoralize witnesses rather than to get at the truth, so that the verdict seems to depend as much on the persuasive powers of the lawyer as on medical errors. Indeed the adversary system is based upon the hypothesis that truth is best ascertained by having both sides of the case forcibly argued; the issue is not whether the client is at fault or not but whether his fault has been proved. Perhaps the dependence upon rhetoric is becoming less but debating prowess is considered a virtue in accounts of distinguished lawyers like Lord Birkenhead (F. E. Smith) of the past, and John Mortimer today (in his book *Clinging to the Wreckage*).

Some doctors think that lawyers, who have no scientific training, tend to see problems as black and white whereas many are in grey areas because of the variables and unpredictable quirks of nature. But anyone who reads the law reports must be impressed by the barristers' grasp of technical problems and the judges' fairness to doctors in these trials. The law itself is a subject where dogmatism is often impossible; as Lord Denning wrote in *The Closing Chapter*, 'I would always strive to do justice. Certainty, I regard, often, as a will-o-the-wisp!'

Constructive suggestions as to how to ease problems arising between the two professions were provided by the report of a working party and lawyers established to consider the matter of medical evidence [8]. In this, an attempt was made to distinguish between proposals which require legislative or similar action, and those which could be implemented immediately by a greater awareness on the part of doctors and lawyers of possibilities in the present system. It includes attendance at court and advises how doctors' time can be saved, and also mentions that recent rules of court provided that in civil cases medical reports shall be exchanged, subject to certain exceptions, and that unless this is done the medical evidence may not be allowed to be heard. This helps to overcome the difficulties caused by insufficient disclosure which often results in wasted time for witnesses.

LANGUAGE OF THE LAW

Legal language provides splendid examples of gobbledegook: it is often longwinded and three or more words are used when one will meet the contingency. Latin phrases are used without translation. Sometimes it seems that the lawyer is fearful of the danger of its being intelligible to the ordinary person. Lord Nathan in his preface to *Medical Negligence* wrote 'I have been anxious to avoid, as far as possible, the unattractive characteristics of so many legal textbooks—obscure language, voluminous footnotes and the rest—in the hope that the book may prove acceptable to members of the medical and nursing professions . . .'[9]. The jibe that lawyers' clerks get paid for the number of words is unfair, but some truth may lie in the fact that the former copying of manuscripts encouraged the traditional language to persist.

Legal jargon may be necessary to avoid ambiguity and some legal documents have to be written in legal language. As Lord Denning stated, 'judgements are sometimes so complicated that they cannot readily be understood at first reading;—they have to be studied and analysed word by word; all this inevitably leads to long sentences and every statement of principle has to be qualified by an exception of some kind or another.' However, he would no doubt agree that this can easily become a habit. Legal writing today is less set in this mould, and simplicity will be further encouraged by the Plain English Campaign and its publications.*

WHY IS THE LAW SO SLOW?

Certain cases may continue for ten or more years: anxiety, worry, and even ill health from compensation neurosis is caused for the plaintiff, and uncertainty and perhaps heartache for the defendant—and enormous costs for the defence body due to the so-called 'tail' where costs after several years hardly compare

* Vernon House, Whaley Bridge, Stockport, Cheshire.

with those at the start due to inflation and legal expenses. Furthermore, essential witnesses or even the defendant may have died.

Just blaming lawyers is unfair, although the cynic could conclude that they have no reason or incentive to hurry and finish the case; after all, there is no financial bonus for early completion. Too many cases have to be handled and a block at the law courts may be partly responsible. Other factors are;

* Statements have to be taken from all those concerned and all the witnesses; some may be difficult to trace.

* Hospitals have to be approached for statements or reports and the staff tend not to hurry to produce these, for there seems to them no reason why they should hurry.

* Discussions have to be organized between legal and medical experts (sometimes six or more people).

* The expert's written opinion has to be obtained.

* Arrangements have to be made for all to attend at court at the same time and this can be daunting: expert witnesses have to be available (but may be lecturing in China or elsewhere), likewise barristers and others.

* Court procedures.

HOW THE LAW AFFECTS DOCTORS

Most doctors are ignorant of even simple legal matters. This was shown by Sharpe and Sawyer in *Doctors and the Law* when they sent a questionnaire in the form of sixty-six multiple choice questions to over 1,800 Canadian doctors; if it had been an examination, many would have failed [10]. Obviously the average doctor need not be familiar with details of legal procedures as with luck he will never need to know, and if brought to court, the solicitors of his defence body will guide him. But some litigation arises because of the doctor's ignorance of the law.

English law developed from two main sources. *Common law* is the foundation of the system. A century or two after the Norman conquest, when the 'King's court' had taken over most of the litigation of the country, it administered the 'common law' in place of the chaos of local customary rules which had previously been enforced by local courts [11]. The common law was created to serve as a standard legal system for the whole country; it originated from the laws of Anglo-Saxon England and of Normandy before the Conquest, but the King's judges created a new and practical body of law with additions of their own and a certain amount of cement from the Roman system. The canon law, which is that of the Roman Church, had some influence for a short time, but the common law in this country has survived the movement whereby many European countries replaced their own systems by canon or Roman laws; this persistence largely explains the wide difference between English law and that of continental countries. Judges make common law but much of it has been enacted by Parliament and thereby changed into statute law; however, a large body of it remains unwritten except in the reported decisions of judges. *Statute law* is given by Parliament by Acts and Regulations made by the Queen in Council and her various ministers. Parliament has complete power to make or unmake any law, and no Act has greater force than any other. The judge has to work within this legislation.

Civil actions concern torts, from the Latin tortum (crooked) meaning a 'wrong', and these result in a pecuniary compensation from the person who caused the injury. Cases concern a breach of duty; a tortfeasor is the person found to have committed a tort. Virtually all medico-legal problems come under this heading and are dealt with in civil courts (see Figure 29); facts have to be proved on the 'balance of probability'. Juries have been abandoned for medical cases: the content is too technical for the lay person and the outcome is often biased by emotion, but a plaintiff or defendant has the right to be tried by jury in defamation cases. Juries still operate in Northern Ireland, Eire (Republic of Ireland), Canada and the USA.

Criminal prosecutions, on the other hand, only rarely involve a doctor: murder, abortion, or sexual assault. The prosecution of offences is mainly defined by statute and the person charged is either guilty beyond all reasonable doubt or not guilty: the first consideration is the protection of society by a penalty which may mean prison.

Scottish law differs from English law, especially in its terminology. Corroboration is required for everything except a claim for personal injury. The difference is fundamental in criminal law: the decision whether to prosecute is made by the Procurator Fiscal, a full-time local representative of the Lord Advocate, the Scottish public prosecutor, and a person entirely independent of the police—so he acts as a buffer between the public and the police. All sudden deaths are reported to the Procurator Fiscal who decides whether to hold a Fatal Accident Inquiry before the Sheriff. There are no Coroners or Inquests in Scotland. A different Mental Health Act applies to Scotland and the procedure for committing patients and for their release is different.

European Economic Community law differs yet again, and a practical problem that may concern doctors who take up posts in Europe is about contracts, and members should consult their defence body, if they are in any doubt.

The subpoena (from the Latin 'under penalty'), which is a writ commanding the person's attendance in a law court, can be a nuisance for the doctor. The committee reporting on medical evidence [8] agreed with the Medical

Protection Society in hoping 'that solicitors will, as they almost invariably do, exercise great caution and restraint in serving subpoenas on professional witnesses'. Any doctor has a duty to assist justice by reading the papers and preparing a report and he may be called to give evidence; however, sometimes an inappropriate doctor has been served with a subpoena, causing an unnecessary waste of time, inconvenience and expense. Regarding this last, agreement may be reached between medical witnesses and solicitors concerning fees for attending court, although an affidavit—the written statement confirmed by oath to be used as judicial evidence—may occasionally suffice:

> A general practitioner was served with a witness summons to attend the High Court at a time when he had arranged to go on holiday abroad. The patient's solicitors were unsympathetic and claimed that his evidence was essential. The patient, a publican, was suing his employers for a broken neck sustained two and a half years earlier when he had fallen downstairs. He had long ceased to be a patient of the member whose only record of him was a hospital discharge report. The solicitors of the MDU were successful in persuading the patient's lawyers that an affidavit could be submitted to the court detailing the member's evidence.

A time limit of three years exists, after which potential plaintiffs are usually barred from commencing legal action according to the Limitation Act, 1980. Without this, potential defendants would be forced to live under the lingering threat of an action from persons they may not have seen for years. Also, after a long lapse of time, there would be the practical difficulty of locating documentary evidence and witnesses whose memories may have become confused. This does not provide an unqualified freedom from possible litigation, and extension of the time limit is possible under the Act: adults may develop unforeseen but significant signs of damage six or more years after treatment and the case can then be initiated, and a child may sue for an injury received at birth for up to twenty-one years. Hence the importance of medical defence bodies covering late claims formulated after retirement or against a deceased member's estate.

NEGLIGENCE

Four circumstances have to be present to give grounds for an action in negligence: a duty of care, a breach of that duty, damage to the plaintiff, and the damage being the result of that breach [12]. (The word 'damage' refers to the harm suffered by the patient whereas the word 'damages' means the amount awarded by the court.)

A doctor owes a duty to any patient whom he attends or advises. He does not guarantee to cure or alleviate or even to be correct in his diagnosis or treatment, but he does undertake to use reasonable skill and care.

Standard of care depends on the experience and position held by the doctor—and not every doctor has or can have the highest degree of knowledge or skill in every specialty. The standard of care required is for the doctor to act as a reasonable man with a comparable professional training would act in the same circumstances. The general practitioner is judged by what would be expected of the average reasonable GP; the consultant or specialist similarly is assessed by what would be expected of anyone of a similar status. Yet he will not be liable if, due to some unexpected occurrence, a treatment which in ordinary circumstances would be successful has unforeseen results; the court may then take the relevant facts into consideration in assessing whether or not there has been negligence. The purpose of the court is not to punish the defendant but to put the patient, as far as money can achieve this aim, in the position he would have occupied had it not been for the negligence. Thus the same act or omission may be met by widely differing awards.

Witnesses will be called from those with a similar status and experience to testify whether or not the doctor's care has been up to the standard of current practice; the law tries to be just in its demands and is prepared to concede that a doctor cannot be expected to be acquainted with every up-to-date minute development, but only with those to which for one reason or another his attention might have been drawn. To quote Lord Denning in an action which revolved around the question of whether an anaesthetist might properly be expected to have read an article published in *The Lancet*: 'it would be putting too high a burden on medical men to say that they must read every article in the medical press'. Nor need the specialist attain to the highest degree of skill and competence but to the ordinary level expected amongst those who specialize in the same subject.

The test for negligence was clearly stated by Mr Justice NcNair in his direction to the jury in *Bolam* v. *Friern Hospital Management Committee (1957)*, the case where a man suffered from a fractured vertebra during electroconvulsive therapy given for depression:

> 'How do you test whether this act or failure is negligent? In an
> ordinary case it is generally said you judge it by the action of the
> man in the street. He is the ordinary man. In one case it has been
> said you judge it by the conduct of the man on the top of a Clapham
> omnibus. He is the ordinary man. But where you get a situation
> which involves the use of some special skill or competence, then the

test as to whether there has been negligence or not is not the test of the man on the top of a Clapham omnibus, because he has not got this special skill. The test is the standard of the ordinary skilled man exercising and professing to have that special skill. A man need not possess the highest expert skill; it is well established law that it is sufficient if he exercises the ordinary skill of an ordinary competent man exercising that particular art.' [13]

The idea of the value of the opinion of the man on the Clapham omnibus, a concept which symbolizes an ordinary man, is to some extent a myth for on most issues there are several opinions possible. So it is that the word 'reasonable' leads to much debate: how does one measure the quality of care dispensed by the average general practitioner or consultant! At the end of the day it is the judge who decides after hearing the facts and circumstances of the particular case and the opinions of the independent expert witnesses called by each party. Suffice it to say that the standard of care now demanded by the courts is very high indeed. It is the experts on both sides who have brought about this situation, not the judges who often are blamed for it.

If, however, a doctor departs from normal practice, he must show that there was some special reason justifying this. Unfortunately, this emphasis on established treatment may hinder new developments—but not so if the new approach is backed by good scientific evidence and when the patient has been fully informed of the treatment's novelty before consenting. Doctors are also at risk if they cling to outdated procedures rejected by the profession as a whole.

THE DOCTOR AS WITNESS

Few doctors like to give evidence in court (Figure 31). Some look upon a request to appear in the witness box with almost as much dismay as if it were a summons to the dock; others are so reluctant that they will go to elaborate lengths to avoid having to attend. Bernard Knight, barrister and professor of forensic pathology, and author of *Legal Aspects of Medical Practice*, in a useful article 'Give Evidence' writes that the days of blood-and-thunder advocacy are thankfully past and that counsel today are almost invariably courteous and considerate, especially to witnesses in a sister profession; but this does not, he states, detract from the penetrating intellect and piercing questions with which they can nail the medical witness to the courtroom wall [14]. So it is not surprising that one specialist, an expert in her field, described this experience as like taking the MRCP examination and she tries not to get angry when the opposing barrister is trying deliberately to make her collapse.

For many doctors their first appearance as a witness will be as a junior member of a hospital staff before the coroner; but in both the civil and criminal

FIGURE 31. Few doctors like giving evidence as a witness in court.

courts at their various levels a doctor's presence may be needed, most commonly to give evidence as to fact, and on occasion to act as an expert witness. These are two distinct categories:

Witness to fact

A medical witness to fact is a doctor who has first-hand knowledge of the case before the court and is called to give evidence of the facts which he knows. If after giving evidence of fact, perhaps about the nature and extent of a physical injury, he also gives a professional opinion, as about the degree of disablement, he does not become an expert witness since his whole evidence is derived from his knowledge of the facts of the case. A witness to fact may be, and often is, subpoena'd to attend court; if this (known in Scotland as a citation) is properly served and conduct money is tendered, the doctor concerned is obliged to go to court, otherwise he could be imprisoned for contempt of court. Conduct money is money handed or sent to the witness to meet the expenses incurred in travelling to the court. He must not give evidence relying on skills or experience which he does not possess and any opinions or inferences should be limited to those which need no special skill and which relate directly to what he saw.

Expert witness

This concerns a doctor who agrees to give medical evidence in a case where he has not had any professional responsibility. He is invited by the parties and not called nor subpoena'd by the court; it would obviously be futile for a solicitor to serve a subpoena on an unwilling expert and force him into court to give an unpredictable opinion, for he wants an opinion from an expert whose testimony will advance his client's case. Usually he will first ask an expert for a report and if that appears useful he will make a bargain with the expert to attend and give evidence. Guidance about the size of fee and other helpful advice can be obtained from the British Medical Association. Giving medical evidence can be a delicate area for the expert witness: the standard of negligence is that of the reasonable man in his field and he should give a detached opinion. But the expert witness, however skilled or eminent, can give no more than evidence and he cannot usurp the function of the judge; nor should he trespass on another expert's domain, such as a general surgeon speaking as if he were a gynaecologist.

ADVICE FOR ANY WITNESS

There has long been a facetious saying that the doctor in court should 'dress up, stand up, speak up, and shut up' and there is much merit in this advice. He should dress like a professional person and not like a disc jockey or lumberjack, for a sober suit is more appropriate to the many cases which have a tragic outcome [14]. He should prepare the case with the same care as when giving a communication at a medical meeting: he must know the case-notes, study the subject, and take the records with him—having sorted them out beforehand. The use of case-notes in the witness box may have to be approved by the judge, who may wish to see them to check that they are the originals and he will always allow the doctor to refer to them for the purpose of refreshing his memory, but it is sensible to make notes on all matters and questions that are likely to arise.

His manner should be confident though not arrogant. He should speak loudly and clearly, for judges especially if elderly can be slightly deaf and mumbled evidence irritates them. Everyone is also confused and irritated by jargon, and medical terms should as far as possible be translated into simple English. Speaking slowly may be important if evidence is being written down in longhand. The witness can play into the hands of the opposition in two ways: by being talkative, as he can easily be encouraged by an expert counsel to 'tie himself into knots', or by succumbing to the temptation to be angry, sarcastic, or even impertinent if loss of face is being suffered for, as Knight again writes, 'not only will this earn a rebuke from the judge, but it delights opposing counsel, who can run rings round an angry witness like a matador around a bewildered bull'.

ATTENDING AN INQUEST

Inquests have changed little except for the implementation of a recommendation of the Brodrick Report [15] which stated that a jury is unnecessary except on rare occasions such as death in prison or after fatal industrial accidents; also without a jury, the occasional committal for manslaughter has also ceased. Inquests may be held in many places like offices or hospital committee rooms (though not on licenced premises) and the business is completed more quickly without a jury. However, the procedure otherwise remains the same and those present will be the coroner, who may be a doctor as well as having had a legal training, and his officer who is usually a full-time police officer with criminal investigation department experience (but sometimes a rural police officer at his first inquest), relatives of the deceased, witnesses of the events leading to death, one or more medical witnesses of the fact and cause of death, and others who will be called and occasionally subpoena'd by the coroner's officer to attend.

The doctor must ask himself whether any complaint about lack of medical care could arise and perhaps consult the coroner's officer. If so, he should inform his medical defence body at once by telephone and be guided by them; a medical witness who is a 'proper interested party' is entitled to be legally represented although there is no absolute need and the presence of a solicitor might needlessly cause suspicion of a mishap in the relatives' minds. Solicitors may be acting for the decreased's family or other interested parties, and there will probably be one or more representatives of the Press present.

Proceedings are usually informal as coroners' courts are not bound by strict rules of evidence and the inquiry may include leading questions and hearsay evidence. Evidence should be given as previously stated under 'The doctor as witness.' There is always much consideration for relatives and often general medical findings are sufficient—with gruesome or harrowing medical evidence being avoided; likewise, coroners avoid publicizing personal tragic details such as suicide notes, and these are seldom read out in full.

Doctors are sometimes asked questions which they can answer only by hearsay evidence, if at all, and if the reply is based upon observations of somebody else who is not in court, this should be stated. An unexpected question suggesting a lack of medical care is unlikely to be allowed by the coroner, or need not be answered. An allegation of negligence without warning can make a doctor a 'properly interested person' and the coroner can allow him to put any relevant questions to witnesses; however, doctors will prefer to claim the right to be legally represented and the coroner may adjourn the inquest. Having a word with the relatives at the end of the inquest may, in appropriate cases, be encouraged and they are often appreciative of the doctor's efforts even if they were unsuccessful.

Another reason for a doctor to report to his defence body is when the deceased patient is well-known or if the mode of death is startling, for publicity by the Press is to be expected; he must make sure that his statements to the coroner do him justice, particularly when he is invited to give it orally to a police officer.

> A house surgeon gave a constable his statement for the coroner about a patient who died shortly after he had discharged him. The young man had been admitted at 3 a.m. after taking an overdose, and his stomach had been washed out. The following morning the doctor concluded that there was no suicide intent; the man admitted that he had been drinking heavily and had made the gesture of taking some tablets because of a row with his girl-friend which sounded like parasuicide. There was no indication for invoking any section of the Mental Health Act 1959 to detain the patient compulsorily. Nevertheless, during the day on which he discharged himself, he stabbed his girl-friend to death and then jumped under a train killing himself. The member was advised that this was a case in which publicity must be expected so the solicitor was instructed to represent him: the considerable publicity which followed the inquest did not reflect well on his management of the case.

WHAT THE DOCTOR SHOULD NOT DO

Medical defence bodies are often hindered in their support by the omissions of doctors. They need to be informed immediately of the possibility of a case having arisen, and not when matters have already developed. They must also be told everything for it can be disastrous if anything is revealed at the last moment, especially in court, of which the lawyers are ignorant. A complete report (p. 162) must next be sent. Junior doctors should also consider seeking advice when asked by their consultants or hospital administrators to deal with approaches by solicitors asking them to make an expert assessment for the purpose of litigation; apart from the fact that an important decision may hinge upon their statement, problems arise because they are a 'floating population' and may have left the hospital.

THE IMPORTANCE OF MEDICAL RECORDS

The lawyers of medical defence bodies spend their time endeavouring to defend that which appears, or perhaps more frequently, that which *does not appear* in the medical records. This subject is seldom far from discussion amongst the secretariats and the need for good notes regularly appears in the annual reports. The doctor's quality of care is often judged by the quality of his notes, inappropriate as this may seem to practising clinicians. This matter is particularly important when cases reach court many years after the event, as reliance has to be placed on the contemporary medical records, but so often the doctor has to fall back on the familiar phrase 'well, it's so long ago I really don't remember the particular consultation, but what I would normally do in such circumstances is . . .'. Weak notes mean weakened defence and no notes may mean no defence.

Medical records should be legible, concise, and capable of being read out in court without giving offence to others or causing embarrassment to the author; so they should not express exasperation (for example, 'Nuts!' or 'A tiresome woman'), invective, criticism or sarcasm; even an exclamation mark may cause trouble—for example, 'he is so uncomplaining!' meaning the opposite. The habit should be to record what has been said to the patient; this also has the advantage of avoiding conflicting diagnoses and statements being given to the patient, as may happen in a group practice of general practitioners and cause confusion with lack of confidence. Every detail should be entered: a man's solicitors wrote to accuse a surgeon of negligence because of an ununited fracture which had occurred six years before; fortunately perusal of the patient's notes showed the letters DNA on two occasions, meaning that the patient did not attend for follow up treatment, so the case went no further.

Medical records in the UK are kept according to a DHHS circular (HC(80)7) for prescribed periods, for example those of obstetric cases for twenty-five years, i.e. till the child reaches adulthood. Notes should not be altered or in any way tampered with retrospectively; if an additional entry is indicated this should be added later in the record, clearly stated to be retrospective and signed

and dated accordingly. Correspondence relating to actual or th
litigation should preferably be kept apart from the patient's notes w
hospital or in general practice. Medical records do not *have* to be pr○○○○
unless there is a court order, but providing the patient's lawyers make out a
proper case for disclosure to their chosen medical adviser, the defendant doctor
may agree to voluntary disclosure in certain circumstances.

HOW CASES ARE SETTLED

Many cases are settled out of court and the following are reasons for this:
* The patient is fully justified and the doctor has no defence.
* Although the lawyers are convinced of the doctor's innocence, there are gaps
in the defence, perhaps due to poor hospital records.
* So many doubtful factors are present that although the doctor was probably
not at fault, the case is settled to avoid the cost of legal expenses. An *ex gratia*
payment may be made on a clear understanding that no admission of
negligence is made and indeed that all criticisms and allegations are
withdrawn.

Some members worry that there is a trend towards easy out-of-court
settlements, but no settlement is made without the member's consent and a
member may insist on going to court; if so, the defence body takes his wishes
into account. Out-of-court settlements take place only when there is a serious
risk that the case will not be won. Some prefer this in order to avoid publicity
even if their innocence is certain; also when a small settlement is made, even
though the case is defensible, a signed declaration by the plaintiff or his
solicitors that there was no negligence is obtained. Other members cannot
stand the prospect and worry of a long trial and again prefer settlement. Often
it is not possible to publish reasons for settling cases out of court without
reflecting discredit upon the doctors concerned. It is a paradox that those
doctors whose behaviour is least reprehensible are exposed to publicity in a
court action whereas those whose error is obvious avoid this as the case is
settled out of court.

When a case is lost in court, the object of damages is not to punish the
defendant but to put the plaintiff—so far as money can achieve this—in the
same position that he would have occupied had it not been for the defendant's
negligence. *General damages* cover intangible losses due to the negligence and
they include items such as pain and suffering, loss of various amenities of life
and loss of life expectancy. *Special damages* are those that can be estimated
precisely, such as the cost of medical and nursing care, other out-of-pocket
expenses, loss of earnings up to the date of judgement, and loss of future
earnings, which is often the largest part of the damages.

Chapter 6

> *Those involved in teaching medical students have a responsibility to ensure that all medical practitioners are aware of the problems and legal hazards of practice, since such an appreciation, without doubt, would reduce the number of potential medical negligence actions.*

Such is the opinion of two lawyers [16].

References

1 Patient voice (editorial) 1983; 22:1 published by The Patients Association, 11 Dartmouth Street, London SW1H 9BN.
2 Klein R. *Complaints Against Doctors*. London: Charles Knight, 1973.
3 *Annual Report*. London: Medical Defence Union, 1971, p. 33–4.
4 *Ibid*. 1982, 58.
5 *A Patient's Guide to the National Health Service*. London: The Consumer's Association and Hodder and Stoughton, 1983.
6 Pearson Commission: *Royal Commission on Civil Liability and Compensation for Personal Injury Report*. London: HMSO, 1978. vol 2 p 67.
7 Mortimer J. *In Character: interviews with some of the most influential and remarkable men and women of our time*. Denning, Lord Alfred Thompson. Middlesex, England: Penguin Books, 1984.
8 *Medical Evidence: The Report of a Joint Committee of the British Medical Association, The Senate of the Inns of the Court and the Bar, and the Law Society*. London: British Medical Association, 1981.
9 Nathan P.C. & Barrowclough A.R. *Medical Negligence*. London: Butterworth, 1957.
10 Sharpe G & Sawyer G. *Doctors and the Law*. London: Butterworth, 1978.
11 Kitchin D.H. *Law for the Medical Practitioner*. London: Eyre and Spottiswoode, 1941.
12 Taylor, J. Leahy. Negligence. In *Dictionary of Medical Ethics*. Ed. Duncan A.S., Dunstan G.R., & Welbourn R.B. London: Darton, Longman and Todd, 1981, p. 304–7.
13 *Bolam v. Friern Hospital Management Committee*. All England Law Reports 2 (1957): 118–128.
14 Knight B. Give evidence. In *How to Do It*, London: British Medical Association, 1985, p. 105–8.
15 *Brodrick Report of the Committee on Death Certification and Coroners*. London: HMSO, 1971.
16 Harland W.A. & Jandoo R.S. The medical negligence crisis. *Medical Science and Law*. 24 (1984): 123–9.

7

Consent

The question as to whether or not a patient has consented to treatment is a relatively new medico-legal problem. Doctors of the past who had a more authoritative approach may have thought it unnecessary to ask whether the patient would agree to their advice. Consent is not mentioned in the Hippocratic Oath (see Appendix VI), which has provided the basic code of Western medical practice, and Professor Polani, in a fascinating historical survey [2], suggests that the Hippocratic doctor required his patient to obey whatever course the physician prescribed for him. However, a discourse on doctor–patient relationships in the Hippocratic writings indicates some discussion with the patient: 'On entering bear in mind . . . your composure, bedside manners, care, *replies to objections* . . .'* Yet later a more dictatorial attitude is conveyed: 'Give necessary orders with cheerfulness and serenity . . . sometimes we reprove sharply and emphatically, and sometimes comfort with solicitude and attention . . .'. The importance of good rapport was emphasized as follows: 'The physician must have at his command a certain ready wit, as dourness is repulsive both to the healthy and to the sick'. [3].

A study by Nathan and Barraclough on medical negligence [4] confirms that there was a paucity of English case law on this subject before the twentieth century. An early example in this century was the case of a medical officer of a football team who, in 1906, was instructed to examine a player suffering from pneumonia whose transfer was in question. When he called at the house, his wife said that he knew nothing about the projected transfer; she feared the knowledge would distress him, and so told him that the doctor had called

* Author's italics.

instead of his ordinary medical adviser. The doctor indiscreetly acquiesced and examined him. When the man discovered the deception he threatened proceedings, but later thought better of it and abandoned his claim [5].

Any intentional interference with another person without lawful justification amounts to an actionable offence for which damages are recoverable by the injured person. The law describes such indiscretions by the doctor as 'assault and battery' which seem quaint and incongruous terms. Assault, which is in common use, covers both and is defined in the Oxford Companion to Law as 'any act done intentionally or possibly, recklessly, which causes another person to apprehend immediate and unlawful personal violence', so that presenting a weapon at another would be an example. Battery means any act done intentionally or, possibly, recklessly by which one inflicts unlawful personal violence on another, actually striking him or, for example, using a scalpel without consent. A battery accordingly implies a prior assault. The following are typical cases:

> *Fractured vertebra during electroconvulsive treatment (Davies* v. *Horton Road and Colney Hill Hospitals Management Committee and Logan, 1954).* The patient alleged that he was not warned that injury might result from the treatment and brought an action for negligence and breach of duties. The claim was defended on the grounds that he had been warned of the risks and had agreed to undertake them. This defence succeeded on the facts [6].

The accusations of lack of consent, and negligence, on the part of the doctor are often combined as in the following instance:

> *A surgeon operated on a woman for varicose veins and noticed a congenital hernia which he repaired. This was followed by intractable pain in the right iliac fossa for which she received an intrathecal injection which caused numbness in the right leg (Chatterton* v. *Gerson, 1981).* Miss Chatterton complained of pain around the scar in the right iliac fossa after the operation though the wound healed normally. No analgesics relieved it, so the surgeon explored the wound and freed any nerve that might have been trapped, but this was of no avail. Every other treatment was tried including injections of local anaesthetic and corticosteroids into the area of pain, but it continued. In desperation, an anaesthetist who specialized in treating chronic intractable pain was consulted and gave an intrathecal injection of phenol. This caused temporary relief but was followed by the feeling of numbness from the lower rib margin on the right side down to

the foot and the severe pain in the original area around the scar returned (though the rest of this area was numb); she also complained of weakness in the right leg and a neurosurgeon was consulted; however, no organic explanation was found for this and tests of muscle function were normal.

Miss Chatterton's action against Dr Gerson did not attempt to blame him for the continuing pain from her scar, nor did it make any allegations of negligence of the treatment she received. Her complaint related only to the condition of her right leg, and she put her claim in two ways. Firstly, since she had allegedly been given insufficient explanation of the procedure to be adopted and its implications, there had been no real consent, with the result that in law the operation had been a battery, a trespass to the person. Secondly, it was claimed that the anaesthetist had been under a duty, as part of his obligation 'to treat Miss Chatterton with the degree of professional skill and care to be expected of a reasonably skilled practitioner, to have given her sufficient explanation of the nature and implications of the proposed treatment to enable her to reach an informed decision whether she should run the risks of the operation or go on living with her pain; that the explanation he had given had been in breach of that duty; that had the duty been performed she would have chosen not to have the operation; and that in consequence the damage to Miss Chatterton flowed from his breach of duty, however wise and skilful his recommendation and performance of the treatment'.

The plaintiff's action was dismissed and Mr Justice Bristow stated, 'In my judgement once the patient is informed in broad terms of the nature of the procedure which is intended, and gives her consent, that consent is real, and the cause on which to base a claim for failure to go into risks and implications is negligence, not trespass. Of course, if information is withheld in bad faith, the consent will be vitiated by fraud'. The judge also said that 'a doctor was required to canvass with a patient the inherent complications of a particular treatment.' [7].

Even minor operations carried out without permission can have unexpected consequences. Some time ago, for example, a surgeon when doing a herniotomy noticed a large sebaceous cyst on the man's scalp which he removed. The patient, however, was a comic in a music hall act and the cyst provided a lucrative prop for his act. He came on the stage wearing a large bowler hat; when he removed it, the audience were amused to see the cyst with a minute hat on the top of it.

Consent is not needed in an emergency or unanticipated condition where immediate action is necessary to preserve the life or health of the patient who is in no condition to give informed consent; the physician or surgeon then has a duty to do whatever the occasion demands. This applies especially when someone is brought in unconscious, is mentally disturbed, or is a child; but the matter should be discussed and consent obtained if possible from a relative or responsible person. Otherwise consent is always necessary. If not, the doctor may in law suffer double jeopardy: straightforward damages and, in theory at least, punitive damages which may be awarded because of the law of assault and battery.

Types of medical consent

Consent may be either implied or expressed; if expressed, it can be in writing or by word of mouth. An expressed consent is more desirable than an implied one and a written one is preferable to oral consent, because it can more easily be proved as evidence.

IMPLIED (TACIT OR EXPRESSED) CONSENT

Any form of physical contact, even taking the pulse of a patient in the absence of consent, can produce a charge for battery and the plaintiff then has an automatic right to damages, though suffering no harm. Most consent is implied, otherwise medical practice would come to a halt. The fact that a patient visits his doctor or goes to hospital or holds out an arm for injection implies acceptance. The doctor states that he wishes to examine a patient who then undresses or lies on the examination couch; this act is a non-verbal consent to examination but—as Leahy Taylor [8] wittily remarked—not to anything else!

ORAL CONSENT

The matter is discussed and consent is by word of mouth. An added precaution is to write this in the patient's notes and, if possible, to have a witness such as a ward sister during a medical round; what has been said can be written down in the sister's office and both doctor and sister can sign it—for the patient may forget or deny having been told.

Consent

This can consist of a simple form which the patient signs, or a detailed one listing exactly what might be done and the possible complications.

WHEN WRITTEN CONSENT IS NECESSARY

Written consent is always necessary for any operation (even minor procedures), for investigations (especially invasive ones such as endoscopy), and for special treatment and indeed any treatment that carries undue risk, including new procedures and research. The consent must apply to the surgeon who is going to perform the operation and is invalid if another surgeon, perhaps a colleague or locum tenens, operates—unless a statement is inserted to this effect. Also, most important is the fact that consent is needed to allow the doctor to disclose confidential information (Chapter 8).

OTHER METHODS

The discussion could be recorded on tape or video tape.

To be an effective answer to a claim for assault the consent must have been fully and freely given and not under avoidable stress such as when it is hastily obtained just before an operation, though there had been time enough to obtain it in a quieter moment. The patient must be told, in non-technical language, of the nature and purpose of the procedure. *This should be done by a doctor.* If an inadequate or misleading explanation is given, the apparent consent obtained may be held to be ineffective.

The writing of consent

A general form of consent for signature by patients was published by the MDU in 1932 and adopted in many hospitals. The case that gave rise to it was as follows:

> A pregnant woman was admitted under a surgeon on the staff of one of the larger county hospitals. He considered that she needed a hysterectomy to sterilize her; for she had been an epileptic for years and during each of her past three pregnancies, her fits had become progressively worse and she had only given birth to one live child. Her own medical attendant had strongly advised termination of this pregnancy but as a natural safeguard he felt that his opinion ought to be endorsed by a higher authority, so he referred her to the

surgeon who definitely supported this view and thought that hysterectomy was preferable because of nodular enlargement of the uterus and the fact that she should not become pregnant again.

She raised no objections and indeed welcomed it. Hysterectomy was successfully performed but on the day after the operation the surgeon was informed that a letter had been sent to the hospital by the patient's own doctor, reporting that—strongly against his advice—the husband had objected to the operation of hysterectomy and merely desired 'curetting' (an abortion); both had, however, undertaken that she should not again become pregnant. This letter, owing to a mistake in the filing department of the hospital, was only shown to the surgeon after the operation. Surprisingly, the patient, when the surgeon saw her in the ward before the operation and explained to the sister in her presence what he was about to do and the reason for it, had said nothing about the altered decision.

An action was instituted jointly against the surgeon and hospital and separate defences were submitted. After a hearing lasting several days, a verdict was returned for the plaintiff, the damages being assessed by the jury as £120 (the amount of special damage only) against the hospital and one farthing against the surgeon. The husband, however, although undoubtedly the instigator, had carefully refrained from joining as a party to the claim, and as the wife had no separate estate it would have been a waste of time and money to seek to enforce the claim for costs.

The claim had little merit and the jury marked their sense of its worthlessness by their verdict. There was undoubtedly a mistake by the administration of the hospital, for this type of operation especially needs the prior consent of the patient, unless after proper explanation the surgeon is given an entirely free hand to perform such operation as is needed. However a surprising fact was that, despite the husband's undertaking that his wife should not again become pregnant, he had the temerity in his letter to the surgeon before the action was commenced to say that he had been deprived of his life's ambition to have a second child; indeed, to give colour to this he even adopted a child before the hearing. This was made abundantly clear in court and it then emerged that the husband was going abroad. His wife, from her previous experiences, feared to go through with pregnancy in his absence. In other words, although it was not represented in this way to the surgeon and their own doctor, they wanted this pregnancy terminated as a matter of convenience and not medical necessity [9].

The reason why nominal damages were awarded against the surgeon is that technically any operation, save one done in emergency in order to save life, which is performed without the consent of the patient is an assault in law, although naturally the damages awarded are governed by the facts of the case and the bona fides of the operator.

Hospital consent forms improve communication, give the patient an opportunity to accept or refuse treatment, and protect the hospital and the doctor against a claim for assault. Yet there is no particular legal magic about a consent form; it does not bar a claim, exonerate a hospital from liability, or prevent a patient making a complaint, although it would help to counteract a claim for assault. Care must be taken to ensure that it is kept in the patient's hospital notes. Needless to say, obtaining a patient's signature should not be allowed to become an end in itself. The most important aspect of any consent procedure should be to explain the nature and purpose of the proposed operation.

OMNIBUS CONSENT FORMS

Consent forms which are like a blank cheque should be obsolete. An example is one signed by a patient which included the following sentences: 'I, ..., of ...., hereby consent to undergo the operation of *whatever is necessary*, the nature and purpose of which has been explained to me'. A form of consent couched in such general terms is open to strong objection and is most unlikely to afford any protection to the surgeon or his employing authority if a claim for assault were made. The nature of the operation should be entered on the form as precisely as is consistent with the best interests of the patient. From the legal aspect, the person consenting must understand to what he is giving consent. Unless the patient is told the nature and purpose of the operation he may afterwards repudiate the consent form on the ground that he did not fully understand its implications.

MULTIPURPOSE CONSENT FORMS

Multipurpose consent forms may tend to result in the form being improperly completed, but do have the advantage of simplicity.

ROUTINE CONSENT FORMS

Consent forms are important in hospital law and practice and indeed have achieved a study on their own as is shown by the booklet *Law on Hospital Consent Forms* by Farndale [10]. Every aspect of this subject is covered including illustrative cases when doctors have been sued for neglecting consent, and it includes discussion of consent forms in different specialties. The standardized consent form approved by the Department of Health and Social Security is shown in Figure 32. No assurance is given that the operation will be done by a particular surgeon; but this should not worry the patient as the standard of surgeons throughout the National Health Service is high; if someone insists that a certain surgeon operates, it may be necessary to go privately and pay a fee. Normally the patient should sign the form shortly before the operation although for elective surgery, such as operations for hernia or varicose veins where no change is expected, there is no objection to the patient's consent being obtained earlier, perhaps at outpatients when the operation is originally recommended. If, however, the condition has changed, a further explanation should be given and a fresh form signed.

In Britain a witness is not required for consent forms, as it is not like a 'contract' or a 'will' which are legal documents. It is merely evidence of consent, and is not legally binding like a contract: consent can be withdrawn at any time before the operation. Another person could be asked to sign as witness to the patient's signature if evidence of the patient's consent needs to be strengthened as, for instance, with someone who has a bad memory or is a difficult person, likely to complain. In Canada and the USA it is customary to have a witness to the patient's signature on the 'operation permit'; this may be the result of the larger number of malpractice claims.

The doctor's role is to explain the nature and purpose of the operation before the patient signs and he also has to sign the form stating that he has given this explanation. He need not necessarily supervise the patient's signature and can leave this to the nurse after he has explained. Her role is to see that the consent form is signed and later filed with the medical records. Any questions which the patient asks when signing should, if important, be referred to the doctor.

RESTRICTIONS ARE PERMISSIBLE

Some hospitals in the USA include a space on their consent forms for 'exceptions, if any', so that the patient can indicate clearly any operation or treatment that is not desired. This is to be encouraged for certain patients and a note could be made when the patient has expressed a desire to restrict the extent of the operation. Naturally a surgeon is not bound to accept someone

Consent

```
                    GENERAL CONSENT FORM

I ............................ of ........................................
...............................................................................
                 (name and address of person giving consent)
*hereby consent to undergo

OR

*hereby consent to ............................................. undergoing
                        (name of patient)
the operation/treatment of ................................................

the nature and purpose of which has been explained to me by Dr/Mr ........

I also consent to such further or alternative operative measures or treatment

as may be found necessary during the course of the operation or treatment and

to the administration of general or other anaesthetics for any of these

purposes.

+No assurance has been given to me that the operation/treatment will be

performed or administered by any particular practitioner.

Date ...................... Signature ...................................
                                                  Patient/parent/guardian*

I confirm that I have explained the nature and purpose of this operation/

treatment to the person(s) who signed the above form of consent.

Date ...................... Signature ...................................
                                                  Medical Practitioner




*Delete whichever is not applicable

+Delete in the case of a private patient
```

FIGURE 32. A standard consent form.

who restricts consent unduly, though legally and morally a patient has the right to do so and the public is learning more about medicine and surgery through, for example, television. As an instance, there is no agreement among doctors at present that the whole breast should be removed when cancer is diagnosed. Increasingly, the tumour and lymph nodes draining it are excised while the patient retains most of her breast tissue; yet some surgeons insist that the whole breast is lost. So the patient may be the victim of conflicting surgical opinion though she has been informed as accurately as possible by one doctor and has consented accordingly. More and more women who learn about this are, not surprisingly, unlikely to be willing to consent to total mastectomy.

> A 36-year-old woman disputed her consent to removal of a breast: she alleged that she had consented only to biopsy and not to mastectomy. The surgeon reported that he had explained both the nature and purpose of the operation as she was worried about the lump in the breast. He had told her that a mastectomy would be performed only if the lesion was malignant and she had signed a consent form which read 'biopsy of right breast possibly proceeding to right radical mastectomy'. After the operation she became upset that her breast had been removed and the surgeon explained the reason for this; the histological report confirmed an intra-duct carcinoma. The consent form was shown to her at this time and when she saw it later she asserted that the wording had been altered after she had signed it, which the surgeon denied. The husband alleged that the consultant had told him that the growth was non-malignant and the patient issued a writ [11].
>
> The claimant's solicitors requested the release of the original consent form so that it could be examined by a handwriting expert and a copy of the expert's report was sent to the MDU. It stated that the signature of the patient was genuine and there was no evidence of alteration or addition to the details of the proposed operation; the handwriting was in all probability that of the doctor who had signed the form confirming that he had explained it to the patient.

CONSENT FORMS—SIMPLE OR COMPLEX?

In an ideal world, treatment and its possible risks are best discussed; writing it down creates fear—and the longer the document, the greater this becomes. The practice in many parts of the USA has been for physicians and surgeons to safeguard themselves by requiring patients to sign documents listing all possible complications even for trivial procedures—an example of 'defensive medicine'. The tendency in Britain has been that complications are not listed and it is left to the surgeon to tell the patient 'the nature and purpose of the operation'. To go into too much detail would cause unnecessary worry; to say too little might lead to an action for damages.

The medical defence bodies and lawyers in the UK considered that the primary purpose of the consent form is to provide evidence of consent to the procedure and of this being done with due care and formality; they have not advised that specific hazards are recorded on these forms, but if an operation carries with it a specific and significant risk which the surgeon has expressly mentioned to the patient, it is wise to record this in the case-notes.

Informed consent—a euphemism?

A cynic could say that informed consent is merely a form of ritual deception and that it is never completely possible except when the patient is another doctor. Indeed, Calnan in *Talking with Patients* does not conceal his scepticism for 'if it takes six years for a doctor to qualify and another ten to reach the level of knowledge of the surgeon who is to carry out a rather complicated operation, how can the patient be so informed in ten minutes!' [12]. Also a readability analysis of surgical consent forms from five Los Angeles hospitals gave disturbing though perhaps not surprising results; all contained sentences of over fifty words. On one readability scale all five scores fell off the graph—indicating 'material written for advanced undergraduates or graduate students' [13]. According to the other formula used, one form was 'difficult'—the standard of an academically orientated magazine; the others were all 'very difficult'—the level of a scientific journal. And how is informed consent meaningfully applied to the mentally retarded or the disturbed, or to people in primitive Third World communities who are unable to read or write, and other such vulnerable groups? In practice consent is given more often on the basis of trust rather than on understanding.

Informed consent has become almost a sacrosanct concept, especially with officials and local ethical committees, and implies that all the information necessary to enable a patient to give consent has been provided. However, it may be impossible or inadvisable to tell everything, so that the term 'informed consent', is usually a relative one.

THE LEGAL POSITION IN THE UNITED KINGDOM

Consent in the United Kingdom has been valid if a doctor tells a patient the general nature of what is concerned in an operation or other treatment but fails to disclose an improbable but serious risk. This has applied even if the patient could prove that, had he been told of the risks, consent would never have been given. The method of judging the case has been the same as that for negligence: the opinion of other doctors of the same status, and working in the same specialty, as to what they would have told the patient in the same circumstances is sought and accepted.

The defence has sometimes been based upon the principle which is legally defined as *primum non nocere* (foremost not to harm) and has been founded upon the belief that telling of all the risks would create harmful anxiety, and might deter a patient from undergoing an operation. However, the Court of Appeal in 1984—for the first time in legal history—raised doubts about this according to Diana Brahams, a barrister-at-law, writing in the *Lancet*. [14]. These arose during the proceedings of the following case:

> *Disablement of arm after operation for prolapsed cervical disc—Sidaway v. The Board of Governors of Bethlem Royal Hospital and the Maudsley Hospital and others* [15].
>
> The plaintiff, an elderly woman who had a history of pain, claimed damages for negligence by a neurosurgeon on the grounds of failure to disclose or to explain to her the risks of the operation advised: the spinal cord had been damaged during an operation for a slipped disc in the neck—leaving her with some degree of paralysis of the arm. Mr Justice Skinner dismissed the claim and in the course of his judgement stated, 'before I turn to the question of law which this involved, I must first deal with the evidence I have heard from four neurosurgeons about their own practices before an operation of this kind and what they conceive to be proper professional practice. They all agreed that they would give the patient some warning of the risks involved. They differed about the nature and scope of the warning they would give and each conceded that it might differ from patient to patient and from surgeon to surgeon. All agreed that there was a certain minimum of information a neurosurgeon ought to give a patient, viz:
> (a) A description of the general nature of the operation.
> (b) A warning that there was a small risk of untoward results and of an increase of the pain the operation was intended to alle- viate.
> The degree to which the surgeon should enlarge on this informa- tion depended, in the witnesses' opinions, on the individual's prac- tice . . . the doctor's duty is to take such action by way of giving or withholding information as is reasonable in all the circumstances,

including the patient's true wishes . . . too much information might hinder rather than help the patient in making a rational choice . . . and the mere fact that a patient asks to be told everything might not mean that he really wants to know the worst'. The judgement in the Court of Appeal was in favour of the defendant.

Later the five Law Lords in the House of Lords dismissed Mrs Sidaway's appeal [16]. She had claimed £67,500 against the surgeon. Lord Scarman gave a dissenting judgement though he joined with the other Law Lords in dismissing the appeal but only because of lack of evidence as to what the surgeon had actually said: he had died and this was not recorded in the case-notes. Dissatisfaction was expressed with the present test used by the courts: this is based on the 'Bolam principle'—the decision of Mr Justice McNair in 1957 (p. 168) where the court ruled that the doctor could not be found negligent if he could show that he was following current medical practice. Lord Scarman, who indicated some support for the USA doctrine of 'informed consent', stated that this principle might be appropriate when dealing with questions of diagnosis or treatment but should not apply to whether a doctor had given sufficient advice about the risks of a proposed treatment: the determination of a legal duty—to provide the advice which the law requires—could not be left to the judgement of doctors but must be decided by the courts.

The opinions expressed during the course of this appeal are important to the medical profession. Any doctor who in the future declines to tell the patient about the risks of an operation might be in trouble, the implication being that a patient has a legal right to know, and the doctor a legal duty to disclose, the risks inherent in any recommended treatment; where there is a conflict over what should be disclosed, the courts could decide what is right. If a patient wished to know about a particular risk in order to make an informed choice about treatment, the court could rule that a doctor had neglected his duty if he did not disclose. it This may depend upon the degree of risk and the urgency of an operation or other treatment. In Mrs Sidaway's case, the chance of paralysis was stated to be 1 per cent but judgement was given against her on reasons other than this. No doubt the courts will also take into account the seriousness of the threatened injury. A substantial risk of death or paralysis would require the patient to be told, whereas the danger of suffering from feelings of numbness or pins and needles would not. Doctors will still have discretion as to what and when to tell, providing that they can show reasonable grounds for the belief that the patient's mental condition or health would suffer as the result of the knowledge.

INTERPRETATION OF CONSENT IN THE UNITED STATES OF AMERICA

The definition of consent in the USA, which was firmly rejected by the Court of Appeal in the case of Mrs Sidaway, is that the patient has an absolute right to know; he or she can determine whether or not to have an operation only after receiving full disclosure of the risks.

The basic elements of information needed in the USA for consent were defined by the US Department of Health, Education and Welfare [18] as follows:

1 A fair explanation of the procedures to be followed, and their purposes, including identification of any procedures which are experimental.
2 A description of any attendant discomforts and risks reasonably to be expected.
3 A description of any benefits reasonably to be expected.
4 A disclosure of any appropriate alternative procedures that might be advantageous for the subject.
5 An offer to answer any queries concerning the procedures.
6 An instruction that the person is free to withdraw his consent and to discontinue participation in the project or activity at any time without prejudice to the subject.

This has resulted in surgeons—to protect themselves from litigation—presenting patients with consent forms sometimes containing several pages which list every conceivable complication, lethal and otherwise (an amusing parody of this is shown in Figure 33) [19].

Yet not all doctors in the USA agree with the need for a complete revelation of all the facts, and one policy that has received considerable attention is known as the 'reasonable person standard' [20]: in legal language 'a doctor should divulge that information which is material to the patient's decision, where the information is understood to be that which a reasonable person in the patient's position would consider to be significant.' The problem with this is that it overlooks the fact that the information needed depends upon the idiosyncrasies of the particular patient—and that a patient can differ from the reasonable person in at least two ways: in being able to decide in a rational manner and in knowledge. Not all, however, wish to make a rational decision and many would leave this in the hands of their doctor, but others would like to know about the alternative courses of treatment as well as risks and side-effects which might affect their life plans and values.

PROPOSED INFORMED CONSENT FORM FOR HERNIA PATIENT

I, ..., being about to be subjected to a surgical operation
said to be for repair of what my doctor thinks is a hernia (rupture or loss of
belly stuff - intestines - out of the belly through a hole in the muscles), do
hereby give said doctor permission to cut into me and do duly swear that I am
giving my informed consent, based upon the following information:

Operative procedure is as follows: The doctor first cuts through the skin
by a four-inch gash in the lower abdomen. He then slashes through the other
things - fascia (a tough layer over the muscles) and layers of muscle - until
he sees the cord (tube that brings the sperm from testicle to outside) with all
its arteries and veins. The doctor then tears the hernia (thin sac of bowels
and things) from the cord and ties off the sac with a string. He then pushes
the testicle back into the scrotum and sews everything together, trying not to
sew up the big arteries and veins that nourish the leg.

Possible complications are as follows:
1. Large artery may be cut and I may bleed to death.
2. Large vein may be cut and I may bleed to death.
3. Tube from testicle may be cut. I will then be sterile on that side.
4. Artery or veins to testicles may be cut - same result.
5. Opening around cord in muscle may be made too tight.
6. Clot may develop in these veins which will loosen when I get out of bed
   and hit my lungs, killing me.
7. Clot may develop in one or both legs which may cripple me, lead to loss of
   one or both legs, go to my lungs, or make my veins no good for life.
8. I may develop a horrible infection that may kill me.
9. The hernia may come back again after it has been operated on.
10 I may die from general anesthesia.
11 I may be paralyzed if spinal anesthesia is used.
12 If ether is used, it could explode inside me.
13 I may slip in hospital bathroom.
14 I may be run over going to the hospital.
15 The hospital may burn down.

I understand: the anatomy of the body, the pathology of the development of
hernia, the surgical technique that will be used to repair the hernia, the
physiology of wound healing, the dietetic chemistry of the foods that I must eat
to cause healing, the chemistry of body repair, and the course which my physician
will take in treating any of the complications that can occur as a sequela of
repairing an otherwise simple hernia.

Patient: ....

Lawyer for Patient: ....

Lawyer for Doctor: ....

Lawyer for Hospital: ....

Lawyer for Anesthetist:...................

Mother-in-Law: ....   Date ....

Notary Public: ....   Place ....

FIGURE 33. Parody on informed consent [18].

THE ATTITUDE OF PATIENTS

Patients' views, not unreasonably, have been sought and several studies have reported these. Dr R. J. Alfidi [21] sent a letter (Figure 34) to a hundred patients before angiography stating, *in reassuring language*, all complications including the risk of death (four in 6,500 angiograms which this team had performed), together with a questionnaire to assess their reactions. Results were so encouraging that this was continued. Most patients wanted the information and only an occasional one refused the investigation; concern that informing a patient of possible complications would result in refusal of the procedure seemed outmoded. Perhaps a little knowledge is more worrying than knowing the full facts: many parents are deterred from having their children vaccinated against whooping cough because of newspaper reports of brain damage but they would probably agree to it if they knew more about its rarity. There is certainly evidence that most patients who are better informed about the details and risks of operations and other procedures have less anxiety but some do suffer apprehension, anger, and anxiety from being told. Reactions probably depend on how patients are given the information.

HOW MUCH TO TELL AND HOW IT SHOULD BE TOLD

The attitude of the public in 1985 must make every doctor consider carefully the dilemma of the doctrine of informed consent; for issues concerning this appear almost daily in the newspapers and much has already been written in medical journals [22–25]. Some patients are no longer willing to be fobbed off with incomplete and inadequate disclosures of the potential risks of treatment. Also, there is generally an emphasis on human rights and on the freedom of the individual; this applies to the liberty of the citizen to accept or refuse medical or surgical treatment.

How much should be told is no easy matter to decide. It depends upon the patient's personality, age, temperament, whether anxious or apathetic, state of the illness—whether he is clear or clouded mentally—on his desire to know, social class, intelligence, knowledge of the language and above all upon the circumstances: the briefest statement will suffice if the patient is desperately ill and needs an urgent operation whereas optional treatment may need discussion of the merits of different methods.

The 'prevention of harm argument' can and has been challenged, as described by Sheila McLean and A. J. McKay [26]. They point out that for a doctor to be in a position to claim that he knows that the withholding of information is in the best interests of the patient, he, the doctor, needs to judge not only that giving information will be harmful but also that withholding information will not turn out to be more harmful. Such judgements require knowledge not only of the patient, but also perhaps of his family or associates—knowledge which extends well beyond any notion of what can be said to be purely medical matters; this cannot plausibly be claimed to be possessed by most doctors in such situations. A valid point like this illustrates the need for careful consideration of the best policy in every case and for not laying down some general rule. Indeed it could be disastrous if it became accepted that every patient should be *fully* informed and that, if not, the doctor has *de facto* acted negligently: costly litigation could increase and create a situation of defensive medicine.

Telling too much can do harm and is the antithesis of ethical behaviour, though no doctor has yet been sued for this. One example is that of the patient with ulcerative colitis who needs an operation to remove the large bowel (colectomy) and the provision of an external opening (ileostomy). There is a small risk of sexual impotence after this operation because of damage to the sacral nerves when the inflamed bowel is removed. Most instances of impotence are nervous, so that telling the patient of this risk is highly likely to cause impotence from anxiety although there is no physical cause. In such a case it must be reasonable to mislead the patient but it would be wise to mention it to the spouse or mistress if one is available. Mason and McCall Smith in *Law and Medical Ethics* [27] mentioned the Canadian case *Hopp* v. *Lepp* which had certain features which seemed to strain the doctrine of consent: the patient alleged that the doctor should have told him that this was the first time he would perform the operation since obtaining his Special Certificate, an argument which the court, not surprisingly, rejected.

The telling of horrific though rare complications could deter the toughest patient, but so much depends on how this is told or written. The author has, when talking to patients, related the risks to those normally accepted in the community, such as driving or flying. Even this can have unexpected results: the risk of an operation on the stomach was explained to a man as being about the same as the chance of him getting run over when crossing the road in front of his house. He looked alarmed and this was because he lived at a particularly dangerous part of a main road where accidents were frequent. In spite of such a misapprehension, the policy of putting risks into perspective is worthwhile and many doctors must already do this. For example the risks of death during an operation for removal of the appendix can be equated with the risk of being killed when driving down a stretch of a motorway. A study of risk comparisons by Sir Edward Pochin [28] makes thought-provoking reading. Vaccination and taking drugs prescribed by the doctor are shown as minor risks compared

Dear Patient,

Your doctor has referred you for an angiogram, which is a study of your blood vessels. This is one of the most accurate studies we can make concerning the condition of your blood vessels. As with all medical procedures, it carries some risks, about which we think you should be informed. Your doctor is aware of these risks and has determined that the benefit in diagnostic information which may be obtained from the arteriogram outweighs the potential risk of the procedure.

In this procedure, a small tube (catheter) is introduced into one or several of your blood vessels. Through this tube, a solution will be injected which will enable us to see your blood vessels on X-rays. This tube is introduced into a blood vessel, either in your arm or your groin, by means of minor surgery under local anesthesia.

Patients, understandably, wonder what complications can occur from this procedure. It does involve some minor surgery and it does involve entering the body and the blood stream. The usual complications which we would consider relatively minor, but nevertheless can be distressing to patients, are accumulation of blood in the tissues where the catheter has been (hematoma) or a small outpouching of the artery at the site where it was entered by the catheter. There are less frequent complications which we consider more serious, which might lead to serious damage or loss of an organ. Surgery may be required to correct the complication.

Very rarely, complications from the procedure have resulted in death. This has occurred four times in the 6,500 angiograms we have performed.

Our overall serious complications rate is approximately one in 500 angiograms.

It would be impractical, and probably misleading to the average person, to describe here in detail all the complications which might possibly result from this procedure. If you would like more detailed information, we will be glad to discuss it with you.

Sincerely yours,

FIGURE 34. Patients' views on how much should be told were sought by letter (*above*) in one study and analysed by a questionnaire (*right*) [20].

Consent

I, ... have read the above and give my consent to
      (name of patient)

have an angiographic procedure performed.

....
(signature of patient)

....
(date)

PLEASE ANSWER QUESTIONS BELOW

1. Do you regard the above information useful?   Yes .....   No .....

2. Do you think all patients should receive the
above information?   Yes .....   No .....

3. Do you desire further information regarding
specifics of possible medical complications
of this procedure?   Yes .....   No .....

4. Has this information caused you to change
your mind as to whether to go through with
this procedure?   Yes .....   No .....

   a. Makes me more comfortable going ahead with it .....
   b. Did not affect me one way or other .....
   c. Makes me less comfortable going ahead with the procedure .....
   d. Has caused me to decide not to go ahead with the procedure .....

with liver biopsy, childbearing or scuba diving—none of which seem hazardous in comparison with hang gliding or sport parachuting.

Professor W. H. W. Inman of the Drug Surveillance Research Unit at the University of Southampton has written about the problems of measuring risks, especially those resulting from drug therapy, though hard data on this subject hardly exist and he regards his ideas as tentative. If drug risks could be classified as acceptable or unacceptable, a doctor might then be happy to prescribe a drug which was 'no more dangerous than aspirin', but alas, no-one knows how dangerous even aspirin is. He prepared a logarithmic scale of risk values and arranged some examples of fatal conditions extracted from the Registrar General's mortality statistics for England and Wales for 1981 (Table 10): for comparison the risk levels for violent or accidental deaths are shown (Table 11)—thanks to seatbelts, car accidents fell to level 5 [29]. To be able to relate the risks of drug therapy or operations to these would be helpful.

Patients who wished merely to know more about their condition could be guided to literature written especially for lay people: for example, the 'Family Doctor' booklets published by the BMA cover almost every illness, both medical and surgical. These could be used to inform patients before operations or special medical treatment; risks and complications could be inserted at the end but, if so, these should be put *into perspective* and written in a reassuring way. Failure to inform is likely to become an increasing medico-legal problem, and a review of the method of obtaining consent may be considered necessary. If so, the consent form could be developed further: not to emulate the complex and frightening consent forms used in the USA but as a compromise between those

TABLE 10. Risk of death from certain diseases in England and Wales. (Reproduced by courtesy of Professor W. H. W. Inman, who extracted these examples of fatal conditions from the Registrar General's mortality statistics for England and Wales for 1981.)

Risk level	Deaths per year	Cause of death
1	1	
2	1 per 10	(any cause)
3	1 per 100	Cancer, coronary disease, stroke
4	1 per 1,000	Peptic ulcer
5	1 per 10,000	Arthritis, asthma, cirrhosis, diabetes
6	1 per 100,000	Pregnancy, venereal disease
7	1 per 1,000,000	Tetanus, measles, whooping cough
8	1 per 10,000,000	Acute rheumatic fever

TABLE 11. Risk of violent or accidental death in England and Wales in 1981. (Reproduced by courtesy of Professor W. H. W. Inman.)

Risk level	Deaths per year	Violent and accidental deaths
1	1	
2	10	
3	100	
4	1,000	
5	1 per 10,000	Motor vehicles, burns, falls, suicide
6	1 per 100,000	Homicide, railways, aircraft
7	1 per 1,000,000	Falling objects
8	1 per 10,000,000	Lightning, animal and plant venom

and the uninformative ones used in the UK. This might list—perhaps in small print—the commonly expected risks of an operation or medical treatment, if possible with an approximate risk level: for example, the risk of failure of tubal sterilization in a woman being perhaps 1 in 250 or a serious side effect of a drug being 1 in 20,000. The patient could sign that he had read it or, having decided not to read it, that he was satisfied that all the information necessary to make a decision had been available to him. This type of consent form would also provide the courts with written evidence as to what the patient had been told.

Special categories

UNCONSCIOUS PATIENTS

Consent should be obtained from the nearest available relative if a seriously injured and unconscious person is taken to hospital and immediate operation is necessary, but the need to obtain consent must not jeopardize treatment. If the consent of a relative is impossible to obtain, the surgeon would be able to plead the defence of 'necessity' provided an immediate operation was necessary and could not reasonably be postponed.

CHILDREN

The age of a child (minor) was raised to sixteen years in 1885 when the Medical Defence Union was born. This change was a landmark in British social history and was promoted by the Salvation Army Chief of Staff, Bramwell Booth, and supported by the ardent journalist W. T. Stead, with Elizabeth Armstrong. The Criminal Law Amendment Act in that year made it an offence to have sexual intercourse with a child and was largely inspired by a revulsion to child prostitution; the concept of lawful sex was still closely allied to the idea of marriageable age and to virginity [27].

Social attitudes have changed since then and school-age sex is commonly practised; therefore, the law may have to be changed. Indeed the National Council for Civil Liberties suggested in 1976 that the age of consent should, in general, be fourteen years but that an overlap of two years on each side of that age should be allowed [30]. Until then many doctors will have problems of conscience as to whether to prescribe contraceptive pills in secret to girls under sixteen years (see Chapter 8).

CONSENT TO TREATMENT

The age of consent to treatment was in doubt till 1969 when the Family Law Reform Act (section 8) settled it by putting it in writing: the consent of anyone aged sixteen years or over without reference to the parent or guardian is effective for medical, surgical or dental treatment, so a person of sixteen or more years can override parental objection and give an independent valid consent. The common law does not exclude a child under sixteen consenting to medical treatment providing the child can understand the issues involved. The parents' consent should, as a matter of prudence, be obtained before an operation is performed on a child under sixteen except in an emergency when the health or life of the child would be put at risk by waiting for consent. Difficulties arise in two fields: contraception and termination of pregnancy. A National Health Service circular (HN(81)5) emphasized the need for the best interests of the patient to be considered for contraception for a girl under sixteen; in respect of abortion, however, the parents should always be consulted unless the girl forbids this and their written consent should be obtained, but refusal should not be allowed to prevent a lawful termination to which the girl consents. Conversely, an abortion cannot lawfully be carried out in opposition to her wishes if the parents demand it.

> A schoolgirl aged fifteen wanted to have an abortion against the wishes of her parents, who said that they would be prepared to help look after their grandchild. She already had a son aged eighteen months and the two lived in a local authority Mother and Child Unit. Mrs Justice Butler-Sloss said in her ruling in the Family Division that she was taking the girl's view into account in allowing

the abortion 'I am satisfied that she wants this abortion, she understands the implications of it . . . as a consequence of that operation [the abortion], a suitable internal contraceptive device shall be inserted, again with the approval and at the request of the girl, and with the hope that that may be more successful than the former methods of contraception she has used . . . I assumed that it is impossible for this local authority to monitor her sexual activities and, therefore, contraception appears to be the only alternative'.

There was an angry reaction from the Society for the Protection of the Unborn Child, 'We regard this as a gross violation of human rights . . . there would be a high degree of risk that as a result of the abortion she might never be able to bear children again . . . it could also scar her mind for life' [31].

Doctors sometimes run into difficulties when treating a child and the parents object: this has happened in cases of leukaemia where blood transfusions or drugs are needed. Procedure can then be as follows:
* A court could counteract the withholding of consent by the parents on the grounds that it was unreasonable.
* The child could be taken into care if the treatment was necessary to save life.
* The treatment could be given if dictated by clinical judgement but the defence body should first be consulted.
Consent can be a problem concerning adopted or fostered children, as in the following case:

A girl of ten needed a tonsillectomy. She lived with foster-parents and was in the care of the social services of a London borough. When the surgeon came to get the consent, he found that the social worker accompanying the child was not empowered by the director of social services to sign the form as the legal guardian of the child, since the director of social services insisted on signing the form himself—but he would not attend the hospital in person so that the surgeon could discuss the operation with him. The girl's father was unknown and her mother was several hundreds of miles away and had little interest in the child.

The answer from the medical defence body was to quote the wording of Section 10(2) of the Child Care Act 1980 as follows: 'A local authority shall . . . have the same powers and duties with respect to a person in their care by virtue of a Care Order . . . as his parent or guardian would have apart from the Order . . .'. So a local

199

authority is entrusted by statute with powers equal to those of the child's parents. In this case the director of social services was delegating the task of obtaining information about the operation to one of his social workers before he signed the consent form. There was no reason why this should invalidate the consent form or put the surgeon at risk if he proceeded with the operation on the strength of it [32].

The British agencies for Adoption and Fostering (11 Southwark Street, London SE1 1RQ) have produced a leaflet on consent to medical treatment for children in care or placed for adoption.

THE MENTALLY SUBNORMAL

Ethical dilemmas haunt the parents of mentally subnormal children or those who look after adults with the mental age of children. They are already worried about what will happen to their offspring when they die and their wish for the girl or adult, especially if sexually active, to be sterilized is understandable: she cannot look after herself let alone a baby, and sometimes an inherited disease may be passed on. The legal position is complicated because the patient can neither understand the procedure nor give informed consent.

Commonsense might dictate that a severely handicapped child should be sterilized, but the decision of Mrs Justice Heilbron in 1976 should be remembered [33]. This arose from the concern of a social worker who managed to get an injunction to prevent a gynaecologist from sterilizing an eleven-year-old girl with epilepsy, dull intelligence and personality problems: she would be unable to cope with a family and might pass on her defect. An application in wardship was obtained. Mrs Justice Heilbron supported the social worker and rejected the opinions of the gynaecologist, paediatrician and the mother who had agreed that a sterilization was desirable. She was persuaded partly because the girl's IQ was roughly 80 which did not necessarily make it impossible for her to look after a family and partly because of some medical evidence which tended to be against the operation. A BBC television discussion about this was recorded in the *Journal of Medical Ethics* [34].

Reluctance to sterilize young patients by operations to block the Fallopian tubes depends upon their virtual irreversibility—though microsurgery may in the future solve this. Children with deficient brain tissue could never improve, assuming that brain transplant will not be possible, but other cases might respond to some future medical discovery.

In practice, these children and mentally backward adults are occasionally sterilized [34]. Doctors will usually consult their defence bodies and the gynaecologist may have problems due to the religious scruples of the medical or paramedical staff, either when considering sterilization or abortion. Pressure groups may object but objectors should ask themselves whether they would be prepared to look after a mentally subnormal person and her baby, or pay for them to be looked after.

Fortunately, the effective reproductive capacity of those with an intelligence quotient below 70 is very limited and below 50 is statistically negligible [35]. There is certainly a case for preventing conception as the offspring are likely to be retarded, according to figures quoted in a review of this topic [36]. The intrauterine device is usually the only possible form of contraception and this does offer a semi-permanent solution.

RESEARCH ON CHILDREN

Medical treatment can be given to unwilling children if the parent or guardian consents, but this is not so for research: the capacity for consent then depends upon whether the child can understand. Various studies have been carried out to determine at what age a child is capable of giving consent; these vary from seven to fifteen years. John Pearn in a useful review in the *Lancet* writes, 'that all children over the age of 10 should be approached for informed consent and that any refusal should be honoured. Most paediatricians believe children over the age of reason should not be involved in research against their will, even though the parents may give informed consent. There may be occasional exceptions to this policy in non-invasive research' [37].

It would be trite to emphasize that special care is needed for research on children who fall into the class of 'captive subjects' like prisoners and medical students. Permission for a project is obtained from the independent Research Ethical Committee. The parents should give informed consent for research where the child may benefit and preferably see the project put in writing; close rapport is important. Views have been expressed that children are essential for some research and it would be unethical not to do this when it advances knowledge of childhood disease and its cure [38, 39].

PSYCHIATRIC PATIENTS

There are two separate issues. First, decisions about confining patients with mental disorders in hospital against their will: these are made on the basis of medical opinions backed up by consents from patients' relatives, social workers or a review tribunal—this issue is not discussed here. Secondly, the difficult matter of the treatment of the mentally sick which is decided by their doctors alone. The Mental Health Act 1983 has defined treatments which need the patient's informed consent and/or a second medical opinion before the treatment can be given.

Professor Bluglass in *A Guide to the Mental Health Act 1983* has dealt with every aspect of consent to treatment [40]. Here two main points are summarized:

Treatment requiring consent and a second opinion
No patient may be given any surgical operation for destroying brain tissue or for destroying the function of brain tissue, or any other form of treatment specified for the purpose of this section (57) unless he has given his consent *and* a medical practitioner appointed by the Secretary of State (not the responsible medical officer) and two other non-medical appointed persons have certified in writing that the patient is capable of understanding the nature, purpose and likely effects of the treatment and has consented to it. Moreover the medical member must certify in writing that, having regard to the likelihood of the treatment alleviating or preventing a deterioration of the patient's condition, the treatment should be given, but before doing this, he has to consult two other persons who have been professionally concerned with the patient and his treatment, of whom one shall be a nurse and the other neither a nurse nor a doctor.

Treatment requiring consent or a second opinion
This section (58) applies to treatment such as electroconvulsive therapy and the prescribing of medicine after the first three months of detention in hospital; for the first three months this can be given without any formalities but the patient must give his informed consent (recorded by the responsible medical officer or appointed doctor in writing) if this is continued. Alternatively a doctor appointed by the Secretary of State must certify in writing that the patient is not capable of understanding the nature, the purpose or likely effects of the treatment and has not consented to it but that, having regard to the likelihood of its alleviating or preventing deterioration of his condition, the treatment should be given. When the treatment is continued after three months, the doctor has to give a report on it whenever the order for detention is renewed—six-monthly or annually as the case may be.

Urgent treatment can be given irrespective of the above restriction: if it is necessary to save the patient's life, or (not being irreversible) is immediately necessary to prevent a serious deterioration of his condition, or (not being irreversible or hazardous) is immediately necessary to alleviate serious suffering, or which (not being irreversible or hazardous) is immediately necessary and represents the minimum interference necessary to prevent the patient from behaving violently or being a danger to himself or others.

Some other treatments not mentioned above could properly be given at the responsible medical officer's discretion. The Secretary of State will prepare, from time to time, a code of practice to guide staff about admitting patients to hospitals, or mental nursing homes, and regarding medical treatment. This will indicate which treatments require the various forms of consent. Psychiatrists have immense powers, for example the use of enforced detention in hospital, and, not surprisingly, many ethical problems have arisen: these are covered well in the book *Psychiatric Ethics* [41].

WOMEN

CONTRACEPTION

Informed consent is necessary for the intrauterine device or oral contraception and freedom of choice is especially appropriate in this area of human fertility control. Information must be given in a way that can be understood but this is especially difficult in the developing world: the social distance between the physician and the patient is greater, comprehension of the technical aspects of medicine is less and traditions of autonomous decision, especially amongst women, vary. In one programme of voluntary sterilization in Thailand, financed by the USA, a woman refused to add her thumb print to the appropriate form because on the only other occasion in her life when she had done this, she had been defrauded of the small amount of land that she held [42].

STERILIZATION

If an operation to sterilize a woman is necessary for a medical reason, then she alone can give consent; or the reason may be social because she already has several children: then although unnecessary in law for the husband to give consent, it is sensible in practice to counsel the husband or lover. The following case illustrates the risk of sterilization without consent:

> *Fallopian tubes tied during a caesarean operation* (*Murray* v. *McCurchy*, 1949) This was a Canadian case where the surgeon when doing a caesarean operation found fibroids in the wall of the uterus and tied off the Fallopian tubes to prevent the patient having further children as there would be a risk in this. He was held liable for assault as

there was not sufficient justification for taking such a drastic step without consent [43].

There are several techniques for sterilizing women. Ideally, according to the book by Potts and Diggory, each woman 'should be able to make an informed choice about the method used, taking into account such competing factors as reliability, length of stay in hospital, post-operative discomfort, morbidity and potential reversibility. In practice the place where the operation is to be performed and the facilities available are commonly the determining factors' [42]. The patient should be told that there is a risk of failure, and this fact must be recorded in the notes. The consent form should also include a sentence about this (Figure 35).

ABORTION

The Abortion Act 1967 requires two doctors to recommend abortion but it is usual, although not laid down in the Act, to have the written consent of the patient. If she is married, the proposed abortion should, with her consent, be discussed with her husband and his agreement obtained too. But if there is danger to her life or a risk to her physical or mental health, it is unnecessary to obtain the husband's consent.

ASSISTED REPRODUCTION

The consent issue concerning the test tube baby and other techniques can become very complex so that special care is necessary in obtaining informed consent. For further details see page 105.

CHILDBIRTH

Obstetricians have not insisted that pregnant women should sign consent forms for antenatal care, confinement and postnatal attention, for consent has been accepted as implied. But consent and a full explanation is as important in obstetrics as elsewhere in medical practice, especially when forceps delivery or caesarean section is needed, or for the more refined methods of monitoring and treatment, because advocates of natural childbirth oppose these develop-ments, and as one put it 'some women would like to opt out of an epidural or high tech birth'—such issues should, if necessary, be discussed during the antenatal period. If the woman's wishes are unusual the obstetrician should record them in the case notes, since he may not be on duty when she is admitted in labour. If she insists on restrictions which he thinks unsafe or terms on which he is not prepared to accept responsibility, he should say so and

Consent

STERILISATION

CONSENT BY PATIENT

I, ... of ....
(name and address of patient)

hereby consent to undergo the operation of ....

....

the nature and purpose of which has been explained to me by Dr/Mr ....

I have been told that the intention of the operation is to render me sterile and incapable of further parenthood. I understand that there is a possibility that I may not become or remain sterile.

I also consent to the administration of a general, local or other anaesthetic.

*No assurance has been given to me that the operation will be performed by any particular surgeon.

Date .... Signature ....
                                                                        Patient

I confirm that I have explained to the patient the nature and purpose of this operation.

Date .... Signature ....
                                                              Medical Practitioner

*Delete in the case of a private patient

FIGURE 35. A consent form for sterilization in women which mentions the risk of failure.

205

refer her to a more compliant colleague if he knows of one. Obviously a mutual understanding should be established so that she agrees to the obstetrician taking any steps considered necessary for the safety of her and the child. If she is incapable, because of anaesthesia or the pain of contractions, of making a decision about some unexpected situation, the position should be put to her husband or other 'labour companion'. If this is impossible and the safety of the mother or child is at stake, the obstetrician proceeds as he thinks best.

STERILIZATION FOR MEN

VASECTOMY

Consent forms should include a statement that, however perfectly performed, vasectomy cannot guarantee permanent sterilization—for occasionally the ends of the vas may join. Also it is wise to have the consent of the wife or mistress; otherwise the doctor or hospital might be open to an action by an aggrieved spouse and the case of *Bravery* v. *Bravery* (1954) illustrates this: a man had himself sterilized to spite his wife; Lord Denning said that the operation was plainly illegal even though performed at his request, since it was without just cause or excuse [44]. In 1960 the Medical Defence Union took Counsel's opinion that non-therapeutic sterilization would be considered legal provided there was valid consent.

TRANSPLANTATION OF ORGANS

There is hardly a more harassing situation for a doctor than having to seek consent for use of a kidney for transplantation from someone whose spouse has died suddenly and unexpectedly: for example, a fit young man, aged thirty, was admitted as an emergency under the care of the author and died of subarachnoid haemorrhage. Approaching his young wife was an unforgettable and poignant experience. Hence it would be helpful if all suitable donors carried a multipurpose consent card. It has been suggested that everybody could be accepted as agreeing to removal of an organ when they die unless they carry a card objecting to this; but the problem might be that such a card was not carried at the time and not found. More propaganda is necessary to convince people of the value of removing organs to save the lives or sight of others. It is ironical when a relative refuses permission for use of an organ but asks the doctor to sign a form for cremation.

Consent arises particularly in the case of brain death in someone on a life-supporting machine. The person lawfully in possession of the body may authorize removal of any part of the body if, having made such reasonable enquiry as may be practicable, he had no reason to believe:

(a) that the deceased had expressed an objection to his body being so dealt with after his death, and had not withdrawn it; or

(b) that the surviving spouse or any surviving relative of the deceased objects to the body being so dealt with.

Some hospitals obtain a form of consent from relatives to authorize removal of a part of a body but the Human Tissue Act, Section 1(2) does not require this to be signed: it is sufficient, if reasonable enquiry is made, that there is no reason to believe that the surviving spouse or any surviving relative objects and circular HSC(IS)156 advises that specific consent is unnecessary, merely a lack of objection. Usually it will be sufficient to discuss the matter with a relative who has been in close contact with the deceased and this could take place on the telephone. Any objection made by patient or relatives must be noted immediately in the patient's notes. The circular also points out that certain specified persons of sufficient seniority should be authorized by health authorities or similar bodies to exercise the important function of ensuring that enquiries for any objections have been made. But it has to be remembered that it will often be necessary to contact this person urgently at night and at weekends; so the person delegated must be known to the local transplantation team and be available twenty-four hours a day, seven days a week. Transplantation teams should have this information from each of the hospitals where they work. If there is any question of having to report the case to the coroner, nothing should be removed from the body without the coroner's consent. Any patient, before giving consent to undergo a relatively new operation such as heart transplant, should be informed of past successes and failures.

RELIGIOUS OBJECTORS

Jehovah's Witnesses will not allow blood transfusion, so this sect presents the doctor in the casualty department and the surgeon with a dilemma. Giving blood in opposition to the wishes of the person is an assault in law whether or not the life is in peril; however, if this did lead to a court action, it would be unlikely to succeed—hence many doctors faced with an urgent situation will be inclined to get on with it and give blood. One surgeon has taken blood from the Witness with his consent before the operation and kept it in the refrigerator for use during the operation; others have used an infusion of dextran instead of blood.

If a child's life is in danger a transfusion could be given despite the parent's opposition but certain precautions should be taken: the doctor should discuss the position fully with the parents and explain the object of the transfusion clearly, and the risk to the child if not given; this should be done in the presence of a medical colleague and religious leader. If the parents still refuse a record should be made of their refusal in the case-notes. If the doctor does decide to transfuse, the parents' signed acknowledgment (or the note recording their refusal to sign it) will be evidence that they were warned of the dangers to their child. Equally, if he should decide to be bound by the parents' refusal, there would be complete evidence to show that the parents knowingly inhibited him from doing what he considered necessary. In some cases when the child is in hospital, advantage has been taken of the power given to magistrates by the Children and Young Persons Act 1969, to remove the child from the custody of the parents; then the necessary consent can be given by the person to whom the magistrates entrust the custody. The Department of Health and Social Security does not favour this method. In the USA, parents who refuse may have to go to court.

A similar procedure should be adopted in dealing with an adult except that the patient himself signs a form witnessed by the doctor and by the witness present at the interview acknowledging the fact that he was informed and warned but nevertheless was unwilling to agree to a blood transfusion.

Operations on Jehovah's Witnesses without blood transfusion have, in fact, proved to have a remarkably low morbidity and mortality in skilled hands: one surgical team performed forty-eight open heart operations upon children of the Witnesses without blood—all did well and only four of the smaller infants needed post-operative transfusions [45].

Other religious objections may have to be taken into account. For example, Roman Catholics often hold strong views against contraception and sterilization and Mohammedans have very special ideas on the subject of the lower bowel contents, so that death might be preferable to an operation such as colostomy. Also religious Jews may not be allowed to donate sperm for the artificial insemination of anyone but their wives, nor Jewish women allowed to use sperm banks.

PRISONERS

Prison doctors who need to sedate patients with anxiety states or personality problems have been subject to much unfair publicity and have been accused of giving 'liquid cosh'. Precautions must also be taken when treatment is offered to prisoners-of-war.

The Council for Science and Society, an independent group of scientists which tries to stimulate discussion of difficult contemporary problems, has produced an invaluable booklet called *Treating the Troublesome* [46]; it concerns the ethical problems of compulsory medical treatment for socially unacceptable behaviour. As well as being relevant for prison doctors, it deals with the possible treatment of these unfortunates whether they are in prison, in the community, or in a psychiatric hospital. 'Society would be glad to be

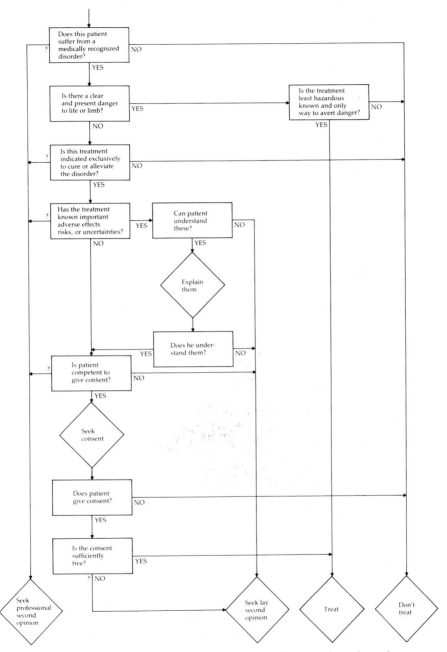

FIGURE 36. Flow chart for decision-taking when consent from psychopaths and prisoners is required (by courtesy of the Council for Science and Society) [46].

delivered from a whole range of murderers, psychopaths, muggers, child molesters and thieves especially as the crime statistics continue to rise. Some would also welcome the disappearance of eccentrics with odd life styles, who do not conform to accepted norms of behaviour and political opinion'. The temptation to manipulate and control deviant behaviour, in the interest of the greater safety of the community, obviously exists in democracies as well as being practised in some totalitarian states. Modern drugs and psychosurgery offer doctors a special power. A flow chart for decisions involving consent (Figure 36) provides a useful guide for handling these patients.

THE NEED TO TELL ABOUT CANCER

A man, aged forty-eight, started an action alleging that a consultant had failed to inform him that he was suspected of having stomach cancer, though he was told, correctly (as the biopsy report had not come back), that he had a gastric ulcer, for which he received surgery [47] . 'I have been denied, apparently deliberately, enough information to make one of the most serious decisions of my life, affecting my future and that of my wife and family', he said. When he died, his wife threatened to continue the case.

THE DYING

'Not to be resuscitated' is a phrase written confidentially in the nursing notes kept in the Sister's office. It saves the dying patient from measures to keep life going if an emergency arises. Surely patients should have an option to decide this when the quality of life becomes unbearable due to a terminal illness. A study in Boston supported this: one-third of all patients who die in the Beth Israel Hospital undergo cardiopulmonary resuscitation. And, of those who received resuscitation one-third stated that they had not wanted to be resuscitated and would not want to be in the future [48]. Allowing a patient to 'die with dignity' is not active euthanasia; it is letting Nature take her course.

Publicity and the patient

Releasing the name of a patient and details of his illness to the Press or other media makes a doctor liable to answer for his conduct if he is reported to the General Medical Council for invasion of privacy, unless he has obtained the written permission of the patient.

The need for consent extends to other aspects of a doctor's responsibilities. No statements or reports on a patient's condition should ever be made voluntarily to a third party without permission, preferably in writing. This requirement applies equally to requests for information whether they come from insurance companies, from employers, or from friends and relatives; the greatest discretion must be exercised for a doctor can easily find himself in a position of some embarrassment. Nor does the right of the individual end with death: no insurance certificate about a deceased person should be completed, nor should any report be voluntarily submitted, without the signed consent either of the executor or of the person responsible for administering his estate.

Research

'Medicine', remarked Sir George Pickering, 'is an advancing science and the best hospitals in the world are not those which merely use knowledge, but those who create it'. So the medical profession has a responsibility, not only for the cure of the sick and prevention of disease, but also for advancing knowledge and this is obtained by investigations and experiments on humans who are, in fact, the only mammals for which a licence to experiment is not required; and using one's fellow beings raises all sorts of legal, ethical and moral issues. Anything done to a patient which is not directly beneficial, or which does not help in diagnosis, is an experiment.

Whereas consent concerning medical practice was derived from case law, that for research stemmed from the Nuremberg Code [49]. The horrific accounts of brutal human experiments in concentration camps by Nazi doctors during the last world war led to serious concern about the use of non-consenting subjects and, since the Nuremberg trials, the matter of informed consent has received more attention than any other ethical issue in research. The Nuremberg Code, which was a direct result of the war crimes trials, stated at the start that the voluntary consent of the human subject is essential and provides principles that are worth reading by any researcher today. The medical profession publicly endorsed the principles expressed in these ten clauses of the code in the Declaration of Helsinki, drawn up by the World Medical Association in 1964 and revised in 1975 (Appendix V).

Distinction must be drawn between research where the aim is essentially therapeutic as in drug trials, and research which is purely scientific and without benefit to the person. If the experiment is carried out solely to acquire knowledge and is of no immediate benefit to the individual, this should be made clear and written consent obtained. Informed consent may, however, be more complex in this field, for experimental procedures are usually too technical for patients or non-experts to understand; so the doctor carries a moral responsibility for the proposed investigations. Nevertheless, every effort should be made to involve the patient in the object of the research and, as far as possible, the practical and theoretical details. In practice, the patients usually receive the greatest care and attention from doctors who may have more time to talk than the busy general practitioner (so the patient may benefit by taking part in a clinical trial of a new drug) and monitoring of side-effects is also more thorough than for other patients.

Informed consent can, however, be a deterrent to research. This particularly applies to assessing of the value of treating cancer, and the report of the Cancer Research Campaign Working Party in Breast Conservation [50] covers this aspect. Informed consent could result in loss of patients to any controlled trial of anti-cancer drugs: firstly, the seeking of informed consent might deter surgeons from participating in the trial and secondly, having recruited the surgeon, the possibility of patients who had been 'fully informed' refusing entry might further jeopardize the trial. Despite this dilemma, the working party did recommend the seeking of informed consent.

Problems especially arise in a prospective trial where patients are allotted at random either to the potentially effective drug or to a harmless inert placebo. Even when comparing two possible effective treatments, the doctor who seeks informed consent has to admit to his patient that he does not know which is the better treatment and may have to explain the reasons for random selection. Undoubtedly randomized clinical trials are the most efficient means of assessing treatment, and unsound research whether in clinical trials or otherwise is unethical—it puts the patient to unnecessary trouble and often leads to wrong conclusions. But the practical aspects of, for example, taking part in cancer trials in real life are distinct from those of the ideal world of trial design [51, 52]. The problem is to inform the patient but to avoid distressing him unnecessarily. Impossible situations can arise, as Professor D. J. Weatherall described: 'a patient is admitted to a coronary care unit with a coronary infarction in severe pain, drowsy with diamorphine, attached to various monitors, and surrounded by worried relatives in a totally strange environment. In rushes the investigator who says that he is doing research and that he wishes the patient to swallow a pill which will either contain sugar or a beta-blocker; a garbled account of the pharmacology of beta-blockers follows and a piece of paper representing 'informed consent' is produced for signing [53].

This is an extreme example but there are other situations where it may be inappropriate to ask patients to give written permission for a particular investigation. In one case a woman aged eighty-four years admitted to a cancer trial was killed by an anti-cancer drug she did not know she was receiving. At the inquest Professor Owen Wade [54] said that fully informed consent to the post-operative drug treatment could only have been obtained from the patients by explaining to them why the drugs were to be given and how unfavourable the prognosis after the operation for cancer would be. 'We thought this would be an unacceptable psychological trauma for many of the patients who had just agreed to a major operation for cancer', he said, 'the trial protocol does not stop surgeons obtaining fully informed consent about the use of drugs, but it does not make it mandatory. We agreed with the protocol because we felt that the quality of the limited post-operative life of many of these patients would be impaired if, in explaining the trial, the grim prognosis was revealed'. Although the patient consent procedure had not been carried out, one might consider that exceptions would be made if it were to the patient's benefit. Lengthy documents that have to be signed can especially distress patients and these, together with the feeling of being guinea-pigs, can easily deter them. Taking part in research could, on the other hand, benefit them and might well advance medical knowledge.

The Research Ethical Committee, created in Britain in 1967, should protect the patient from unwarranted or ill-advised research and the doctor from ethical complications. Each committee may consist of six people, which may include a nurse, a lay member of the Community Health Council, and a non-medical scientist. Details of all types of research are submitted for approval.

Too tight a control—when written consent is needed to obtain a sample of blood or urine—inhibits research. This did happen in the USA as innumerable ethical watchdogs apparently convinced workers that invasive, non-thera-peutic studies on patients with brain failure (Alzheimer's disease) were unacceptable without the patient's consent. So this produced a classic paradox: if the patient had the disease then by definition he was incapable of giving valid consent; if he could give consent he was most unlikely to have the disease [55].

An analysis of 105 inquiries about consent received from members by the MDU in 1983 showed that ten concerned sterilization, particularly whether the spouse should give consent. Eleven were questions about mentally retarded children or adults: sterilization in eight, oral contraceptives in two and abortion in one. Four were asking about consent in children—the rest covered a wide range of topics: consent forms—for research, whether a patient under sedation was capable of giving consent, and whether a consent form could be signed three months in advance. Dentists had some problems: one extraction and one filling without consent and a counter-claim when an account was sent, alleging extraction of four teeth instead of two.

Chapter 7

Consent: its relevance to doctor and patients

The consent issue *by itself* is unlikely to be a legal problem for the doctor, for accusations concerning lack of consent more often complicate some cases. The lawyer's attitude, according to Mason and McCall Smith, is that 'British courts are clearly cautious, even if not all judges are as favourable to doctors as was Lord Denning. Actions based on lack of consent are generally seen by lawyers as a last-ditch attempt to obtain damages when no more obvious medical negligence is evident. In this light, consent actions may well be regarded as back-door attempts to extend the scope of medical liability and may, therefore, expect to encounter both judicial scepticism and powerfully voiced policy objections' [27].

Nevertheless, consent remains a matter which is likely to trouble doctors more and more in the future. Due to advances, the age of dangerous medicine may be replacing that of dangerous surgery—except for pioneer operations such as heart transplants. So today, the array of different treatments—both by drugs and by operation—and their risks lays an additional burden on the doctor to inform patients. The evidence of expert medical witnesses as to what is established practice has hitherto played an important role in deciding whether or not there has been a failure to inform adequately but this may not necessarily apply in the future.

Hard data obtained by questioning patients usually indicate that doctors should not insist on getting 'fully informed consent' from anxious patients—but nor should they deny detailed information to inquiring ones [56]. Hence the doctor has to consider the personality of the patient and few patients are alike, but it is well to have in mind the following two classes [57]:

1 *The patient who decides to place himself unreservedly in the hands of his medical advisers and who signifies his willingness to accept any decision that they may make as to his treatment.* Here the only question which arises is the extent of the medical man's duty to volunteer explanations of the proposed treatment, its probable outcome and the risks concerned.

2 *The patient who makes it clear by questions about the nature of the treatment and its consequences or risks, that he does not wish to surrender himself entirely into the hands of his medical advisers, but desires to exercise his own judgement as to the type of treatment he is to undergo.* The patient should have his questions answered in a full and accurate manner. The doctor should explain to him, if he desires, the various factors to which consideration ought to be given in exercising a choice as to the form of treatment. The risks of an operation, investigation, or treatment should be explained.

Dr Samuel Johnson—author, compiler of the dictionary, critic, conversationalist and poet—seemed to belong to the second group for, in 1784, he

Consent

stated 'I deny the lawfulness of telling a lie to a sick man, for fear of alarming him. You have no business with consequences; you are to tell the truth . . . Of all lying, I have the greatest abhorrence of this, because I believe it has been frequently practised on myself' [58]. No doubt; but the doctors may well have been justified, for he suffered from cardiac asthma for some years and also had attacks of severe depression; when sick he was, according to Boswell, oppressed by the fear of death—so they might have bent the truth or told a falsehood to hasten his recovery on these occasions. When he said this, he had reached the end of his life and died that year.

References

1 Quoted by Strauss M.B. (Ed.) *Familiar Medical Quotations*. London: J. and A. Churchill, 1968, pp. 157–8.
2 Polani P.E. The development of the concepts and practice of patient consent. Ch 6 in *Consent in Medicine: Convergence and Divergence in Traditions*. Eds. Dunston G.R. & Seller Mary J. Oxford: Oxford University Press, 1983.
3 Jones W.H.S. (translater of Hippocrates). Vol 2. *Decorum XII*. London: Heinemann, 1967, pp. 294–5.
4 Nathan P.C. & Barrowclough A.R. *Medical Negligence*. London: Butterworth, 1957.
5 *Annual Report*. London: Medical Defence Union, 1937, p. 45.
6 *Davies v. Horton Road and Colney Hill Hospitals Management Committee and Logan*. British *Medical Journal* (1954) 1–88.
7 *Chatterton v. Gerson. All England Law Reports* 1 (1981): 257–67.
8 Taylor J.L. *Medical Malpractice*. Bristol, England: John Wright & Sons, 1980.
9 *Annual Report*. London: Medical Defence Union, 1933, p. 16–18.
10 Farndale W.A.J. *Law on Hospital Consent Forms*. Beckenham, Kent: Ravenswood Publications, 1979.
11 *Annual Report*. London: Medical Defence Union, 1974, pp. 49–50.
12 Calnan J. *Talking with Patients—A Guide to Good Practice*. London: Heinemann, 1983.
13 Grunder T.M. On the readibility of surgical consent forms. *New England Journal of Medicine* 302 (1980): 900–2; 917–8.
14 Brahams Diana. The surgeon's duty to warn of risks: translantic approach rejected by Court of Appeal. *Lancet* 1 (1984): 578–9.
15 *Sidaway v. Board of Governors of Bethlem Royal Hospital and the Maudsley Hospital and others. Weekly Law Reports* 2 (1984): 778.
16 Law report. *The Times* February 22 (1985): p. 28, col. 1–8.
17 What should a doctor tell? (medicolegal). *British Medical Journal* 289 (1984): 325–6.
18 United States Department of Health, Education and Welfare. Code of Federal Regulations, title 45. Public Welfare part 46. 103, p. 142. 1978.
19 Burnham P.J. Medical experimentation on humans (letter). *Science* 152 (1966): 448–9.
20 Strong C. Informed consent: theory and policy. *Journal of Medical Ethics* 5 (1979): 196–9.
21 Alfidi R.J. Informed consent. *Journal of the American Medical Association* 216 (1971): 1325–9.
22 Consent re-examined: explaining risks to the patient (leader). *British Medical Journal* 1 (1980): 574.
23 Rennie D. Informed consent by 'well-nigh abject' adults. *New England Journal of Medicine* 302 (1980): 917–8.
24 Meisel A. & Roth L.H. What we do and do not know about informed consent. *Journal of the American Medical Association* 246 (1981): 2473–7.
25 Kirby M.D. Informed consent: what does it mean? *Journal of Medical Ethics* 9 (1983): 69–75.

26 McLean S.A.M. & McKay A.J. Consent in medical practice, Ch 8 in *Legal Issues in Medicine*. Ed. McLean Sheila A.M. Aldershot, England: Gower Publishing Co, 1981.

27 Mason J.K. & Smith McCall R.A. *Law and Medical Ethics*. London: Butterworth, 1983.

28 Pochin E. Risk and medical ethics. *Journal of Medical Ethics* 8 (1982): 180–4.

29 Inman W.H.W. Risks in Medical Intervention. (Wolfson College Lecture, Oxford) *PEM News*. No 2 (1984): 15–36. Drug Surveillance Research Unit, University of Southampton, Botley, Southampton, SO3 2BX.

30 National Council for Civil Liberties. *Sexual offences*. 1976. Report no 13.

31 Butler-Sloss Mrs Justice. *The Times* 14 May (1982): 24 (col 1 and 2).

32 Extracted from correspondence arising from an inquiry from an ENT surgeon. London: Medical Defence Union, 1983.

33 Heilbron Mrs Justice. *All England Law Reports (Family Division)* 1 (1976): 326.

34 Porter G. Child sterilisation (a BBC television discussion reproduced). *Journal of Medical Ethics* 1 (1975): 163–7.

35 Kirman B. & Bicknell J. *Mental Handicap*. Edinburgh: Churchill Livingstone 1975, p. 77.

36 Chakraborti D. Contraception and the mentally handicapped (leading article). *British Medical Journal* 289 (1984): 1095–6.

37 Pearn J.H. The child and clinical research. *Lancet* 2 (1984): 510–2.

38 Editorial. Research involving children—ethics, the law and the climate of opinion. *Archives of Disease in Childhood* 53 (1978): 441–2.

39 Dworkin G. Legality of consent to nontherapeutic medical research on infants and young children. *Ibid*: 443–6.

40 Bluglass R. *A Guide to the Mental Health Act 1983*. London: Churchill Livingstone, 1983.

41 Bloch S. & Chodoff P. (Eds). *Psychiatric Ethics*. Oxford: Oxford University Press, 1984.

42 Potts M. & Diggory P. *Textbook of Contraceptive Practice*, 2nd edn. Cambridge University Press, 1983.

43 *Murray v. McCurchy*. Dominion Law Reports 2 (1949): 422.

44 *Bravery v. Bravery*. All England Law Reports 3 (1954): 59–68.

45 Kawaguchi A., Bergsland J. & Subzamanian S. Total bloodless open heart surgery in the pediatric age group. *Circulation* 70 (1984), part 2: 30–7 (Cardiovascular Surgery 1983).

46 *Treating the Troublesome: Report of a Working Party of the Council for Science and Society*. London: Calverts North Star Press, 1981.

47 Prentice T. Cancer man to sue consultant. *The Times* July 12 (1984): 3 (col 8).

48 Bedell Susanna & Delbanco T.L. Choices about cardiopulmonary resuscitation in the hospital. *New England Journal of Medicine* 310 (1984): 1089–93.

49 Beauchamp T.L. & Childress J.F. *Principles of Biomedical Ethics*, 2nd edn. Oxford University Press, 1983.

50 Cancer Research Working Party in Breast Conservation. Informed consent: ethical, legal and medical implications for doctors and patients who participate in randomised clinical trials. *British Medical Journal* 286 (1983): 1117–21.

51 Dudley H.A.F. Informed consent in surgical trials (leading article). *British Medical Journal* 289 (1984): 937–8.

52 Brahams Diana. Informed consent to clinical trials in cancer. *Lancet* 2 (1982): 275.

53 Weatherall D.J. Commentary on research, consent, distress and truth. *Journal of Medical Ethics* 8 (1982): 63–4.

54 Wade O.L. Informed consent to clinical trials in cancer (letter). *Lancet* 2 (1982): 275.

55 Kolata Gina. Alzheimer's research poses dilemma. *Science* 215 (1982): 47–8.

56 Fraser A.G. Do patients want to be informed? A study of consent for cardiac catheterisation. *British Heart Journal* 52 (1984): 468–70.

57 Hawkins Clifford F. *Speaking and Writing in Medicine: The Art of Communication*. Springfield, Illinois: Charles C. Thomas, 1967.

58 Quoted by James Boswell in *The Life of Samuel Johnson LID*. Ed. Edward Malone 1807. London: William Paterson, p. 526 (June 13 1784).

8

Confidentiality

*'I will respect the secrets which are confided in me, even
after the patient has died.'*
The Declaration of Geneva [1].

Secrecy is needed in some consultations, but confidentiality in most—for few patients like their complaints or conversations with doctors broadcast. Those with marital problems or venereal disease might wish to see their doctor alone, but the majority who suffer from symptoms such as bronchitis, indigestion or rheumatism, are seldom concerned whether or not others—the general practitioner's receptionist or students in hospitals—know of their problem; however, trouble can arise if certain of these matters gets outside medical confines. The importance of this subject is highlighted by the publicity given to breaches in the assumed confidentiality of information given to doctors and because of the use of computers for dealing with information storage and retrieval.

Confidentiality provided no problem in the days of the simple relationship of patient and doctor, a system that lasted until the twentieth century. Then there were virtually no specialists, or ward rounds with their entourage, or paramedical groups—e.g. physiotherapists, dietitians, and occupational therapists—or social services and other elaborations of a highly developed society such as medical boards and appeal tribunals concerned with compensation for industrial or other injuries. Now case-notes may be exposed to all of these so that a system with a guarantee of confidentiality is impossible to conceive.

The ethical laws of doctors have had to change with these developments. Originally the Hippocratic Oath, written five centuries BC, guided doctors (see Appendix VI). It stated 'whatsoever things I see or hear concerning the life of men, in my attendance on the sick or even apart therefrom, which ought not to be noised abroad, I will keep silence thereon, counting such things to be as sacred secrets'. This has become obsolete as, incidentally, has the recommendation that a successful pupil should share his wealth with an impoverished teacher. In 1948 the newly formed World Medical Association (WMA) produced a modern restatement of the Hippocratic Oath: the Declaration of

217

Geneva (see Appendix VII). This was amended by the WMA in 1983 and emphasizes the importance of confidentiality.

A legal action in 1896 (*Kitson v. Playfair and Wife*) [2] showed the financial perils of departing from the rules. An obstetrician undertook the medical care of his sister-in-law who was a guest in his house. When she was recovering from an anaesthetic, she thought that she heard him say to a colleague that she might have been 'playing hanky-panky'. Subsequently she found that the doctor had told his wife of his suspicion. Because of this indiscretion, which affected the family honour, the obstetrician was ordered to pay £12,000 damages, his plea of privilege failing. This was an astonishingly high award in those days, the explanation being that the events occurred in the top ranks of high Victorian society. The evidence included this passage:

Counsel: Suppose a gentleman did not want to serve on a jury and came to you for a certificate and you found that there was nothing the matter with him. If you were afterwards asked what was the matter with him what would you say?

Defendant: I should say that there was nothing the matter with him.

Counsel: Then you would be betraying his confidence.

SHOULD A DOCTOR TELL?

Dear as confidentiality may be to doctors and patients, it does not enjoy the benefit of legal privilege [3]. Confessing before Roman Catholic priests is confidential, and editors of newspapers have sometimes chosen imprisonment rather than reveal their source of information. All that passes between solicitor or barrister and client enjoys absolute legal privilege, for no lawyer can be compelled to reveal his client's secrets. Yet a court of law can compel a doctor to disclose details about patients and can order him to produce his notes; if he refuses to obey an order of the court, he runs the risk of being found in contempt of court and is liable to a possible term of imprisonment. The argument is that the interests of justice override all other considerations and therefore protests of the medical profession should be brushed aside. In practice, the solicitor seeking the information applies to the court for a subpoena or a witness summons to serve upon the doctor and compel him to attend court, usually with the medical records.

A solicitor is, technically, bound to let his client see documents collected on the client's behalf; this applies to all medical reports, though doctors are sometimes unaware of this when writing them. The solicitor does not have to disclose his own notes and these do not appear at any time in court.

Confidentiality

Confidentiality as a legal matter is a problem that has mainly arisen in this century. There are few references to it in the early annual reports of the Medical Defence Union and these usually refer to three relatively simple 'run of the mill' queries:

* Enquiries by insurance companies for information to which they are not entitled because no consent has been given by the patient. If deceased, consent must be obtained from the executors.
* Requests to doctors from solicitors in cases where the solicitor is not acting for the patient and has not got the necessary consent.
* Requests by the police, usually to general practitioners or junior hospital doctors, for information about patients where consent is also missing.

Telephone calls can be a particular hazard. Information should be given warily and only after certainty about the identity of the caller. Revealing an illness to an employer may result in the patient losing his job even though full recovery is expected. Patients are often sensitive about certain illnesses, for example a slight stroke which also might interfere with their employment. A Christian Scientist, for instance, who held an important position in this church which holds the principle of rejecting medical attention, was most anxious that no-one—neighbours, friends or others—should know that he was in hospital.

> *When information about a patient is requested consider:*
>
> *By whom*
> *To whom*
> *What is to be disclosed*
> *For what purpose*

In some countries, France and Belgium for example, a law is in force which positively obliges the doctor to maintain confidentiality, with criminal sanctions for a breach. There is no general legal duty in English law but some people argue that there should be and that there ought to be some uniformity in the law within the European Economic Community. The issue has never been tested in court in the UK and so confidentiality remains an ethical rather than legal principle—thus there is much scope for honestly held differences of view.

EXCEPTIONS TO THE CONCEPT OF CONFIDENTIALITY

Circumstances where secrets may be revealed without the consent of the patient are as follows (from the General Medical Council *Professional Conduct and Discipline* [4] and British Medical Association *Handbook of Medical Ethics* [5]):

* Confidential information may be shared with other doctors and other people, nurses and other health care professionals, who are assisting and collaborating in treating the patient.

* If the doctor thinks it undesirable on medical grounds to seek the patient's consent, information may sometimes be given in confidence to a close relative or someone in similar relationship to the patient.

* If, in the doctor's opinion, disclosure of information to a third party other than a relative would be in the best interests of the patient, he can then feel entitled, in exceptional cases, to disregard the refusal of a patient who cannot be persuaded to allow such information to be given.

* To satisfy a specific statutory requirement such as notifying an infectious disease.

* For the purposes of medical research, when approved by a local Research Ethical Committee or in the case of the National Cancer Registry by the Chairman of the BMA's Central Ethical Committee or his nominee.

* When the information is required by due legal process.

* When the doctor believes that he has an overriding duty to society.

A DOCTOR'S DUTY TO SOCIETY

Doctors, whether trying rigidly to observe the rule of secrecy or deciding to use discretion, can find themselves in complex moral predicaments. Someone's illness may endanger the public: the typhoid carrier, or an ill airline pilot or car driver. So the doctor may have to adjudicate between the requirements of the doctor–patient relationship and those of the community. The question as to whether or not to tell the police may arise. If a doctor knows that patient is likely to commit a crime which could injure people (e.g. murder), he should inform the police (Figure 37). Here are some examples:

> *Railway signal man suffering from incapacitating attacks.* This early case in 1906 provided a dilemma for doctors as shown in the correspondence columns of the *British Medical Journal* [6] and it appropriately occurred in the same year Bernard Shaw wrote *The Doctor's Dilemma*. A general practitioner was treating a railway signal man for asthma but the attacks were sometimes so severe that he fell on the floor and was unable to do anything for more than one hour. He was often alone in his signal box but so far had not suffered an attack while on duty. The man would not tell his employers about his condition for fear of being dismissed or being

FIGURE 37. If a doctor discovers that his patient is about to commit a crime that will injure others, he should tell the police.

transferred to another job at a lower wage. Horrified letters stated that it would be a breach of confidence between doctor and patient for the doctor to inform the railway company of the man's illness and the editor of the *British Medical Journal* stated 'in our opinion the circumstances, extreme though they be, cannot be held to justify a breach of the law of professional secrecy . . . the doctor ought not to write direct to the railway company without the patient's consent, and unless he fully understands the nature of the communication to be made'. Later letters dissented violently from this advice. This attitude of not breaking confidence under these circumstances would not hold sway today.

CAR OFFENCES

(i) There are particular circumstances when the doctor must tell police the names of road offenders. For example, a car was involved in an accident, and the driver and passengers hurried away. It was alleged that the driver was guilty of dangerous driving. On the same day a man was treated by a GP at his surgery and in the evening at the man's request the doctor treated a girl who said she had been involved in a car accident. Later the police asked the doctor to disclose the names and the addresses of the man and the girl or to give them information which would enable the police to discover them. He declined to do so on the grounds that the information was confidential, having been obtained through the relationship of doctor and patient. He was subsequently convicted of contravening the Road Traffic Act 1972 [7]. This states that where the driver is alleged to be guilty of an offence, the person keeping the vehicle has to give as much information about the identity of the driver as the police need and that any other person must give any information that he has which may lead to identifying the driver. It was held that the words 'any other person' included a doctor acting within his professional capacity and carrying out his duty and responsibility and that a doctor in the circumstances in which the GP felt himself had 'power' to give the information required.

(ii) Physically unfit drivers. A man under the care of the author suddenly developed loss of the left side of his vision (left homonymous hemianopia) which prevented him seeing anyone stepping off the kerb when he was driving. The risk to pedestrians and other traffic was explained to him but he refused to stop driving. The wife was interviewed and, with her agreement, a letter was sent to the licensing authorities to withdraw his driving licence.

PROBLEMS WITH BABIES

(i) In one area the police had received many reports of mothers coming out of shops to find that the bedding of their babies in their prams had been disarranged or even that one side of the baby's reins had been unclipped [8]. Finally one mother came out of a shop to find that her baby had been taken. There was an immediate police alert and within hours the baby was found on some waste ground, unharmed. The police suspected a particular woman and they approached her general practitioner for information which might help them. When he rightly refused to give information without her consent, the police persisted and pointed out the danger to other babies in the neighbourhood. The doctor consulted the MDU whose solicitors arranged for suitable information to be given to the police after having obtained the woman's consent. It transpired that there was a history both of infertility and of mental illness; so it was possible to help the police in their enquiries with all speed and at the same time to ensure that the interests of the patient were protected against any disclosure to which she had not fully consented.

(ii) When the body of a baby was found in a lorry, the police asked local doctors the names of recently delivered women under their care. Several members asked about the legal position and were told that there is no duty to report even patients known to have committed an offence, let alone to give the names of potential suspects [9].

> *A doctor must be able to justify his decision to disclose information*

POSSESSION OF DRUGS

An unusual case of 'Pot Belly'. A man aged thirty-three attended the accident department and told the casualty officer that one month earlier he had swallowed eighteen condoms filled with hashish to prevent discovery that he had them in his possession. He had recovered only twelve, two being vomited and ten having passed rectally. He had attended accident and emergency departments in two other hospitals but stated that nothing had been done since his story was not believed. There was slight tenderness in the epigastric region. Plain X-rays were normal but a gastrografin meal (Figure 38) showed six filling defects in the stomach and a deformed duodenal cap suggesting that the foreign bodies were unlikely to go further. A duodenal ulcer had been diagnosed two or three years earlier.

The surgical registrar, before operating, consulted the MDU about professional secrecy, and asked whether he had any obligation to notify the police. He was advised that he owed a duty of secrecy to the patient and that even his knowledge that the foreign bodies contained drugs did not place him under a duty to report to the authorities, however strong the inference of a breach of the drugs regulations. Any drugs should be handed to the theatre superintendant for transmission to the hospital pharmacist.

To forestall possible disintegration of the contraceptive sheaths and a potentially lethal overdose, the registrar, with the patient's written consent, operated and not only removed the six packets but

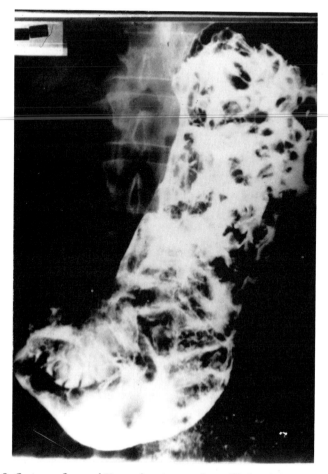

FIGURE 38. Gastrografin meal X-ray showing condoms filled with hashish in stomach. These were swallowed to evade Customs officials.

also performed a vagotomy and pyloroplasty. Although he had taken no steps to inform them, the police brought charges against the patient who had given written permission for the registrar to disclose his medical history to them. The police expressed surprise that the registrar had not reported the facts to them and that the MDU had advised this, but as there was no threat to 'life or limb' of others, the doctor had no duty to break confidentiality with the patient [10]. (This also applies to burglary and damage to property but, in contrast, would not be acceptable if arson or rape were committed as both are a risk to people.)

Doran and Amar reported this case in 1977 and referred to previous ones in the medical literature; but this was probably the first where the smuggler came to grief because of pre-existing gastrointestinal disease—the narrowed gastric outlet due to a healed duodenal ulcer [11].

THE ILLNESSES OF POLITICIANS

Our lives and futures are guided, for better or for worse, by decisions taken by political or military leaders in positions of power. The duty of a doctor towards a person in such a position if—for medical reasons—he considers that the patient is not fully competent to make sensible and informed decisions, has not been defined. The advice may be take a rest and hand over decision-making to a colleague but this advice is often rejected; in fact the suggestion of weakness to a strong-willed person may increase the determination not to give in. For the doctor to inform the leader's colleagues would be a breach of medical etiquette and confidentiality unless it was done with the patient's consent. Even when close associates know the diagnosis, it may, for political reasons, be concealed from the public: the Chairman of the Communist Party in Russia, Mr Andropov, was reported by the mass media as suffering from a cold for six months, whereas he was really dying from renal failure and being treated on a dialysis machine.

The President of the United States, Franklin D. Roosevelt, made important decisions about the future of Europe at the end of the Second World War though he was ill with hypertension. Mr Winston Churchill, when Prime Minister after that war, suffered a slight stroke. His physician, Lord Moran, gave a bulletin to the Home Secretary, Mr R. A. Butler, stating that he had suffered from defective cerebral circulation. Mr Butler changed this and concealed the fact, reporting to his colleagues in the Cabinet that Churchill was overtired and needed a rest. Today, the harm that a sick leader can do is potentially much greater and an extreme example might be that a nuclear war could be triggered off by an error of judgement.

Special groups

CONTRACEPTIVES FOR CHILDREN

Some lay people harbour the belief that doctors prescribe the contraceptive pill to children (those under sixteen years) too casually and irresponsibly. This is seldom, if ever, the case. The doctor usually has no option and the matter is often more a social than medical responsibility. This is shown in the following

Chapter 8

letter written to the Medical Defence Union by a general practitioner with children of his own, and in the reply from the MDU:

November 1976

Dear Sir,

I am sorry that I have to write to you about a matter which no doubt you have had extensive correspondence on before. This is the matter of prescribing oral contraceptives to girls under the age of 16.

Yesterday, I had a 14-year-old girl attend the surgery requesting tablets to regulate her menstrual cycle which was rather erratic. It transpired that she was having regular sexual intercourse with her 16-year-old boy-friend without adequate contraceptive precautions, and she felt that the pill would be a good idea. I reminded her that her boy-friend was breaking the law and also suggested that she discussed the matter with her parents. Her parents, however, dislike him and this was, therefore, out of the question. I felt duty bound to prescribe the pill, as obviously an unwanted pregnancy would be an even worse situation.

The two points I would like you to clarify for me, however, are (1) should one insist that the girl tells her parents before prescribing the pill or, alternatively, tell the parents oneself, thus breaking one's confidentiality with the patient, and (2) if the girl's parents were to question me directly, should I divulge this information? My reason for asking the second question is the fact that the girl may well tell her parents that I have given her the pill to regulate her periods which is, in fact, one of my reasons for doing this.

If you are able to clarify these points, I would be very grateful, as I am quite sure the situation will crop up time and time again, in the so-called permissive society. It really is a rather disturbing situation; when I was 14 I think I was more interested in reading comics than sex!

With many thanks,

Yours sincerely,

Dr...

Confidentiality

Reply from the Medical Defence Union:

December 1976

Dear Dr..

Your letter of 24th November has been passed to me and I refer to your problems connected with a fourteen-year-old girl who appears to have got beyond the stage of reading comics.

You can, if you consider it correct, withhold the prescription of the pill for a girl of fourteen until you are satisfied that her parents have agreed to the prescription. The snag is that if the girl is adamant that her parents are not to be informed, with the result that the pill is withheld and an unwanted and potentially disastrous pregnancy follows, you may feel you have let the patient down. It is a matter for your judgement which path you follow. If, in good faith, you explain to the parents, against the daughter's wish, that the pill was about to be prescribed, you could destroy your professional relationship with the girl, again with harmful result.

If the parents of a girl of fourteen ask you directly whether or not you are prescribing the pill for the child then I think you must give the correct answer. It is always possible, if you prescribe the pill for a girl under sixteen, to warn the patient that you would have to tell the truth if you were questioned by the parents.

The legal as well as the ethical background to these questions is often unclear and the practitioner is thrown back on his or duty to consider the patient's welfare to be of prime importance. Please write again, or speak to me over the telephone, if you run into particular difficulty.

Yours sincerely,

Deputy Secretary..................................

Medical confidentiality should be respected in consultations with those under sixteen years. The decision whether or not to prescribe the pill depends first of all on the doctor's clinical judgement; but if he has a conscientious objection to this, he should tell her and suggest another doctor who could look after her—an approach that could also apply when a doctor has a religious objection to abortion.

This approach to the moral dilemma was upturned in 1984 by the case *Gillick* v. *West Norfolk and Wisbech Area Health Authority and DHSS.* Mrs

Victoria Gillick, a Roman Catholic mother of ten children, had written to the AHA asking for an assurance that none of her daughters would be given contraceptive or abortion treatment while they were under sixteen without her prior knowledge and consent. Not having received any assurance satisfactory to her, she sued the AHA and the DHSS claiming two declarations:

1. That the health service notice concerned with family planning and abortion services for young people issued by the DHSS in 1980 (HN(80)46) had no authority in law and gave advice which was unlawful and wrong and which did, or might, adversely affect the welfare of Mrs Gillick's children, her right as a parent, and her ability effectively to discharge her duties as a parent.

2. That no doctor or other person employed by the health authority either in the family planning service or otherwise might give any contraceptive or abortion advice to any child of Mrs Gillick under the age of sixteen without the prior knowledge and consent of the child's parent or guardian.

Mrs Justice Woolf dismissed her claim but Lord Justice Parker in the Court of Appeal summarized his view of the law as follows: 'Any doctor who advises a girl under sixteen as to contraceptive steps to be taken or affords contraception or abortion to such a girl without the knowledge and consent of the parent, save in an emergency which would render consent in any event unnecessary, infringes the legal rights of the parent or guardian. Save in emergency, his proper course is to seek parental consent or apply to the Court'. The Court in question would be either the Juvenile or High Court. The DHSS immediately sent a revised version of the health service notice and appealed to the House of Lords against the decision [12]. The function of the five Law Lords is, however, to interpret the law. If the decision of the Court of Appeal is upheld, doctors might—through the BMA—attempt to have the law altered.

THE DILEMMA FOR DOCTORS

The decision was a fundamental threat to confidentiality and to the freedom of doctors to advise and to prescribe treatment, which in their clinical judgement, is best for the patient; it also put them at risk of prosecution under the criminal law. Any idea that doctors encourage sexual proclivity by giving contraception to girls under sixteen without the consent of their parents is mistaken. These girls are usually already sexually active and few are deterred from intercourse by the thought of unwanted pregnancies. One-third at least have already told their parents before they visit a clinic; many of the rest decide to 'talk to mum' after two or three visits. This leaves a small group who find it impossible to talk to their parents or who live in an intolerable family situation.

Although allowed to provide information without giving advice, clinics found this to be impossible: one could not be given without the other, and lessons about sex at school were curtailed. The judgement did not close the door completely: it allowed doctors to give contraceptive advice in cases of emergency, and the risk of pregnancy in a girl under sixteen can come into this category. For example, a fifteen-year-old girl goes to her general practitioner's Friday evening surgery saying that she has been thrown out of her home by her parents and that evening intends to live with her boy-friend. Assuming that her story is true and she cannot be persuaded into any other course, contraceptive advice and treatment over the weekend—until application could be made to Court in 'Care' on wardship proceedings—would be viewed by most as an emergency. This matter is obviously also a social problem and both medical and lay people hold strong views as to the moral, religious or ethical issues arising out of the case.

VENEREAL DISEASES

Confidentiality is a special problem in venereology. Failure to keep confidences will dissuade patients from seeking attention or volunteering information about their sexual actions and contacts. Patients must realize that their diagnosis or, indeed, any other information is never given to their sexual partners when they consult or to anyone else outside the clinic service. This creates problems: for example, a man with syphilis may refuse to allow his wife to know or to be checked; persuasion and rapport is the only possible way as there is no law of compulsion; sometimes a cover-up story such as a search for familial anaemia can be invented so as to persuade him and to 'save his face'.

Family doctors are informed of the diagnosis and treatment if the patient has been referred by them. Any enquiries, for example from solicitors or doctors undertaking life assurance examinations, are not answered unless the patient gives written permission and it is in his own interest. Similarly, the police are never given information unless a court orders it, or the doctor considers that it is in the patient's best interests.

Medical secrecy became statute law for the first time in the Venereal Diseases Act of 1917 which states that all information from persons treated for these diseases shall be regarded as confidential. This was repeated in the National Health Service (Venereal Diseases) Regulations 1974 (Statutory Instruments 1974/29) which state that any information capable of identifying the patient shall not be disclosed except:

(a) For the purpose of communicating that information to a medical practitioner, or to a person employed under the direction of a medical practitioner in connection with the treatment of persons suffering from such disease or the prevention of the spread thereof.

(b) For the purpose of such treatment or prevention.

A record-keeping system separate from the rest of the hospital records secures the confidential nature of such information.

From the practical aspect, Dr Jennifer C. Clay, director of the VD department at the General Hospital, Birmingham, finds that many 'con tricks' are likely to be tried: telephone calls are always regarded with extreme suspicion and the caller's identity must be checked—usually no information is given over the telephone but the number is taken and rung back if it belongs to a person with the right of access to the information requested. Case-notes are kept in the department and are not allowed out but information is of course given when referring patients to other specialists or to the general practitioner and no consent from the patient is needed for this; consent may be inferred in these situations but many doctors would still prefer to have the written agreement of the patient. Those in need of care and protection are a problem and social

FIGURE 39. In a department of venereology, the doctor wished to see a prisoner alone and the latter agreed to be secured to a waterpipe for the consultation.

workers can unwittingly break confidentiality. Children who have absconded may have to be checked medically, and coercion can easily be used; so it is better to see the child alone to check whether the child has agreed and needs an examination anyway. Prisoners in custody are usually seen with an escort, as happens in prisons where patients are seldom seen alone. However, it may be possible to negotiate a solution where privacy and security are compatible; in one exceptional case the patient elected to be attached to a waterpipe for the consultation (Figure 39) but the more usual solution would be to have the police escorts guard possible escape routes.

Dr Clay believes that the best way of ensuring confidentiality in her department is to explain the need for this and to educate all her staff and medical students accordingly.

MENTALLY ILL PATIENTS

Doctors in charge of patients with mental illness may face considerable problems. If there is doubt about the patient's ability to handle his own affairs, his consent to disclosure should not be relied on. His solicitor, relatives, or even the Court of Protection should be contacted. In particular, a doctor should not disclose information about the condition of a patient to the spouse who is contemplating divorce—even when the object is to prevent the spouse from being worried.

HUSBANDS, WIVES AND SECRETS

Every day husbands ask doctors how their wives are progressing. The wife's doctor takes for granted that he can keep her husband informed—an example of implied consent, rather than that the wife's permission is unnecessary. When there is a marital dispute, the only safe rule is to insist upon the patient's permission before telling the other spouse. Solicitors acting for the partner who requests information when divorce proceedings are imminent must produce the patient's written permission. One member once reported a case that illustrates the tendency of some patients to read notes about themselves:

> A young married woman discharged herself from an acute psychia-
> tric ward after taking an overdose of aspirin. She had done this
> because her husband had physically ill-treated her for flirting, he
> said, with a foreign student. In the discharge letter to the family
> doctor the woman psychiatrist wrote 'she admits to being unfaithful
> to her husband on at least two occasions in the past'.
>
> Later the family doctor referred her to a gynaecologist with a view
> to sterilization. The patient was given an envelope containing copies

of hospital reports including the recent one from the psychiatrist. At the gynaecological clinic, she offered the envelope to a member of staff who indicated that all the hospital records were available and that the copies were not necessary. She then put them in her handbag and read them at home. Subsequently her husband took them from her handbag and read them. When he confronted his wife she denied the statement about her alleged infidelity and stated that this must have been a misunderstanding by the psychiatrist. The husband sought an interview with the psychiatrist to discuss the matter further; but the MDU advised her to reply to the husband that she could not discuss the wife's clinical affairs with him and so must refuse to meet him. [13].

GENETIC COUNSELLING

Some guidance about genetic counselling is given in the *Handbook of Medical Ethics* issued by the BMA but this is a difficult area. Certainty about an individual's genotype could affect his attitude to life, and society's attitude to him, with the possibility of considerable medical, economic and social repercussions. A problem occurs when someone, who is found to be carrying an abnormal gene, is reluctant to allow this knowledge to reach other family members. Does the information belong only to the individual in whom the abnormality was found, or does it, because of the shared nature of genetic material, belong to all members of the family who could be affected? The importance of such information, states the handbook, probably outweighs the importance of complete individual medical confidentiality, providing that this is kept to the medical profession and to those entitled to it because of their potential carrier state. The spouse, or the potential spouse, of a carrier may have to be informed because of the responsibility for passing such genes on to future generations. This area of medicine is growing in importance and practical help is provided by P. S. Harper in his *Practical Genetic Counselling* [14].

DOCTORS WITH DUAL LOYALTIES

Difficulties arise because of dual loyalties. For example, the occupational physician (or employment medical adviser) may be asked to advise by either management or unions—the latter perhaps because of possible risks to health in a factory. A medical report (after consent by the employee) may have to be provided for the management on the employee's health; then he should give a fair and conscientious opinion even if it means the employee's dismissal.

Confidentiality

Problems occur in the collection, transmission, storage and use of information obtained during epidemiological surveys. For example, inclusion of named data in cancer registration at a national level allows identification but stringent control must be maintained of information provided without the patient's knowledge—particularly because some may not know that they actually have cancer. Further aspects of this are given by M. Alderson in his *An Introduction to Epidemiology* [15].

FIGURE 40. A patient can sometimes be identified even if the eyes are covered. Then a consent form agreeing to publication should be signed.

233

Chapter 8

All doctors know of the importance of concealing the identity of the patient when writing, lecturing, and broadcasting. This can easily be overlooked when preparing videotapes, and also when using photographs of patients to illustrate articles or make slides for lectures. Usually, though not always, the identity of the person is concealed when the eyes are covered (Figure 40); if not, the patient should sign the consent form agreeing to the publication. Parents should be consulted in the case of a child. The confidentiality of illustrative clinical records was dealt with thoroughly in a report by C. C. Gilson generated by the Audiovisual Advisory Committee of the North East Thames Regional Health Authority [16].

Confidence was breached on one occasion when a medical textbook, which cost £70, was published showing a full frontal nude photograph of a patient without his permission; it also gave his initials, hospital record number and an extract from his medical records. The man borrowed the book from the library and asked the Health Service Commissioner, Sir Cecil Clothier, to investigate his complaint. The publishers temporarily suspended sales of the book and replaced the offending page without the patient's face [17].

A grey area can arise in the writing of biography, as, for example, with the publication of Lord Moran's *Churchill: The Struggle for Survival*. It appeared only a year after its subject's death and described the illness and decline of a great national figure. It aroused stronger feelings in the national press about the ethical issues than it did even in medical journals although Lord Moran claimed that his book had been written with Sir Winston's knowledge and approval. A later example was when the editor of the *British Medical Journal* received a complaint from the General Medical Council when he wrote a follow-up obituary tribute about the distinguished General Orde Wingate of the Chindits. Further evidence had suggested that his depression and attempted suicide in Cairo during the Second World War was due to cerebral malaria and not mental instability [18]. Much correspondence followed and no definite conclusion was reached on whether there should either be clearer guidelines on time limits for publishing or whether the GMC should set up a tribunal or committee to adjudicate on such material. (Guidance was issued later by the GMC [4].) Sir Christopher Booth wrote that 'there must be occasions, admittedly rare, when the interests of history outweighed those of confidentiality. History . . . is part of the soul of a nation, and the views of the public are at least as important on this issue as those of historians or of the guardians of the conscience of the medical profession' [19].

Fashions and conventions about the art and practice of biography change, and the degree of permissiveness which is necessary, proper, and acceptable is difficult to calculate, especially in medical matters. Biography has become franker and is likely to become even more so [20].

Medical records

'Records have been kept by doctors for thousands of years', said Professor Neil McIntyre in a lecture to the Medico-Legal Society [21], 'details of medical conditions and treatments have been chipped in stone, carved on wood and in the form of hieroglyphics on parchments . . . The reason is clear; lawyers keep notes for the same reason. The doctor needs an *aide-mémoire* to remind him of what was wrong with the patient on the previous occasion, what his own opinions were at the time and what he did for the patient. This information is essential if the doctor is to see if his condition has changed, whether treatment needs to be altered, or whether there are social or psychological factors which are affecting the course of his illness'. Medical records even a hundred years ago were simple. Now, with the advances in medical science and treatment, they can be complex and very bulky—and, for the sake of the patient, be available to various people and departments. They are of paramount importance for the patient: information concerning the particular illness together with technical reports about blood tests, X-rays, etc. make up the most part but doctors are interested in caring for the whole patient and not just in treating the disease itself—thus it is necessary to record risk factors such as smoking and alcohol consumption, to check whether there are any serious sexual or pyschological problems or financial worries, or the risk of an occupational disease. Patients occasionally object to such wide-ranging questions but rarely sustain this objection if the reasons for asking the questions are carefully explained.

The average person is not much interested in what happens to his case-notes and whether anyone reads them. Indeed, illness is a popular subject for conversation: ailments and operations are discussed with enthusiasm on buses, in bridge clubs and anywhere. Certain diseases, however—mental trouble, venereal disease and formerly tuberculosis—have a stigma in the public mind and secrecy is often necessary. In contrast, the duodenal ulcer is widely regarded by the layman as the penalty for tension, pressure and worry, and the prerogative of the successful business man, though there is virtually no evidence for this. Gout is also considered to be a high-status disease; in fact, when the author told a factory worker that he had got this and that it was easily treated, the man appeared worried and wittily remarked, 'No doc, please not gout—I can't go back to my workmates and tell them that I have got a Tory disease. Can't we call it syphilis or something like that?'

SHOULD PATIENTS KEEP THEIR OWN RECORDS?

Some people have suggested that patients should keep their own records at home and carry them with them when they come to hospital. The reasons given for this are twofold:

* *Secrecy.* Any information being released without the patient's consent would scarcely be possible.

* *The patient would be fully informed.* Anyone, however, who has looked through, say, a hundred case-notes for research purposes would view this as a forlorn hope because of hieroglyphics, the technical jargon, and sometimes bad handwriting.

Some patients do already carry their own records; it happens in private practice, and patients going overseas or visiting doctors here are often given a summary of their condition together with X-rays and results of investigation. The same idea has been carried out on a small scale within the National Health Service: patients at St Mary's Maternity Hospital, Portsmouth, have been given custody of their own obstetric records and are responsible for taking them along when they visit the antenatal clinic [22]. This has been successful: administrative time has been saved, records have been kept in good condition and very few have been lost—although many of the women admitted that they were not able to understand what was written. However, these and casualty case-notes are usually ephemeral from the patient's aspect. Points against extending this approach to all medical records are:

* Case-notes of patients (especially medical cases) are often bulky and doctors could not rely on patients carrying them around with them, and they might be unavailable at times when they were most needed—as in emergency admissions.

* The entire notes with the vital information could easily be lost—as not a few households are somewhat disorganized, a fact illustrated by the loss of so many National Insurance Cards.

* Patients might remove material from the records. Some do, after all, deliberately withhold information from doctors under certain circumstances, though rarely; but it would be dangerous to act from inaccurate or misleading data.

* Patients' records are essential for research and the task of retrieving perhaps 500 case-notes from patients' homes might well deter any research worker.

* The patient might read them and be distressed.

SHOULD PATIENTS SEE THEIR OWN RECORDS?

There is a good case for allowing patients access to their own notes if they wish;

in practice, it has improved doctor–patient relationships; but a problem arises with those who have malignant disease. It is the policy of many doctors personally to tell the patient the truth and this can be done in a caring way—to cause the least distress and to give a ray of hope. Fortunately it is uncommon nowadays for insulting remarks or words like 'neurotic' to be used ('nervous' or 'psychosomatic' mean the same but do not offend). Hypochondriacs or others may get the wrong impression whatever they read; one read a chest X-ray report as 'no chance' and thought that the end was near whereas it was really 'no change'.

Many patients probably read their case-notes anyway. For example one of the author's first patients was a man of fifty years who needed an operation for a duodenal ulcer: as the surgeon was making the incision, he had a cardiac arrest and the wound had to be sewn up without the operation being done, but fortunately he recovered from coma a day or two later without brain damage. Courage was needed to go and tell him about this. However, when the author approached in trepidation to the bedside, the man held out his hands and shaking hands warmly said 'Doctor, I must apologize, I read my case-notes and am so sorry to have caused you all this bother!'

A suitable compromise would be to keep records at the hospital but to let the patient have a copy of the discharge summary, after explaining the details, to keep at home. This could be taken on holiday, or shown to a doctor visiting the patient at night from a deputizing service who otherwise would have no access to the case-notes.

Letters given to patients may sometimes be opened and read:

> A GP practised in an area where gynaecologists did not interpret the Abortion Act liberally, accepting only those women who had been thoroughly investigated by doctors whose opinions they respected. He gave a patient a sealed envelope marked 'confidential' and addressed to a gynaecologist, telling her to hand it to him when she attended hospital. Shortly after she had left the surgery, her husband telephoned and said that his wife had opened the letter and that he had read it. As a result he was going to take the doctor to court, and bring him before the Executive Council (now the FPC) and insist that he would be rendered unemployed—also that the letter was on its way to a popular daily national newspaper.

> The letter went: '. . . her husband is an impossible fellow—the most impossible in the practice. He's always "ill" though evidence of organic disease has not been found. Last year he had a laparotomy when nothing was found. He has been in and out of the courts in

237

the past. At present he's drawing unemployment benefit as well as doing a job. I have discussed the case with my partner and his comment was that anybody pregnant by Mr A. should be terminated without hesitation. She has two young children. She took the pill for a month after the last baby but did not continue taking it as she says she could not afford it. Should you agree to terminate the pregnancy I will arrange for her to be seen at the family planning clinic. She has left him twice but he has the charm of a psychopath and she always comes back.'

The statements were relevant and true, written without malice and addressed to a person entitled to receive them. So the doctor had a good defence against a legal action; but he had no redress against the offensive threat from the irate husband—except by the embarrassing method of giving evidence in a local court against him for fraudulently drawing unemployment benefit [23].

PUTTING MEDICAL RECORDS ON THE COMPUTER

The information explosion has placed a tremendous strain on the recording of medical data and on the ability of doctors to deal with it. Information is the life-blood of their work, but the problems of handling it are very great [21]. The computer offers a solution to this problem and the saving of time is obvious when dealing with a bank or buying airline tickets. Computers are already used in some hospitals for handling laboratory data, plotting graphs of changes in biochemical results, giving information about drugs and drug interactions, as well as for administrative purposes: to schedule out-patients, to monitor bed occupancy and so on. Help might also be given to doctors for diagnosis as a computer could cover every possibility including rare diseases. It increases the accuracy of diagnosing patients admitted as emergencies with acute abdominal pain; however, the reason for this may be that doctors have, even in the middle of the night and under stressful conditions, to get all details of the patient's symptoms to feed into the computer so it increases their thoroughness in taking a history [24].

An appreciable minority of patients—17 per cent—are opposed to doctors using computers, according to a postal survey of 350 patients from two rural practices [25]. This, however, may be due to neophobia—the fear of new things. Most of the general concern was accounted for by ninety-one patients, of whom 31 per cent feared that confidentiality of information would be reduced. Smaller proportions were found to oppose computers on other grounds: impersonality, economy and general anxiety. When patients actually face a computer, many prefer being questioned by this than by a doctor [26]—a poor reflection on the bedside manner of some doctors. The patient does, however, feel more private and may give answers which would otherwise be embarrassing. Computers could save time for doctors and give them more time to spend talking to patients.

THE DATA PROTECTION ACT 1984

The fear that confidential matter will be more easily available from a computer without the patient's consent is probably unjustified: records held in a computer are likely to be more confidential than records in paper envelopes. Indeed, the Chairman of the Patients Association, Dame Elizabeth Ackroyd [27], has remarked that computerized records would probably be more secure than manual records which are commonly passed to a number of people within the hospital. Computer-held records should be less accessible to the ordinary person than are manual records: passwords and checks are used to protect them against unauthorized use and only a very determined and skilled person could gain access to the records—and a deliberate act of burglary like this would be extremely rare.

The Data Protection Act of 1984 regulated the use of automatically processed personal information and was based on two fundamental concepts: the need to know and the person's right to confidentiality. An important principle was that information about a patient should be kept only for the purpose of health care and that release of personal data must not be allowed except for the purpose of health care [28, 29). However exceptions to this occur under the following circumstances:

* To notify infectious diseases under the Public Health Act.

* If a court of law, or a person empowered by statute to require its disclosure—for example the coroner's court—orders disclosure.

* When disclosure is authorized by the appropriate research ethical committee. Provisos are that no distress or damage will be caused to the patient and that his anonymity is preserved when the research is published.

* To prevent or control communicable diseases if there is a serious risk to public health.

* To help prevent or detect serious crime or bring the person to justice. The crime has to be sufficiently serious and the value of the personal health data for this purpose undoubted. Rarely, personal health data might have a bearing on national security and then convincing evidence of the importance of such a disclosure must be given and a certificate has to be signed personally by a cabinet minister, the Attorney-General or the Lord Advocate.

Normally, the health-care professional and the patient will be notified and their permission obtained. This may not always be practical. Any person who controls the contents and use of automatically processed personal health data is required to register as a data user and to comply with the data protection principle set out in schedule I of the Act. Patients and doctors can inspect the register which provides details of the use to which this data is put. Bodies outside the Health Service (including the police) are excluded from consulting patients' records held in computers. Thus, the Act has not affected existing arrangements within the National Health Service governing the use and disclosure of manually kept case records.

TYPES OF INQUIRIES FROM MEMBERS

A computer print-out gave details of ninety-six inquiries from members of the MDU during 1983 which were specifically related to confidentiality. Fourteen concerned police inquiries; thirteen were questions about the release of medical records; twelve related to the writing of medical reports; three were about child abuse; two about sterilization and another two about drug addicts. Fifty covered a range of topics, many of which concerned disclosure of information:

* Patient who refuses to see a psychiatrist plans to commit suicide on her fortieth birthday if she is not married by that date.
* Confidentiality in Department of Venereology: break-in and disturbance of records and index cards.
* Father of 26-year-old mentally retarded patient has threatened to kill him should he, the father, become too ill to look after him, rather than have him admitted to a home—advice concerning action.
* Information to insurance company *re* duration of deceased patient's illness.
* Pregnancy—twelve-year-old girl.

Abuse of professional confidence has fortunately been only a small problem so far but increasing publicity about breaches in the assumed confidentiality of information given to doctors may cause this subject to become more important. When in doubt, consider the following:
* A doctor will be wise, the General Medical Council advises, to seek advice from a medical defence body or professional association.
* Consult a colleague.
* Discuss matters with relatives of the patient, if the patient agrees.
* Think what a court of law might decide—remembering that lawyers are often governed by a commonsense approach.

References

1 Declaration of Geneva. *Dictionary of Medical Ethics*, Eds Duncan A.S., Dunstan G.R. & Welbourn R.B. London: Darton, Longman and Todd, 1981, p. 132.
2 *Kitson* v. *Playfair and wife. British Medical Journal* 1 (1896): 882–4 and *The Times*, 28 March 1896.
3 Palmer R.N. Defamation, assault and confidentiality. In *Medical Malpractice*. Ed. J. Leahy Taylor pp. 59–82. Bristol: John Wright, 1980.
4 *Professional Conduct and Discipline: Fitness to Practice*. London: General Medical Council, 1985.
5 *Handbook of Medical Ethics*. London: British Medical Association, 1984.
6 Railway signalman. Professional secrecy. *British Medical Journal*. Dec 15 (1906): 1753.
7 *Hunter* v. *Mann. All England law Reports* 2 (1974): 414–20.
8 *Annual Report*. London: Medical Defence Union, 1973, p. 23.
9 *Ibid.* 1972: 24.
10 *Ibid.* 1977: 11–12.
11 Doran J. & Amar S.S. An unusual case of 'pot belly'. *British Medical Journal* 2 (1977): 1630.
12 Teenage confidence and consent. *British Medical Journal* 290 (1985): 144–5; Treatment without consent—intervention by the court. *Ibid.*: 1408–9.
13 *Annual Report*. London: Medical Defence Union, 1972, 25–6.
14 Harper P.S. *Practical Genetic Counselling*, 2nd ed. Bristol: Wright, 1984.
15 Alderson M. *An Introduction to Epidemiology*, 2nd ed. London: Macmillan, 1984.
16 Gilson C.C. Confidentiality of illustrative clinical records. *Journal of Audiovisual Media in Medicine* 7 (1984): 4–9.
17 *The Times*. 11 June (1984): 5 (col 2 and 3).
18 Lock S. A question of confidence: an editor's view. *British Medical Journal* 288 (1984): 123–6.
19 Booth C. A question of confidence (letter). *British Medical Journal* 288 (1984): 398.
20 Keynes M. Medical sense and nonsense in biography. *British Medical Journal* 286 (1983): 1023–6.
21 McIntyre N. Medical records: computers and the patient. *Medical-Legal Journal* 4 (1982): 159–170.
22 Murray F.A. & Topley L. Patients as record-holders. *Health and Social Service Journal* 84 (1974): 1675.
23 *Annual Report*. London: Medical Defence Union, 1972, 55–6.
24 De Dombal F.T. Leaper D.J., Horrocks Jane C., Staniland John R. & McCann A.P. Human and computer-aided diagnosis of abdominal pain. *British Medical Journal* 1 (1974): 376–80.
25 Pringle, M., Robins S. & Brown G. Computers in the surgery: the patients' view. *British Medical Journal* 288 (1984): 289–91.
26 Card W.I. & Lucas R.W. Computer interrogation in medical practice. *International Journal of Machine Tool Design and Research*. 14 (1981): 49–57.
27 Ackroyd Dame Elizabeth. Patients' voice. 8 November 1983. Minutes of the Annual General Meeting. *The Patients Association*, 11 Dartmouth Street, London SW1H 9BN.
28 Ashbury A.J. Confidentiality of personal health information. *British Medical Journal* 289 (1984): 1559–60.
29 Steering Group on Health Services Information. *The Protection and Maintenance of Confidentiality of Patient and Employee Data*. London: HMSO, 1984.

9

Litigation in the United States of America and in other countries

> 'Discourage litigation. Persuade your neighbors to compromise whenever you can . . . As a peace-maker the lawyer has a superior opportunity of being a good man. There will still be business enough . . . Never stir up litigation.'
>
> ABRAHAM LINCOLN, 1850 [1]

'Litigation', an American stated, 'has become a mania in the USA—against everyone.' This judgement may be considered unfair by other Americans, for the USA is a vast country, a continent, and to generalize can be misleading. Nevertheless, doctors in the United Kingdom have for some years been looking uneasily over their shoulders at medico-legal developments in the USA where settlements in millions of dollars are no longer news; but this desire to seek compensation in the courts is not surprising, for the patient must often bear the financial burden of disability in a free market economy with minimal welfare support.

Awards to patients continue to rise. Those of one million dollars or more rose to forty-five in 1981 from only four in 1976; in the same period the average award climbed to $840,396 from $192,344. Some broke records: in Brooklyn, New York, a baby girl was awarded $29·2 million when made blind and deaf from meningitis and in another tragic case an out-of-court settlement provided annual payments that could exceed $120 million if an infant lived to seventy-eight years. When citing these figures an editorial in the journal *Pediatrics* in 1984 [2], reported that obstetricians were particularly vulnerable because juries were likely to recommend big awards in malpractice cases concerning infants; and 25 per cent of Florida's obstetricians had stopped practising their specialty because of malpractice liability. These astronomical sums awarded were probably due also to several factors including inflation and the sympathetic attitude of juries.

Studies of medical malpractice in the USA

A formidable list of studies has been carried out in the USA. Any self-respecting state, whether it had a malpractice crisis or not, had to have a study, and the two most informative ones were one by the Secretary of Health's Commission on Medical Malpractice [3] and the report of the National Association of Insurance Commissioners [4]. The Secretary's Commission was set up in 1971 by the President; it was hoped that the medical malpractice problem might be solved by a Federal Commission but, as with other commissions, the result hardly justified the cost in time or money; members started work in 1971 and reported in January 1973 and millions of dollars were spent on it. The secretary of the Medical Defence Union and the senior partner of the MDU's lawyers were called to the USA and submitted a memorandum on medical malpractice in Britain. Weighing $5\frac{1}{2}$ lbs (2·5 kg), its 1,000 pages covered every aspect of medical malpractice and provides a mine of information. Unfortunately nobody discovered anything not already known; the relative risk of different specialists was interesting (Figure 41) but not new knowledge.

One member of the commission wrote a minority report and stated 'as a commission we failed to even approach an overall solution of the malpractice crisis. We did, however, dispel some myths around the subject'. These were as follows:

* *That doctors who stopped to treat patients in an emergency are in great danger of being sued.* The commission said that there was no evidence of that. The idea had been perpetuated by the American Medical Association survey which showed that 50 per cent of their members would not stop if called to an emergency for fear of being sued. The Secretary's commission dispelled that notion and, although many states had enacted 'good Samaritan' laws to

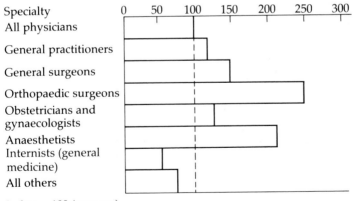

Index = 100 (average)

FIGURE 41. The relative risk of different specialists in the USA. (Data derived from the USA Secretary's Commission on Medical Malpractice [3].)

243

FIGURE 42. The good Samaritan: contrary to popular myth, a doctor who stops to treat a patient in an emergency is in no danger of being sued.

protect doctors, it considered that there was no need for these as there was nothing to legislate against (Figure 42).

* *That there were a lot of unjustified claims in the USA.*
* *That the increase in litigation was due to nurses and other ancillary staff doing doctors' work.*
* *That it was all the fault of the lawyers.* Doctors particularly were very suspicious of one or two lawyers who ran courses for lawyers on how to sue doctors; these were comprehensive and covered all phases of trial practice. But some fault only was due to irresponsible lawyers.
* *That it was all the fault of the contingent legal fee system.* The commission criticized inflated damages in very large cases and examined figures in law firms, but found that they did not make any undue profit on medical malpractice cases; most were small and only in the occasional very big case did the lawyers gain.

The Commission wrote a follow-up report in 1976 which was smaller (only about 200 pages). In it was a review of all claims against doctors which had been closed between July and October in 1976. Unfortunately, this report was also unproductive, the opening paragraph reading: 'No broad conclusion can be drawn about the nature and extent of medical malpractice in this country'. There were, however, three positive though self-evident conclusions: that most events which led to claims took place in hospital (not surprising as most medical work in the USA goes on in hospitals); that the way to handle the problem was to launch accident prevention programmes, and that the average award was surprisingly small. The reason that awards had risen by 100 per cent during a time when inflation had only gone up by 50 per cent was that juries were over-compensating for inflation.

Dr J. W. Brooke Barnett, Secretary of the Medical Defence Union, discussed these facts in a lecture to the Medico-Legal Society entitled 'Medical malpractice: the American disease. Is it infectious?' [5]. He quoted the geographical distribution of malpractice claims (Figure 43). Figures provided by the National Association of Insurance Commissioners [4] showed the areas where the largest claims had been made: California and New York State were the worst and $6 million had been paid out by the insurers in each of the states of Arizona, Florida, Illinois and Pennsylvania. Other areas were graded as those where $1–3 million had been paid out, and others where the amount was less than a million dollars. Distributions were the same when enormous

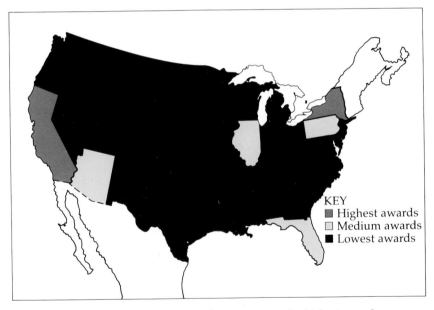

FIGURE 43. Geographical distribution of litigious areas: the highest awards were made in California and New York State. (From figures taken from the National Association of Insurance Commissioners [4].)

single awards were taken out and when figures were adjusted to allow for the number of doctors working in each state; for example California and New York State contained the greatest number of doctors—about 42,000 in each. The red areas on the map were bad for the doctors but good for the lawyers and vice versa; Dr Brooke Barnett facetiously remarked that he would sell this map to anyone going to practise in the USA either in law or medicine.

Factors responsible for the increasing frequency and costs of litigation

Some doctors can be careless and some lawyers behave as rogues, but there is no evidence that either is more common in the USA where both professions are advanced, especially in the top centres. Nor can the insurance companies alone be blamed as the culprits. Several factors are responsible.

THE LAW

Plaintiffs' attorneys are seldom enthusiastic to sue doctors, according to an experienced American lawyer, William L. Thorp, who gives the following reasons for this: medical malpractice cases are very expensive to prepare and the odds of winning are poor (only one out of four)—and lawyers, mainly ignorant of medical matters, have to rely on professionals. Generally they play no role in encouraging people to make claims and indeed spend much time in talking people out of taking actions against doctors and hospitals.

The *legal process* in the USA is an adversary system, as in the UK, though probably more so, and the object is to reconstruct what happened and put this before the court; but the result depends on the skill of the lawyers and the experience and performance of the plaintiff, defendant and witnesses. The judge or jury decide what they think has been proved rather than what actually happened. So, even when negligence is not clearly established but the injury is severe, a skilful lawyer may persuade a sympathetic jury to decide for the plaintiff although, in practice, judgement does not go against the doctor in many cases even when negligence is proven, and a skilful lawyer can protect an incompetent doctor. The judge cannot alter the amount of compensation awarded by a jury; he can only set the verdict aside.

Contingency suing—called the poor man's door to justice—where the lawyer will take on a case free of charge and send in a bill (taking up to 40 per cent of the award) only if he wins, has been an advantage for the public. Without this the average person could not afford to sue, but it has probably increased the number of cases due to irresponsible lawyers though, according to Thorp, they soon learn. So it may not have influenced the position greatly, for most American lawyers must be shrewd enough not to take on a case if facts indicate that they are unlikely to win; even so the system does provide an incentive to ask for larger awards.

Other factors are that occasional members of the American Bar may not possess the honesty and integrity of their fellows: unwarranted lawsuits may be started and assistants may be encouraged to go into hospitals and solicit patients if they notice anything has gone wrong or become 'ambulance chasers and accident watchers'. Also a more business-like approach than elsewhere may exist and some personal injury plaintiffs' attorneys may live off contingency fees that are often not a third but sometimes a half of the award. This accounts for the gibe 'support a lawyer, send your son to medical school'. Finally high legal costs are a problem in the USA as well as in the UK.

SOCIAL ASPECTS

Legal education services in some states enlighten the lay person who then is tempted to seize any opportunity for litigation when reading about the large awards proclaimed in newspapers. Patients' expectations of cure are heightened by seeing the remarkable advances in medicine and surgery on television. Several states have brought in laws to restrict publicity of high awards, rather like restricting publicity on football pool wins, but this has not had much influence.

An important social consideration is *the lack of a health service.* If a patient is injured and has to stay in hospital for another two or three weeks the bill grows quickly and may only be partly covered by insurance, if at all. The awards are high because of the high standard of living; the amount would, for example, be considerable for a Californian with two or three Cadillacs in the garage living in a house worth $2 or 3 million. Dr Peter Ford made an important point when he facetiously remarked that the average American citizen who is aggrieved with his treatment has two possible remedies under the constitution: either he can reach for his gun or file a suit, whereas in the United Kingdom several safety valves are available to let off disapproval: such as through the Family Practitioner Committee, the Health Authorities of the National Health Service, the ombudsman, members of Parliament, and the Community Health Councils [6]. As there are few formal complaints procedures in the USA, patients are, as Jane Smith wrote, forced to 'sue or be silent' [7].

C. T. M. Cameron, a surgeon in New York State, when discussing why so many doctors were sued for malpractice, imagined or real, pointed out that the lawsuit for damages, for any reason whatsoever, was 'as much a part of US life as baseball. The USA is the most litigious land on earth; there are, so far as can be determined, more lawsuits of all kinds than in the rest of the entire world' [8]. Also lawsuits were instituted on grounds that would be considered unethical or unfriendly or immoral in some other countries. For example, 'if a guest gets drunk at a party at my house, falls and breaks his ankle, there is every likelihood that he will sue me. He reasons, quite correctly, that my household insurance policy includes a rider to cover such accidents and that I, personally, will suffer no financial loss (except, possibly, an increase in my premium). The fact that we may have been close friends for years will probably not enter into the matter. The same philosophy extends to all aspects of US life, including particularly medical practice'. This was a personal view, and perhaps a caricature of some aspects of American life with which many may not agree.

MEDICAL CAUSES

Most financing of medical malpractice insurance has been done by insurance companies and the American doctor, when threatened by litigation, has to go (with few exceptions) straight to a lawyer rather than to a doctor who is an expert on medico-legal matters as in the UK. Hence the advice which can often abort a case is lacking.

Doctors too can be at fault: they may fail to communicate with the patient or family after a bad or tragic result or fail to tell what really happened: they tamper with the case-notes and keep information back instead of co-operating fully with the attorney. The image of the doctor may have suffered, as some regard him as more business-like than professional—particularly in sending in his fee—and when things go wrong he is less likely to admit it and more likely to press for his money. No doubt only a few act like this but, as in other fields, they tarnish the image for others. *Depersonalization* has affected the medical system and some patients have to fill up so many forms that they feel 'like a digital computer' and have long waits in the waiting room. Few patients see the same doctor on each attendance, and this may echo practice in some parts of the National Health Service in the UK.

Information about negligence of doctors may come from the *paramedical staff*. Nurses in the UK are anxious to improve their status and function, and in the USA nurses also want increased status and to feel part of the team and not to be treated as underlings. The gap between doctors' and nurses' salaries is wide and angry nurses would not want to cover for doctors if their work is not appreciated.

Health costs have spiralled because there is no limit to what doctors, dentists and hospitals can charge for their services other than what the public is able to pay, and their fees may be increased to cover rising insurance costs. Big private insurance groups such as Blue Cross, Blue Shield and the twin government schemes of Medicare for the elderly and Medicaid for the less well-off protect many, but doctors can still charge as much as they like knowing that these organizations will foot the bill.

MEDICAL MALPRACTICE INSURANCE

Large awards provoked insurance companies to put up premiums and by 1975 physicians' premiums were increasing three times in one year. Surgeons in the following year found that they were increased ten times. At that time the Secretary's commission report had come out and the figures showed that of whatever doctors paid in their insurance premiums, only a little ever reached the patient. It was estimated that in 1970 the insurance industry received $300 million in premiums but only 20 per cent of that ended up in the hands of the claimants.

The high premiums demanded by insurance companies were partly due to large awards in medico-legal cases—partly also, it is claimed, because of substantial losses in the stock market; to recoup their losses, horror stories about excessive jury verdicts and frivolous malpractice claims were created to justify excessive increases. The 'claims made' policy, developed around 1975 and which only insured against claims *during* the policy year, reduced their losses but adversely affected doctors.

A problem for insurance companies is the long time between the incident and settlement of any claim. If a claim could be settled immediately for $10,000 the premium would be easy to calculate but, as many of the larger claims take four or five years, guesswork is needed as to how much to allow for inflation and other unknown factors such as a change in attitude of the courts, how much to set aside in the year of the incident to meet the claim four or five years later, and how much to charge the doctor in premiums. Another complaint is that their insured doctors do not stay with them, so they have to add a considerable amount to the premium to allow for the fact that doctors will have moved, leaving claims to be settled later.

Many small insurance companies are engaged in medical malpractice work and also one or two very large brokers—national and sometimes international; some American doctors fear that these powerful brokers may become too powerful and get control of professional insurance. Insurance companies load a doctor's premium if he makes a claim, whereas a doctor's defence society believes that this may happen only once in a lifetime to a doctor, so why must he be penalized by a loaded premium for the rest of his life? That is a corporate responsibility which obviously the insurance companies cannot accept because they are individual insurers, whereas the doctors' societies can, as professional bodies, maintain the same premium in spite of claims.

Insurance premiums vary, not only according to specialty but according to the area where the doctor practises—the three highest areas being California, Florida and New York State. At one end of the scale, as in North Carolina, the neurosurgeons and orthopaedic surgeons pay between $20,000 and $30,000 and the obstetricians who are probably the next most sued doctors for what is known as 'wrongful death' cases pay from $9,000 to $11,000. Elsewhere some premiums reach as high as $75,000 or more a year and a few big insurance companies will not accept doctors even with such premiums. Indeed, a 52 per cent increase in medical malpractice insurance rates was approved in January 1985 for an insurer serving some of New York State's 45,000 doctors. This was the highest increase approved by the state in ten years, with most of the added cost expected to be passed on to patients in higher doctors' fees and to the public through higher health insurance costs for Blue Shield, Medicare and Medicaid. The new rates meant, for example, that the amount that a Long Island obstetrician would pay for malpractice insurance would rise to $82,500 a year from $55,282. For a neurosurgeon on Long Island, which had the highest regional rates for medical malpractice insurance in the States, the annual rate would rise to $101,000 from $66,468. But the increase for paediatricians was much lower—rising to $16,200 from $10,689. In New York City, which was considered by insurance actuaries to be less litigious than Long Island, the rates for malpractice insurance were about 20 per cent less.

A statement by the New York State Medical Society said that the magnitude of the 'skyrocketing increase threatens the state's health care system'. There had been a correspondingly sharp rise in the amount of damages awarded by juries. According to the state, the average malpractice award was $100,000, a figure that was projected to rise to as much as $450,000–$600,000 in eight years [9].

One of the biggest problems faced by doctors who wish to fight malpractice claims is the tendency of insurance companies either to settle cases before trial, despite the doctor's opposition, or to exert pressure upon the doctor to permit such settlements. Apparently in some cases, the insurance companies, having their own interests at heart rather than those of their clients, simply take the line of least resistance: it is cheaper to pay than to fight. The doctor, who in many cases is guiltless of malpractice, is not given the chance to clear his name [10]. To avoid the out-of-court settlement, he would have to dismiss the company attorney and hire another at his own expense and pay the damages.

Effects of litigation in the USA

Many American doctors are much concerned by these medico-legal developments. One remarked that a doctor might be presented with a subpoena in public by a sheriff, and that his name might appear in the news media whether or not he was guilty; much time would have to be taken off practice with many sleepless nights and it might take seven years for the case to come to trial. The reactions to this may be as follows:

* Defensive medicine. The American Medical Association (AMA) made a survey in 1977 and showed that 75 per cent of their members took unnecessary X-rays and did needless tests to protect themselves in case they were sued. In 1984, it was estimated that defensive medicine added $15·1 billion dollars to the country's medical bill which was already around $300 billion a year [11]. In the attempt to avoid litigious patients, surgeons may avoid doing operations where any risk is involved as, for example, a neurosurgeon who will not operate on cervical spondylosis; so treatment of the patient is affected (for further details about defensive medicine see later).

* Some doctors have formed their own insurance companies.

* Countersuings. This is a development which has not reached the UK although some doctors might like to sue litigious patients. In 1976 a Chicago radiologist was sued for having failed to diagnose a minor finger injury. The finger had been splinted which, anyway, would have been the appropriate treatment. The jury ruled that the suit had no merit. The radiologist then brought a countersuit against the patient and her attorney and was awarded $8,000 in damages. Within the first year after the countersuit the incidence of malpractice suits in the Chicago area was said to have fallen by about 75 per cent and many doctors were encouraged to mount countersuits [8]. Another case was in Nevada in 1977 when a physician sued the plaintiff's lawyer claiming that the action brought against him was unjustified, and the doctor, surprisingly, was awarded $85,000. Since then, countersuits have been overturned by superior courts and the Supreme Court has refused to hear appeals.

* 'Going bare' is the term used when a doctor takes a chance and stops insuring himself because of the high costs, believing that litigants will be deterred on the grounds that stones do not bleed. All his assets are then at risk and transfer of these to another member of the family can be voided by the court. It is also unfair to the patient in cases of true liability.

* Some insurance carriers in 1975 withdrew from the professional risks field.

* A surgeon has been known to arrange a separate insurance with each patient for certain operations, protecting himself—he hopes—by a detailed informed consent form.

The insurance system for doctors almost collapsed in 1975 and many private insurance carriers withdrew from the field. The remaining companies increased their premiums by 750 per cent. William J. Curran described the effect of this: arbitration methods were adopted and pre-trial screening panels designed to direct the handling of claims away from courts and to eliminate frivolous complaints; a financial limitation, usually $500,000 on the total award was imposed by many states (under American law a plaintiff may sue for a specific sum); and amongst other measures, reforms were enacted concerning informed consent, expert testimony and the burden of proof [11]. All these were designed to make malpractice trials fairer and more evenly balanced between the parties in litigation. These various tort law reforms probably had only a temporary effect in reducing the number of claims, this being noted in the three years after 1975. Curran quotes the study by the Rand Corporation [12]: neither screening panels nor limitations imposed on contingency fees for plaintiffs' lawyers had affected either the frequency or severity of claims; the density of lawyers increased the severity though not the frequency of claims but physician density did correlate positively with the frequency of claims though not their severity—the opposite of the findings on lawyer density. The Rand Report concluded that urbanization is the most important factor; lawyers and physicians are clustered and awards are higher in urban court houses than in rural ones, largely because of the higher cost of living and the varied style of urban dwellers in general.

Other positive steps were taken in the USA to counteract the rising number of negligence actions against doctors. Some states developed a *Peer Review* and somehow medical reports of these Peer Review committees were not to be disclosable in any court, so all were free to state their worries, concerns and suspicions about the mishandling of a case without its being revealed outside. *Relicensing* has operated in California since 1977, and sounds rather like the Department of Transport Test for older cars. Every four years a doctor has to apply to get back to the Register by producing evidence that he has done a hundred hours of approved studies. One doctor remarked that when the same proposition was put up to the Bar Council in California they turned it down—the statement revealed an occasional enmity between the two professions at the time.

Another interesting development was a system for *periodic payments*, because large payments, perhaps for a brain-damaged child, could end up in being paid to the parents or relatives because the child died shortly afterwards. In one $2·3 million failed forceps case, $1·6 million was awarded as an annuity. Although it was only $2·3 million, the newspapers came forward with a heading '$21 million award'; the paper had to be studied carefully to find out that only if the annuity had been fully paid out at the age of seventy years would the child have got $21 million.

Several states tried, usually unsuccessfully, to abolish *punitive damages*, but juries only rarely awarded such amounts. The celebrated and most quoted case was in Sacramento in 1973 (Sacramento Superior Court No. 228566) when the judge added on $2 million to the ordinary award; this concerned a man of twenty-seven years injured in a car crash. The orthopaedic surgeon carried out an operation on the spine (laminectomy) but this was unsuccessful. The patient sued. When the surgeon got to court he found thirteen of his previous patients there, all of whom testified that they thought that they had had unsatisfactory laminectomies. Just as the case was closing, a witness got up and said that he thought the orthopaedic surgeon had been under the influence of drugs for two years—and there was some truth in both of these accusations. That led the judge to award $1·7 million general and $2 million punitive damages; this was certainly a high award for a man who was suffering from testicular cancer and had made three attempts at suicide. The judge seemed to attribute all this to the unsuccessful operation. Perhaps juries are sometimes an advantage because in this trial the parties elected to have the case tried solely by a judge. In certain states, plaintiffs had to declare collateral sources, for example, if they were getting any money from insurance companies which might reduce the damages. Statutes of limitation, which are different in every state, have had little effect on the malpractice crisis.

Medical defence societies were developed in some parts of the USA, controlled by doctors as in the UK. All of the subscription was retained in the society; it did not go out in profits as it would do in an insurance company, and all surpluses were ploughed back for the benefit of members. Doctors felt a loyalty to these societies which saved them from the terrible increases in insurance premiums at the height of the crisis in 1975 and they tended to stay with them. Dr David Rubsamen, who was one of the medico-legal advisers to the Secretary's commission, directed one of these defence societies in northern California. He confirmed that they were run exactly as defence societies in Britain, with no unnecessary expenses. He compared the way that he worked with the way an insurance company functions; he knew when to work up a case and when it was unnecessary to do a lot of administrative work on it.

The problem facing defence societies in the United States is that they are parochial, without a broad enough base, and so are too exposed. If they could be spread all over the USA, covering both the high and low risk areas, they would be much safer and indeed they may eventually coalesce.

Defensive medicine: will it spread elsewhere?

The moral behaviour of man has always depended upon fear of punishment; indeed, retribution for sins is a feature of most religions. The humanist will dispute this view and point to the inherent nature of many to do good without thought of heaven or hell. Yet most doctors, like everyone else, will perform better if a penalty exists for misdeeds—providing this is not too great. The penalty was somewhat excessive when an ancient king named Hammurabi (about 2000 BC) drew up a code of laws which was engraved on a pillar of stone and set up in the temple at Babylon [13]—the oldest code in existence (it is now in the Louvre). It dealt with property, criminal offences, marriage laws, and with laws relating to medical practice. It stated that 'if the doctor shall treat a gentleman and shall open an abscess with a bronze knife and shall preserve the eye of the patient, he shall receive 10 shekels of silver; if the doctor shall open an abscess with a bronze knife and shall kill the patient or shall destroy the sight of the eye, his hands shall be cut off'. The penalty was less drastic for a slave: 'he shall replace the slave with another slave'. Such reprisals could have deterred an ambitious surgeon in Babylon, and might have resulted in conservative rather than surgical treatment of an abscess. No statistics are available as to the intake of medical students after this law was passed, but Herodotus, some years later, reported that 'there were no physicians in Babylon' [14].

Defensive medicine results in the doctor's professional judgement being influenced by legal instead of clinical considerations, so that he orders investigations for fear of litigation. The financial risks which doctors and hospitals could face in the courts if anything went wrong is the cause of X-rays being taken of every injury however minimal, batteries of laboratory tests in case something is overlooked, the more hazardous operations not being performed, and the length of stay in hospital extended 'to be on the safe side'.

Defensive medicine probably accounts for caesarean section being four times more common in the USA than in some European countries: the obstetrician does this to avoid the rare risk of brain damage if delivery through the vagina proves difficult. Another example is the preservation of life in a brain-damaged infant because of pressure from 'pro-life' lay groups. The legal and political climate which obliges American doctors to engage in such practice is partly created by areas of medical advances where the law is imprecise; hitherto ethical and professional standards have guided doctors' decisions but now an active vociferous, well-organized pressure-group (for example 'The Right to Life') or lobby may seek 'clarification' of the ethical problem in terms of moral and religious principles.

'Medicine', said Sir William Osler in 1906 'is a science of uncertainty and an art of probability' [15] and this is still largely true today. Every new treatment is a form of experiment however carefully it has been tested on animals or in the laboratory; so defensive medicine could result in no new treatment, no new operation and no research—medicine comes to a standstill.

The legal doctrine of informed consent has been developed almost to an absurdity in the USA so that occasionally written permission may be needed for minor procedures such as taking samples of blood—just to protect the doctor. Patients suffering unexpected harm have been successful in suing their doctors when the doctors have not been at fault. Professor Ian Kennedy, the lawyer, when recounting this in *The Unmasking of Medicine*, based on his 1980 Reith lectures [16], gave as an illustration the fictitious case of an otherwise healthy woman about to undergo an operation for a leg injury caused by jogging. The surgeon visits her and tells her in general terms what the operation involves. He does not mention—who would?—two reported cases in the literature of complications following this operation; after all, it has been performed many hundreds of times. Her operation becomes the third to be followed by complications. She sues her surgeon, claiming she did not consent to the operation because she was not informed. This infuriates the surgeon who has done all that anyone would expect. Mercifully, Kennedy thinks it unlikely that this type of negligence litigation will develop in the UK.

Fears have, however, been expressed that defensive medicine could spread to the UK as some of the American ingredients are already present here. But some reassurance also came from the Pearson Commission (1978): 'There is no such thing as a contingency fee system in the UK nor does jury trial (which leads to higher awards) occur in civil cases here and although the number of claims has increased, the practice of resorting to the courts is still not widespread—the total of claims is so far insignificant compared with the number of people who received treatment' [17]. Each year, the Commission stated, some six million in-patients were treated in National Health Service hospitals and some nineteen million people attended out-patient or accident and emergency departments; yet in a year probably no more than 1,000 claims were made against doctors, dentists, pharmacists or health authorities in respect of negligence. However, the final word about this was that we should not be complacent.

Medical defence in the British Commonwealth of Nations

The defence bodies in the UK have often acted as the prototype for many similar bodies elsewhere and the history of these is now dealt with briefly in the chronological order of their dates of origins (Table 12).

AUSTRALIA

The New South Wales Medical Defence Union (Sydney) and the Medical Defence Association of Victoria (Melbourne) were both founded in the 1890s. The foundation president of the latter was Dr, later Sir, George Syme, the

TABLE 12. The growth of medical defence bodies.

1885 Medical Defence Union
1892 (London & Counties) Medical Protection Society
1893 Australia: New South Wales Medical Defence Union (Sydney)
1896 ,, Medical Defence Association of Victoria (Melbourne)
,, Medical Defence Society of Queensland (Brisbane)
1897 Le Sou Médical (Paris)
1900 Canadian Medical Protective Association
1902 Medical and Dental Defence Union of Scotland
1925 Australia: Medical Defence Association of Western Australia (Perth)
1953 Australia: Medical Defence Association of South Australia (Adelaide)

distinguished surgeon; practically every medical association of which he was a member elected him as president.

The early years of the council's activities were mainly 'the ever-encroaching movement of Benefit Lodges', and the medical service fees payable to lodge doctors; lodges followed the system of friendly societies, being transplanted from the UK to Australia. At first the medical profession welcomed them as they promoted sensible attitudes of thrift and self-reliance amongst the working classes as well as enabling doctors to have access to a source of patients and income not possible from purely private practice—as few people could afford private consultations. Lodges also reduced the load of the free out-patient clinics of hospitals and, as in England then, members paid a monthly amount and doctors were paid a fixed capitation fee; by 1890 at least 20 per cent of the population was insured in this way. Later, Australian doctors became dissatisfied: the system made them employees of the lodges who had to tender for contracts and patients, and more and more of the middle classes joined lodges instead of seeing doctors privately.

Other fields of activity at the start of the MDU of Victoria included the following and these were probably common to other defence bodies in Australia:

* Medical ethics.
* Quackery.
* Fees for police cases.
* Disputes concerning abuse of public hospitals.
* Medical services in state schools.

Twenty-eight honorary secretaries managed the affairs of this body, the reason for this number probably being the difficulty of transport and communication in those days as the secretaries were spread throughout Victoria.

New Zealand had a form of health service long before the National Health Service in Britain, and it resembled that proposed in the Lloyd George Health Insurance Act of 1912; it concerned everyone and the state paid 80–90 per cent of the doctor's fees. Apart from the usual matters of mishap and malpractice, doctors have had problems concerning their contracts and consultants were dismissed from hospital, and doctors were accused, rightly or wrongly, of fiddling the state money. New Zealand pioneered the no-fault compensation for medical injuries (Chapter 10) but most doctors in New Zealand still belong to medical defence bodies in the UK.

The Canadian Medical Protective Association (CMPA) resembles the defence bodies in the UK and has hardly been influenced by the medico-legal situation in the USA but juries still exist in Canada (though seldom function in medico-legal cases) and a differential subscription rate was introduced for CMPA members in 1983.

Its birth in 1900 resembled that of the Medical Defence Union. A few doctors in Quebec had already started a local Defence Union but this seemed doomed to failure because its appeal was so local that it would remain too small. Then Dr R. W. Powell, an influential and highly respected doctor, persuaded them to form the nucleus of a Canada-wide association: the Canadian Medical Protective Association. This was achieved with the help of the Canadian Medical Association of which he was President. He had a similar tenacity to that of Mr Lawson Tait, the architect of the MDU, and without this the Association could have died shortly after birth; it had few members, no funds and no experience.

Surprisingly Dr Powell was able to persuade doctors to join an association that simply promised to give its members advice if they were threatened by a legal action and said that at some time in the future they might receive help with defence costs of legal action. Dr Powell was President of the CMPA until his death in 1935 and lived to see the time when the privileges of membership included the payment not only of legal costs but also of awards and settlements. A second driving force was Dr John Fenton Argue, secretary–treasurer for twenty-nine years starting in 1906. He succeeded Dr Powell to the Presidency and guided the CMPA until 1956; he regarded it as the 'doctor's own', as an arm of the profession, bound to give every doctor all the help possible, and his favourite phrase was 'mutual medical defence union'. It

257

seems that his achievements were partly due to his forceful character and unyielding belief on matters of principle.

Many Canadian doctors remember Dr T. L. Fisher who was widely known for his writings on medico-legal subjects and because of his work in the CMPA, as secretary–treasurer from 1935 to 1972 and as consultant to Council until his death in 1976. He was occasionally intolerant of apparent casual indifference of some unrepentant erring doctors who showed lack of concern for their patients, but always insisted that a doctor who has done nothing wrong must be staunchly defended regardless of any other considerations.

The CMPA has, like the MDU and MPS, adapted to the evolving needs of members. Advice and help are given to matters that pose a serious threat to a doctor's professional integrity: these vary from support at a coroner's inquest—which although not intended to attach blame to anyone can provide a problem because of the manner in which evidence is adduced and the publicity given to the hearings—to attendance at disciplinary committees. But the primary function is to offer assistance in lawsuits for alleged malpractice and negligence.

INDIA AND ELSEWHERE IN THE COMMONWEALTH

Protection through insurance companies is generally used by those doctors who are not members of the British defence bodies. Cases of alleged negligence are not so likely to concern doctors in less developed areas of the world, and this applies particularly to some parts of Africa where a large percentage of the population is underprivileged and unlikely to sue.

Europe

The same upward trend in litigation which is so marked in the USA is happening on the other side of the English Channel and it is curious, as Dr Brooke Barnett has remarked [5], that alarming judgements in the German and French courts occur yet no one gets as excited as they do about the American awards—probably because of the lack of a common language. But the medico-legal situation in Europe does not reflect the American scene and in Germany, when there were signs of 'the accident lawyer phenomenon' developing, the courts came down very severely on any lawyer who attempted to use this technique. There are, however, not the same channels for complaints that the patient has in the National Health Service in the UK.

FRANCE

An organization in Europe that could truly be called a medical defence body is

Le Sou Médical, the Medical Defence Union's counterpart in France. Established in 1897, its original objects were:

* To establish an emergency fund for doctors who required it in the form of advances, loans and gifts.
* To provide for the general and medical education of the sons of doctors.
* To establish a fighting fund for the struggle against the exploitation of doctors by certain mutual organizations.
* To institute proceedings in cases of illegal practice.
* To propose and promote desirable improvements in medical jurisprudence.

At that time the subscription was one sou per day which explains the name which might otherwise appear surprising if the history of it were not known. It adopted the structure of a trade union for various legal reasons and deliberately went to work on virgin territory: the individual defence of the right of its members in the name of medical solidarity, and payment of indemnity in matters of professional liability—a subsidiary aim because of the rarity of cases at that time; only in 1904 was a special fund officially established for this purpose, the limit of guarantee being 2,000 f. At the same time, the other aspects of medical mutual help were handed over to the assistance and mutual help societies which existed then.

Defence of the general interests of the profession as a whole was always combined with the defence of the rights of the individual doctor, and in this 'Le Sou' was different from the more or less profit-making organizations which existed in other fields. In 1942 'Le Sou' turned itself into a mutual insurance company in order to reflect the increasing emphasis on that aspect of its work. A link exists between its services and *Le Concours Médical*—an independent weekly medical journal—which makes it possible occasionally to use the information gathered and to reflect it in articles. In spite of its changed status 'Le Sou' remains today, as before, the professional body that it was at the start: a non-profit making mutual organization which, as at the outset, relies on the trust of its members.

An important difference between French and English law is the degree of competence a doctor might be expected to show in treating a patient. Under English law this is limited by the word 'reasonable' which allows the courts in this country to take a more lenient attitude than under French law.

A close rapprochement has existed between 'Le Sou' and the Medical Defence Union for at least twenty years. The first joint meeting of the two defence bodies was held in Paris in 1964 and these meetings are held annually. Both bodies have conducted the occasional case for the other organization and some day there could be a genuine reason to mould them more closely; then the friendship will be given a practical form.

Chapter 9

References

1 Stern P. Van D. *The Life and Writing of Abraham Lincoln*. New York: The Modern Library, 1940. (Quotation from the chapter 'From Notes for a Law Lecture' p. 329.)

2 Malpractice problem continues to grow (annotation). *Pediatrics* 73 (1984): A50.

3 *Report of the Secretary's Commission on Medical Malpractice*. Department of Health, Education and Welfare. Washington DC. Dhew Publication No (OS) 73–89. 1973.

4 *Report of the National Association of Insurance Commissioners*. Malpractice Claims 1975–1978. Wisconsin 1980.

5 Brooke Barnett J.W. Medical malpractice: the American disease. Is it infectious? *Medico-Legal Journal* 48 (1980): 63–75.

6 Ford P. In a discussion. *Medico-Legal Journal* 48 (1980): 73.

7 Smith Jane. Negligence and defence. *British Medical Journal* 1 (1979): 140–1.

8 Cameron C.T.M. Some aspects of US medical malpractice insurance. *British Medical Journal* 2 (1977): 877–80.

9 Medical malpractice insurers win 52% rise. *New York Times*. 15 January (1985): A1–2.

10 Defensive medicine (editorial). *Journal of the American Medical Association* 252 (1984): 1002.

11 Curran W.J. Medical malpractice claims since the crisis of 1975: some good news and some bad. *New England Journal of Medicine* 309 (1983): 1107–8.

12 Danzon P.M. *The Frequency and Severity of Medical Malpractice Claims*. Santa Monica, California: Rand Corporation, 1983.

13 Guthrie D. *History of Medicine* (revised). London: Nelson, 1958.

14 Buck A.H. *The Growth of Medicine From the Earliest Times to About 1800*. New York: AMS Press, 1979.

15 Osler Sir William, 1906. *Aphorisms from his bedside teachings and writings*. No 256. 2nd edn. Ed. Bean W.B. Springfield, Illinois: Charles C Thomas, 1961.

16 Kennedy I. *The Unmasking of Medicine: a Searching Look at Health Care Today*. London: Granada Publishing, 1983.

17 *The Pearson Commission* Royal Commission on Civil Liability and Compensation of Personal Injury) Vol 1; para 1323–4 p. 283. HMSO, 1978.

10

No-fault compensation

The victims of medical mishaps of the present kind should be cared for by the community, not by the hazards of litigation.'
Lord Justice Lawton when concluding his judgement in the case of a brain-damaged baby [1]

No-fault compensation provides a patient who is a victim of a medical mistake with an appropriate award without the need for a court action against the doctor or health authority. The burden of proof is reversed: instead of trying to prove that the doctor has made a mistake, the claimant has to show that he has suffered an injury. So *no-fault compensation* is the antithesis to *fault liability*. A complaint, such as amputation of a wrong finger, should be settled quickly but many such matters are less clear cut. The principle of no-fault compensation is not new: it is almost universal for accidents at work in the developed world. New Zealand and Sweden extended this to medical accidents and have now had ten years' experience of their schemes.

This approach may appear to be a panacea for the patient and a blessing for the doctor who will no longer be at risk of lawsuits, afflicted by guilt, or suffer the slings and arrows of outrageous publicity—or even know that he has committed a mishap or malpractice. But, like everything else in life, it is not without its problems.

WHY NO-FAULT COMPENSATION CAME ABOUT

Few people would argue that the present legal system for dealing with medical mishaps is perfect. It is similar to the one that existed in New Zealand and which was criticized by Justice Woodhouse's Royal Commission of Inquiry (1967) as a 'fragmented response to a social problem that cried out for coordinated and comprehensive treatment' [2]. Too many injured people went uncompensated, the Commission said; the common law system was slow, inefficient and unrealistically difficult for many of the injured; and rehabilitation was hindered by a prolonged, adversarial system. Many of these criticisms could apply to the current British system. A cynic might even regard

261

the law as a lottery. It is not so much concerned with the rightness or wrongness of a particular act as with its defensibility under the circumstances: this relies upon the debating ability of the barristers and depends partly on the judge—and there is no standardization of judges. Some have the reputation of being more severe than others.

A leader in *The Times* [3], when discussing the recommendations of the Pearson Commission (1978) [4] on compensation for injuries, described the present system of justice as capricious, haphazard and inconsistent. An example is the problem of a baby born with a brain defect. Medical experts often find it impossible to decide whether this was congenital or due to injury caused by the obstetrician when delivering the baby. The case may not be settled for many years: the court makes one decision; this is reversed on Appeal and the final verdict is pronounced by Judges in the House of Lords who, though distinguished, are hardly more competent than the 'man in the street' to decide these technical matters. Their object and training is, of course, to balance the evidence of the expert witnesses; and the contrary legal opinions are explained by the fact that evidence is not something that can be measured or expressed in numbers.

The New Zealand scheme

The first comprehensive no-fault compensation scheme for personal injury by accident was introduced in New Zealand in 1974. It covered work and road traffic accidents, those occurring at home or during sporting activity, and also the results of medical mishaps and malpractices.

The categories covered were:
* The physical and mental consequences of 'personal injury by accident'.
* Medical, surgical, dental or first-aid misadventure.
* Incapacity resulting from an occupational disease or industrial deafness.
* Actual bodily harm, including pregnancy and mental or nervous shock, suffered by any person by an act or omission of any other person.

The Act excluded:
* Damage to the body or mind caused by a cardiovascular or cerebrovascular episode unless the episode was the result of effort, strain or stress that was abnormal, excessive or unusual for the person suffering it.
* Damage to the body or mind caused exclusively by disease, infection or the ageing process.

The government, through the Accident Compensation Corporation Scheme, provides the money, and funds come from general taxation, employers' contributions, and a levy on the self-employed. Compensation consists of lump sums for loss of function, and continuing payments based on earnings before the accident. It may also include reasonable medical expenses and other out-of-pocket expenses; in fatal cases funeral expenses are payable. At first, it was thought that doctors would no longer need indemnity insurance against claims of negligence, but the Accident Compensation Corporation, which administers the scheme, interpreted 'medical injury' in restrictive terms. The natural progression of a disease or foreseeable complications of treatment were excluded, and the Commission has tended to distinguish between acts of commission and those of omission. Hence wrong treatment would allow the patient to benefit from compensation but failure to diagnose would not; also lack of 'informed consent' is not covered and so can cause an action for negligence. Hence, doctors continue to subscribe to the defence bodies though at a reduced rate. If a claimant is dissatisfied with the amount of compensation awarded or the refusal of a claim, he can appeal to the Accident Compensation Corporation. Further appeals lie in the courts of law. If the Commission rejects a claim, the plaintiff may bring an action for negligence; if, however, compensation is accepted, the right to go to court is lost. Judge A. P. Blair in his book *Accident Compensation in New Zealand* [5] describes all details of the law relating to compensation for personal injury by accident.

The Swedish patient insurance scheme

The Swedish patient insurance scheme started on 1 January 1975 when the health authorities (the county councils) pledged that they would, through a special commitment, accept liability for certain kinds of injuries associated with health and medical care; the liability was insured by a consortium of Swedish insurers. Previously, very few patients had received compensation by going to court, damages being awarded in only an average of (at most) ten cases per year, according to Carl Oldertz [6] of the Skandia Insurance Co, Stockholm, Sweden, from whose account much of the following information is derived.

Decisions are made on objective facts, as in New Zealand—the circumstances or consideration that led to the injury being of little or no importance. Injuries which can be indemnified are as follows:

* Genuine treatment injuries.
* Diagnostic injuries (meaning lack of or delay in diagnosis).
* Accidental injuries (this covers falling on slippery floors, injuries sustained by epileptic or senile patients, etc.).
* Infection injuries (although it is difficult to determine if an infection injury is indemnifiable and whether the patient was likely to develop an infection or not, for example after an operation).

* Injuries caused by diagnostic investigations (an example of this is paralysis caused by thrombosis as a result of angiography).

If an injured patient is not satisfied with the decision of the consortium of insurance companies which administers the system, he can turn to a specially composed consulting claims panel. This panel has six members, three of them (one is the Chairman, one represents the patients' interests and one is the medical expert) being appointed by the government; two are appointed by the authority in charge of medical care and one by the consortium. If the plaintiff then does not accept the judgement of the board, he can have his case decided by arbitration as stated in the law on arbitration. About 40 per cent of the reported injuries cannot be compensated. The amount paid is based on tables prepared from a compilation of indemnity cases on which judgement was passed by the Swedish Supreme Court before 1975; this creates standardization. A claimant has no absolute right to indemnity and he must, before making a claim from his insurance, have claimed compensation from, for example, social insurances, health insurances, workman's compensation, and employer's no-fault insurance. Injuries to patients volunteering for experimentation and drug trials in hospitals have also been covered since July 1982.

The greatest problem is that costs have been higher than originally thought, perhaps because too liberal an attitude has been taken about conditions that can be compensated. It ought to be possible, writes Carl Oldertz [6] to obtain reliable statistics on the causes of medical injuries and their treatment as all are dealt with, whereas a conventional liability system only gives information on injuries caused by negligent or unacceptable treatment carried out by individuals; also by consistently compiling claims statistics different treatments might be compared and improved; some might even be replaced by safer methods. A project has been started to investigate why certain injuries occur and whether they could be avoided: this includes damage to nerves during hip surgery, infectious complications resulting from other prosthetic surgery, damage to nerves during anaesthesia, complications related to urological surgery and sterilization, and accidents caused by defects in hospital material or appliances.

Disadvantages of no-fault compensation

In an ideal world, the system for compensation should be based purely on need. It is unjust that someone having an accident at work should be fully compensated but receive nothing if disabled from the same accident at home. In practice, many medical problems are so complex that it is no easy matter deciding either about the cause or effect: distinguishing the effect of a medical accident from a natural progression of the disease is often as great a problem as deciding the cause in the tort system, and some medico-legal cases may continue just as long.

Words like 'expected' or 'foreseeable' are used to define suitable cases for compensation but, in practice, confusion is common. For example, rare side-effects such as damage from vaccines not caused by negligence are often foreseeable in the sense that they are well known to medical science; if these injuries were to be included in a no-fault scheme, it would be difficult to draw a line between them and the accepted risks of treatment. If they were to be excluded, the scheme would do little more than convert the negligence test of tort into a statutory formula, thereby making it easier for the victims of negligence to obtain compensation though doing nothing for those suffering medical injury from other causes [4]. The completely unexpected result is easy to distinguish from that which was expected but, in medicine, grey areas are the problem. Some circumstances that are described as 'accident' could, as Harland and Jandoo [7] noted, be described as self-inflicted (injured while drunk at work), or a 'planned risk' (brain damage as a result of boxing), and those which could properly be described as 'true accidents' (congenital blindness) might be ignored. A heart attack, in order to count as an accidental injury, must have occurred under stressful conditions.

No-fault compensation would probably make it easier for a patient to establish a case but compensation for everyone would mean less for most; those awarded high damages at present would find the standard rate much less and a contrast to the situation where the fortunate few who succeed in an action for damages often achieve awards in line with winning the football pools, whilst others find that they have only enriched the lawyers. (Some lawyers have expressed concern about the damaging effect the scheme would have upon their livelihood but, in fact, lawyers' work in New Zealand has increased.)

Doctors would be free from the fear of civil negligence actions—a fear that encourages every precaution against mishaps and malpractice. In Sweden, for example, no importance attaches to questions concerning incomplete or insufficient information about the risks involved in a particular treatment. So some other means of supervising professional standards is needed. In New Zealand, most matters of professional discipline have traditionally been in the hands of the New Zealand Medical Council Subcommittee—the Medical Practitioners' Disciplinary Committee—which has acted like the Professional Conduct Committee in the UK. Slowly and painfully, this disciplinary committee has expanded its field of activities so that it now deals with a whole variety of complaints brought under one umbrella: complaints which, in the UK, would be associated with the General Medical Council, Family Practitioner Committee and with many hospital enquiries. So great has been the increase in work that this has led to problems in finding funds to run the proceedings. The State or the New Zealand Medical Association is unlikely to continue to pay for the developing disciplinary machinery, so that the defence bodies may have to contribute largely to the cost as well as continue to support members on the various problems which still cause them to appear before the Medical Council.

Cost is another hindrance to the introduction of no-fault compensation. This would involve two aspects: the overall cost of any scheme, and the machinery for financing it. In Sweden, minor injuries and complications of treatment are excluded and there has to be some incapacity for work for longer than fourteen days. In the UK, finance would probably come through the National Health Service but the question of what to do about medical accidents occurring in private practice would remain. Expense has been the main argument for not introducing a no-fault scheme into other countries. However, Dr Richard Smith, who made a special study of this subject [8, 9], asked the question whether a no-fault scheme where awards are comparatively small and administrative costs minimal, was really more expensive than a tort system, where some awards were enormous and most of the money available was swallowed up in running the system. It could be more expensive only if more people were compensated but the costing of a compensation scheme is certainly complex [10]. Furthermore a special bureaucracy has to be set up to decide about causation and this would place a considerable burden on the available medical manpower. Introduction of a no-fault compensation scheme would be a far greater problem in the UK than in New Zealand where the population is small—just over three million in 1983 which, from the administrative aspect, compares with the West Midlands region in Britain.

THE POSSIBLE EFFECT UPON THE DEFENCE BODIES OF INTRODUCING NO-FAULT COMPENSATION

Most doctors in New Zealand still belong to the Medical Defence Union or Medical Protection Society, as legal advice is needed concerning interpretation of legislation, inquests, and for health authority tribunals; furthermore lawsuits still arise and representation is needed at the new disciplinary committee. The annual subscription has been reduced but this may have to be increased because expenses for investigating complaints are paid for and these are more expensive than in the UK. The need may also arise to contribute towards the costs of the new committee.

If a no-fault scheme were to be introduced in the UK in 1985, there would be no immediate redundancy of the staffs of the medical defence bodies. All the litigation of the preceding years would still go forward and the reduction in work would be felt sooner in the solicitors' offices than in the defence bodies themselves. This reduction might involve some early retirements rather than sackings. The impressive work-load which is not litigation would continue and it is inconceivable that a no-fault compensation system would be introduced world-wide in the same year or so.

Thus the alternatives to our fault-based system have drawbacks and, in the present economic climate, the government is unlikely to accept the financial burden of no-fault compensation. The Pearson Commission [4] (Royal Commission on Civil Liability and Compensation for Personal Injury) which reported to Parliament in 1978 studied the New Zealand system but concluded that it was not appropriate at that time to recommend the introduction of this for medical accidents in the United Kingdom. Moreover, the medical profession would find it difficult to convince the government that it is a 'special case' and that special provisions should apply to medical mishaps and not to accidents in general, for a major problem in no-fault systems is the difficulty of defining what constitutes the result of a medical mishap as medical cases are more complex than road or other accidents. The Pearson Commission suggested observing the situation in New Zealand and Sweden, and the British Medical Association working party in 1984 came to a similar conclusion [11].

A useful contribution to this subject has come from the Centre for Socio-Legal Studies at Wolfson College, Oxford, as their members have published the results of a comprehensive survey of the ways in which different systems of compensation and support function for the injured, ill, or congenitally handicapped and their families [12].

References

1 Lawton Lord Justice in *Whitehouse* v. *Jordan. All England Law Reports.* 1 (1981): 267.
2 Royal Commission of Inquiry. *Compensation for personal injury in New Zealand.* Wellington: New Zealand Government, 1967.
3 A neglected reform. (leader) *The Times* Aug 21 (1981): 13 (col 1–3).
4 Pearson Commission. *Royal Commission on Civil Liability and Compensation for Personal Injury Report.* London: HMSO, 1978 (Cmnd 7054).
5 Blair A. P. *Accident Compensation in New Zealand*, 2nd edn. Wellington, New Zealand: Butterworth, 1983.
6 Oldertz C. The Swedish patient insurance system—8 years of experience. *Medico-Legal Journal* 52 (1984): 43–59.
7 Harland W. A. & Jandoo R. S. The medical negligence crisis. *Medical Science and Law* 24 (1984): 123–129.
8 Smith R. The world's best system of compensating injury? *British Medical Journal* 284 (1982): 1243–5; Problems with a no-fault system of accident compensation: 1323–5; Compensation for medical misadventure and drug injury in the New Zealand no-fault system: feeling the way: 1457–9.
9 Smith R. Compensation: making the best of a bad job. *World Health Forum.* Vol 4 pp. 51–6. World Health Organisation, 1983.

10 Palmer G. *Compensation For Incapacity: A Study of Law and Social Change in New Zealand and Australia.* Wellington: Oxford University Press, 1979.
11 British Medical Association Working Party on No-Fault Compensation. *British Medical Journal* 1 (1984): 1469.
12 Harris D., MacLean M., Genn H., Lloyd-Bostock S., Fenn P., Corfield P. & Brittain Y. *Compensation and Support for Illness and Injury.* Oxford: Clarendon Press, 1984.

11

Causes of complaints and their prevention

> '*I would make it compulsory for a doctor using a brass plate to have inscribed on it, in addition to the letters indicating his qualifications, "Remember that I too am mortal".*'
>
> From the Preface to
> *The Doctor's Dilemma* by BERNARD SHAW

Complaints against doctors are not new; they have existed for centuries. The sayings of famous writers and wits have immortalized them.

The inability to cure was a common gibe:

> A doctor is a man who writes prescriptions till the patient either dies or is cured by nature. (JOHN TAYLOR, 1694–1761) [1]
> God heals and the doctor takes the fee.
> (BENJAMIN FRANKLIN, 1706–1790) [2]

Treatment—bleeding and purging for example—could hardly have been beneficial and must have added an iatrogenic component:

> The doctor is often more to be feared than the disease
> (French proverb) [3]

> The Parson shows the way to heaven,
> and then with tender care
> The doctor consummates the work
> and sends the patient there
> (JOSEPH JEKYLL, 1754–1837). [4]

Roger Bacon the scientist wrote an essay [5] in the thirteenth century about the mistakes of doctors (*De Erroribus Medicorum*) and some of this has a modern ring: 'Medical men don't know the drugs they use, nor their prices', and few today would deny some truth in the remark by Voltaire:

> Doctors are men who prescribe medicine of which they know little
> to human beings of which they know nothing [6].

Modern technology today is advanced but treatment lags behind. Patients may be intensively investigated in order to reach a diagnosis though no treatment is possible, so the aphorism of Immanuel Kant (1724–1804) the philosopher is apt:

Physicians think they do a lot for a patient when they give his
disease a name [7].

Complaints are now frequent because the public expects more from doctors,
and the medical scene has changed. False expectations of cure are raised; lay
pressure groups may highlight misconceptions; the increased power over life
and death provided by modern technology creates new moral dilemmas for the
doctor; and ethics is in the front line of medico-politics, for barely a week passes
without the media portraying some ethical predicament and perhaps pillory-
ing the medical profession, although the issue is likely to remain grey rather
than black and white.

The changing public

The public is better informed about medical matters through education, and by
radio, magazines and medical books written for lay people, so that many can
'take on' medical experts in a discussion. Thus the doctor, traditionally a
person of authority, has his opinions questioned; and the ethical implications
of his actions are under scrutiny as never before—not surprisingly, because of
the general tendency to challenge authority, to criticize the establishment and
to be sceptical of elitism. There is therefore less willingness to accept that a
complication of an illness or its treatment does not necessarily mean that the
doctor has erred.

Doctors have to accept that their actions have become the subject of public
debate. The topic of medical mistakes makes good television viewing and the
appearance of a patient alleged to be the victim attracts uncritical sympathy
from the audience though often only half the story is shown. Richard Smith [8]
described the attraction of these themes:

> 'Firstly, there is always human drama—invariably a loved one is
> snatched away or horribly disabled. Secondly, as in all the best
> myths, a small man fights against almost insuperable odds: gunned
> down, he battles against the might of doctors, the intransigence of
> lawyers, penury, and his own dreadful afflictions. Usually he loses,
> but just sometimes the cavalry of the media takes an interest and he
> triumphs. The media enjoy being the saviours of the small man, and
> it is indeed one of their essential functions; what is more, the small
> man and his millions of brothers and sisters are just the people who
> make up the viewers . . .'.

The sensation-seeking news media tend to over-elaborate medical matters to
the point of fantasy. A doctor who is criticized may be unable to answer
because of his ethical position concerning patients or from fear of doing
anything which might advertise himself and result in a report to the General
Medical Council.

Consumerism—the movement to protect and promote the interests of the consumer—is playing an increasing role in medicine. The idea is not new: an annotation in *The Lancet* in 1961 entitled 'Patients as consumers: wants and needs' reported the findings of a study of a political and economic planning group which investigated the patients' opinions of their general practitioner, and the various aspects of the National Health Service [9]. Since then there have been numerous other studies to determine patient satisfaction arranged by the government and by various voluntary organizations. An increasing emphasis on consumerism is bound to affect the doctor–patient relationship.

Professor Ian Kennedy, the lawyer, dealt with this subject in his Reith lectures *The Unmasking of Medicine* [10]. His view was that 'in the practice of medicine the consumer is the patient. His interests, which consumerism would seek to assert, are those of self-determination and the power to participate responsibly in decisions made about his life. The challenge to that power comes from the doctor, who, in the exercise of his professional role, threatens to infantilise his patient, to undermine his power of self-determination, to act in a paternalistic manner. Consumerism has a role to play in establishing standards which doctors must meet in their practice, in measuring the doctor's performance in the light of these standards, and in creating means of redress for the patient and sanctions against the doctors if these standards are breached'. The themes that he developed concerned audit and that of telling the patient: 'informed consent is a doctrine far more highly developed in the United States than here in the United Kingdom. Doctors and lawyers here seem to delight in ridiculing it, and preaching strongly against any movement towards it. The ridicule, in my view, is unwarranted and born largely of the sort of chauvinist and lofty ignorance which the English have developed into a higher art form'. However, he also wrote critically of the extent to which informed consent has been taken in the USA.

Some people have argued that the public's attitude has changed since the introduction of the National Health Service, the idea being that the patient was merely suing the state instead of the former voluntary hospital, and that the doctor was insured, so that getting compensation would not cost him anything. The provision of legal aid was also suggested as a cause for increasing legislation. There is no way of proving these ideas and any graph would be affected by several variables; furthermore the NHS and the legal aid scheme started at about the same time, in 1948 and 1950 respectively, so that any possible effect could not be plotted separately.

The changed medical scene

The dear old family doctor—friend and counsellor, available day and night—

has almost disappeared. Some doubt whether he ever existed. Anthony Moore has described how he dipped into the novels of the early part of this century and found that doctors did not fare too well. 'They made Virginia Woolf and her characters feel uneasy. Somerset Maugham's Dr Tyrell "had a patronising air, and from dealing always with the sick he had the healthy man's jovial condescension". And Sinclair Lewis' Dr Arrowsmith "did not, could not, develop the bedside manner" and saw patients "as a mass of drab pain". One of Thomas Mann's doctors "did not receive the patients who came to his waiting room in the order in which they arrived, but took the most influential first, letting the humblest sit and wait". A. J. Cronin's Dr Andrew Manson compromised his idealism for advantage. And we all know what G. B. Shaw thought about the medical conspiracy. All literature cannot be lies.' [11]

Whatever was the truth about the practitioner of the past, the patient did at least have one doctor looking after him and, indeed, this is so today since many general practitioners provide an excellent personal service; but this is not always so, as the family doctor's place has been taken by a group practice doctor in some areas and the patient may not see the same doctor each time; if taken ill at night, he may have to call in a new doctor, through the deputizing service unconnected with the practice, who does not know him nor has access to his clinical records. Different diagnoses (though often different names for the same condition) given by different doctors confuse patients. Fortunately a movement towards continuity of care has started, as research has shown—not surprisingly—that this improves the compliance (co-operation is a more personal word) of those who are prescribed drugs.

The one-to-one relationship between doctor and patient has suffered in hospital as well as in general practice. Specialization—the natural consequence of expanding knowledge—has resulted in the patient often being looked after by a team which includes non-medical scientists as essential members of the team. The lack of a personal physician may be felt and each may think that the other has explained matters to the patient. At out-patients, the six-monthly changes of trainee doctors who often see follow-up cases may result in the patient seeing a different person each time.

Doctors may seem so busy that they can hardly talk to patients and in some practices they allocate too little time to each consultation. This busyness is not confined to the UK, for a distinguished American physician, Dr James Means, stated that 'the most conspicuous change in the behaviour of the doctor is that nowadays he is usually in such a hurry that he is less accessible and less communicative' [12]. Perhaps some general practitioners in the UK, isolated from hospital medicine and dealing mostly with minor and often trivial complaints, become bored with the monotony of their work. Paramedical staff are increasingly being used to deal with the less important matters, even with suturing cuts and taking blood and this, carried too far, can result in the patient seldom seeing the doctor himself. Doctors' complaints of being too busy are not new, for an editorial in the *Lancet* in 1899 stated, 'the pressure and pace of life are unprecedented. We live through as much in a month as our forefathers did in a year . . .' [13]. However, the medical scene has changed and conditions are much improved for doctors so that pressure upon them may not be the sole reason for many patients feeling that they are given too little time and being obliged to start a consultation saying 'I'm so sorry to trouble you'.

Specific complaints against doctors

Generalizations are unavoidable and may be resented by the many doctors whose attention to patients is above reproach. Complaints and grumbles are usually about the behaviour of doctors and not about any technical incompetence. J. R. A. Mitchell, Professor of Medicine at Nottingham University, aptly wrote that tragedies arise, 'because doctors don't communicate clearly, can't be bothered, or are ill, and few problems arise because doctors don't know' [14].

The studies of Rudolf Klein, Professor of Social Policy in the University of Bath, provided hard data about complaints [15]. A profile of grumbles against general practitioners is shown in Figure 44, the shaded area (just over a third) being formal complaints that were then dealt with by the Executive Councils (now the Family Practitioner Committees). The clear areas were grumbles that

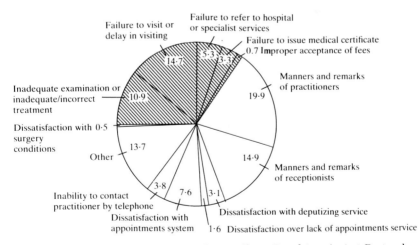

FIGURE 44. Profile of grumbles against doctors (from *Complaints Against Doctors* by Rudolf Klein [15]).

were potential complaints and only half seemed to be a direct criticism of the technical competence of the doctor: 10·9 per cent about inadequate examination, 5·3 per cent alleging failure to refer patients to hospital, and 14·7 per cent about the failure to visit or delay in visiting due to a lapse either in organization or judgement of the GP. Nearly a fifth were about the manners and remarks of GPs—a possible aggravating factor in the bringing of formal complaints or even legal action—and complaints about the attitude of receptionists were then on the increase. Klein wrote that personal friction was inevitable in any service involving a large number of face-to-face contacts on every day of the week and at most hours of the day, but he stressed the point that it was not the technical quality of the service which mattered most to patients—in fact it seemed to matter least of all. Some cases fell into the stereotyped categories of the 'bad' doctor or 'vexatious' patient but most involved a far more subtle play of personalities and clash of conceptions about the role of the doctor and of the patient.

Professional misconduct has hitherto been confined by the General Medical Council to the more serious offences but in 1984 the decision was taken to include the behaviour of doctors if it is incompetent, inconsiderate, unacceptable or obvious misconduct [16]. Guidelines issued by the GMC stated that doctors should assess a patient's condition conscientiously, give a sufficiently thorough examination and 'competent and considerate' professional management. Many of these points were considered in Chapter 4. Ann Cartwright, from the Institute for Social Studies in Medical Care, London, pioneered the study of doctor–patient relationship by the methods of professional interview and facts about the problems of general practitioners and of their patients are well documented in the book *General Practice Revisited* [17].

The aim of a perfect doctor–patient relationship is as difficult to achieve in hospital as in general practice and the problems are well described in Ann Cartwright's *Human Relations and Hospital Care* [18]. This book is full of statistical data but is also garnished with anecdotes and statements by patients, such as the following:

> 'The consultant came round with an assistant and student explaining cases. The doctor looked at me, said nothing and asked the student to examine me and find out what was the matter. They seemed to find out but they did not tell me.'

> 'They examine you and wander off in the distance without telling you how you are getting on.'

> 'They leave you in the dark too much; if only they treated you as if

you could understand something. The doctors especially were very superior; they did not tell you anything.'

'You're an entity and you are known by name and you call the doctors "doc". It's very easy to get to them, none of these formalities. You can always have an interview and can have a man-to-man talk with them. They told you step by step what was wrong and what they were going to do.'

'A little black doctor. He had a lovely smile. It made you feel better just to see him. He seemed to have more patience. He was bright and cheerful. Others would come and look stern, you expected the worst.'

'What a lovely fellow. Is he a proper doctor? He talked to me as if I were a real person.'

Many other studies have been carried out in the last two decades. One compared the approach of hospital doctors with that of general practitioners [19]. General practitioners were better at greeting the patient by name and more patients felt able to talk freely with their GP (Table 13). Seventy-one per

TABLE 13. A comparison of the approach to patients of general practitioners with that of hospital doctors [19].

	General practitioners	Hospital doctors
Greeting patients by name	65%	38%
Easy to talk to	76%	51%

cent liked to have a detailed account of their illness but only 40 per cent were satisfied in this manner by hospital doctors and, in general, the GP was found to be more friendly and helpful. Hospital doctors—who fared worse—could take comfort from the fact that the population sample was hardly big enough as there are so many variables: country or town practice, the number of patients that each doctor is responsible for, and the type of hospital—apart from variations in the doctors themselves.

POOR COMMUNICATION (FAILURE TO LISTEN OR TALK)

The failure of doctors to listen or explain causes the greatest disruption of the doctor–patient relationship. Unfortunately the word 'communication' is used too commonly today and often so loosely that it risks losing its impact and meaning. This would be a pity as many of the world's problems are caused precisely by failure of communication. In medicine, it mainly covers listening and talking. 'Words', wrote Lady Violet Bonham Carter, 'may act on man like dynamite, lull man to sleep, lead and mislead' [20]. It is also true that the misuse of words may spoil a patient's life by creating unnecessary anxiety (iatrogenic illness), although more often *lack of words* creates worry or even a medico-legal situation.

Failure of communication is the most common complaint that reaches the Patients Association and there are three aspects of this:

* Failure to pay much attention to what the patient is saying about himself and his symptoms and health problems.
* Not telling the patient in simple and clear terms what the diagnosis is and why a particular treatment is being given.
* Clamming up (along with other colleagues) when the patient considers that something has gone wrong with the diagnosis and treatment. In the experience of the Patients Association, most patients are not seeking compensation but a frank explanation of what went wrong; a defensive attitude causes a lot of anxiety and resentment [21].

It is, indeed, only too easy for the general practitioner to write a prescription to keep the queue of patients moving instead of listening to the patient, or for the hospital doctor at the out-patient clinic to write a form and send the patient off for an X-ray. A bank clerk once asked the author to give him the name of a family doctor to whom he could go. 'What I really want', he said, 'is a homely doctor whom I can talk to . . . I know so many are so busy.' In hospitals, an obstacle to communication is the inaccessibility of the consultant on his formal round when usually accompanied by the sister, resident doctor and students. Some patients are embarrassed or confused by groups and need an atmosphere of intimacy and privacy to overcome the diffidence which they feel. Others become inarticulate in the presence of a white coat or a stethoscope. Nearly everyone who lies half-naked in bed is completely disarmed whatever his social status. It is easy to underestimate the desire for information of the modern patient or to assume that he knows: in a study of 504 patients and their reactions to investigations [22] it was found that patients were told about unusual, complicated procedures such as cardiac catheterization but often nothing about common ones such as taking a sample of blood or a barium meal examination, as the staff thought that they would know; simple tests like venepuncture or an electrocardiogram without explanation caused worry but this could be avoided by the simple statement that such tests were routine investigations on most patients.

Sometimes the doctor says nothing to avoid worrying the patient, though knowledge is more likely to allay anxiety—even for those with cancer. It is easy to overlook the fact that patients forget or do not listen properly; hence the frequent unfair accusation that 'I was told nothing' when the doctor had in fact taken time to talk and to explain. Important matters concerning life and death or prescriptions of dangerous drugs are often discussed cursorily whereas information must be repeated and the patient invited to come back with questions.

An architect once told the author that we were the only profession with whom you cannot talk. If he planned a house for his doctor he would give him details, but neither his GP nor other doctors spoke to him about his illness. No doubt a surveyor would explain dry rot, and accountants may talk, though some clients prefer to leave themselves in their hands and not to hear about income tax—like some patients and their disease. The problem of communication in most other professions is trifling compared with the need to translate medical jargon into the vernacular and the sensitivity required when dealing with the sick.

Doctor–patient communication is important, but so is doctor–spouse and doctor–relative communication, for in all these areas silence breeds dissatisfaction. Unfortunately many hospitals have been built without proper facilities for talking: there is no special room for seeing patients privately or for interviewing relatives, so that intimate matters concerning life or death have to be discussed in a corridor or within the hearing of others.

> *The problem of communication lies at the heart of medicine: diagnosis and successful doctor–patient relationships depend upon the art of listening and speaking to patients.*

Finally, poor doctor–doctor communication can be a source of trouble for the patient. Sir John Walton, President of the GMC in a preface to the booklet *Doctor to doctor; writing and talking about patients* wrote

'while communication between doctors on the one hand and patients and their relatives on the other is clearly a fundamental aspect of clinical medicine in all its branches, there is no doubt that communication between individual doctors often leaves much to be desired. Stories about misunderstandings and mistakes caused by careless clinical requests, notes, and letters are often recounted by doctors when they meet and talk 'shop' and are attributed, with some merriment, to curious idiosyncrasies of other doctors from which the gossipers feel themselves to be free. The fact that it is usually the patient rather than the doctor who may be most inconvenienced or even harmed by these mistakes is often overlooked' [23].

The era of lay pressure groups

Informed public opinion is an asset for doctors, and so are some lay pressure groups; others are not helpful, especially if they are ill-informed, suspicious of new advances in technology, and anti-doctor as well. The Patients' Association [21] was at first viewed with suspicion by the medical profession, but anyone who reads their publications (and it is a pity that doctors seldom do) will realize that they are an ally and not an enemy, as the approach is one of understanding as well as criticism; indeed, as doctors become patients from time to time, enlightened self-interest should be an incentive to support any efforts to improve the quality of care.

Life, the anti-abortion organization, is less acceptable to doctors and an anathema to many of the lay public. It is disturbing that a moralist group like this tries so hard to enforce its views. This happened when the Director of Public Prosecutions (DPP) prosecuted a doctor for attempted murder after allegations by Life. The case was that of Dr Leonard Arthur [24], a Derby paediatrician, who allowed a three-day-old handicapped baby suffering from Down's syndrome to die; he was put on trial on a charge of murder, reduced subsequently to attempted murder, and was then acquitted. Life has also encouraged nurses throughout the country to act as informers by reporting their cases to Life who will call in the police if protests to the hospital or district health authority are ineffective. If doctors were to be placed in continuous danger of prosecution, medical decisions would become influenced by legal considerations—defensive medicine (see Chapter 9)—and if this were allowed to happen, it would be the patients who would suffer.

The remarkable 'Baby Doe' case in the USA illustrated some bizarre political actions due to a lay pressure group [25]. The baby had Down's syndrome and a fistula (perforation) between the oesophagus and trachea as well as possible other congenital abnormalities. After discussion with the local doctor, the parents decided that no corrective surgery was to be carried out and it died on the sixth day. An uproar was created in 1982 and the President, needing something visible to satisfy his 'right-to-life' constituents, allowed the following: the federal Government notified all hospitals that it was unlawful to deny medical care to a handicapped baby; an order was sent requiring hospitals to post a notice in a conspicuous place in delivery rooms and nurseries stating that discrimination against handicapped infants was prohi-

278

bited and warning that federal funds would be witheld from offending hospitals; an investigative agency in Washington was set up with a 24-hour free hot-line telephone number and with 'Baby Doe squads' ready to descend on maternity units to check on the treatment of the newborn—monopolizing the time of doctors and nurses. All this unleashed a storm of criticism by the public and judges also disagreed with the way that the government had approached the matter. Eventually, in a court case brought by the Academy of Pediatrics, the regulations were overturned. Judge Gerhard Gesell described the effect of a seriously handicapped child on the marriage or on the siblings, the cost of a life support system needed to keep it alive, its poor quality of life and stated that 'the parents . . . in many ways are in the best position to evaluate the infant's best interests' [26].

Complaints against doctors were carried to their extreme limit when clinics in the USA performing abortions were bombed in 1984 by anti-abortion groups.

Sans Everything [27] was a book that resulted from a letter [28] which appeared in *The Times* in 1965 about the plight of old people in hospital; it protested about the evil practice in certain hospitals of stripping geriatric patients of their personal possessions. Dissatisfaction with the attitude of the Ministry of Health to complaints prompted the ten writers of *The Times* letter (several Lords with other distinguished figures and a consultant geriatrician) to collect evidence of the ill-treatment of geriatric patients. Their request for detailed information from those who had encountered such malpractice was answered and contributed to the book. Three of the distinguished signatories, having tried and failed to get the practice stopped by official action, formed an association called Aid for the Elderly in Government Institutions (AEGIS).

The book consisted of articles written by nurses and social workers who supplied sworn affidavits about the bad conditions they observed in geriatric wards of general hospitals as well as in mental hospitals. These confirmed that some patients were stripped of their spectacles, dentures, hearing aids and other civilized necessities and so were left to vegetate in utter loneliness and idleness. The Government set up a group of official hospital investigations where lawyers represented the hospitals and also the individual doctors, and the medical defence bodies were much concerned. Some of the accusers came across as unreliable and irresponsible but the result was a Report in 1968 which was presented to Parliament by the Minister of Health [29].

A BBC play called 'Minor Complications' by Peter Ransley illustrated the influence of television. Focusing attention on probable and unrecognized medical mishaps, it caused numerous calls from doctors to the medical defence bodies seeking their advice. It also resulted in the group Action for the Victims of Medical Accidents (AVMA) being set up as a registered charity in 1982—the object of which is implicit in its title. This has become a watch-dog and some doctors have feared that it might hinder research and the advance of medicine; for example, an article appeared in the *British Medical Journal* entitled 'Confidential paediatric inquiry into neonatal deaths in Wessex, 1981 and 1982' [30]. It was a valuable audit by doctors as it dealt with factors responsible for such deaths, one of which included 'possible adverse factors in medical care'. A letter appeared in the *British Medical Journal* from the treasurer of the AVMA suggesting a further inquiry and stating that 'the problem of medical negligence (that is, accidents due to 'adverse factors in medical care') is far larger than the complacency of some sections of the medical profession, and certainly the medical defence organizations, suggest' [31]. The matter of equating 'adverse factors in medical care with medical negligence' was discussed in further correspondence. It would be a sad day for medicine if audits like this were inhibited for fear of provoking litigation. This is unlikely to happen, for the literature produced by AVMA is responsible, informative and professional. In one sense the AVMA and the medical defence bodies have a common purpose: that patients who have suffered definite medical accidents should be compensated, and this is done as rapidly as possible by the latter who settle such cases out of court. The problem is that many cases are in grey areas and are not black or white, so that it is difficult to decide whether a case is due to negligence or natural causes and then the defence body does its best to prove the doctor's innocence.

False expectations

Wonder cures are reported in newspapers, but the accounts of them are hardly recognized by authors of articles about the relevant drug trials. The ideal operation is shown on television with, so said a surgical colleague, no mention of operations where 'all hell is let loose' when the surgeon has to meet the unexpected and deal with almost uncontrollable bleeding and collapse of the patient.

Alistair Cooke, in an address to the BMA Congress, stated, when discussing the increasing litigation in the USA, 'but many of these suits reflect rather the bitter disillusion of a generation lulled by the popular education we have been talking about into believing that doctors can cure any disease, and that almost any organ of the body can be replaced as readily as a punctured tyre or a shock-absorber' [32]. Hence is born the belief that all things are possible in modern medicine if only the doctor would try harder. Perhaps doctors, when they appear on the media, tend to act as if their treatment is a breakthrough when obviously it is not, and are reluctant to tell of failures; for, in practice, some diseases have no effective treatment and few treatments can be guaranteed successful. Certainty is elusive in spite of the remarkable advances. The effect of too rosy a view about doctors and their power over disease was well put by Professor Ian Kennedy: 'We, the public, have been led to expect too much and have been more than willing partners in the process. We have come almost to believe in magic cures and the waving of wands. The reality is a constant disappointment' [10]. Public expectation has been set too high.

Prevention

Doctors aim, of course, to avoid the causes that will provoke complaints from patients. Such a spate of literature has been published in the medical journals in the last two or three decades that anyone might think that the matter of doctor–patient communication had been solved. A computer retrieval search suggested that at least a hundred books have appeared in the world literature in the last twenty years on this subject. Many articles also have appeared on specific areas of communication: talking to cancer patients, to the terminally ill, to those with strokes, and to couples facing death; or about the 'grieving process' when a spouse has died, or breaking bad news, to mention just a few. Also much research has been done on the views and reactions of patients on, for instance, the psychological effect of the removal of a breast (mastectomy), or the fears aroused in patients by migraine.

The medical defence bodies advise doctors how to prevent an increase in medico-legal problems. For example:

* Awareness of the increasing possibility of these problems arising is necessary.
* The next point is that it is essential to keep up to date with the literature, with clinically relevant Health Department circulars, with the law as it affects medicine, and with warning notices issued by the Committee on Safety of Medicines and the drug manufacturers.
* An excellent doctor–patient relationship at all times still goes a long way to avoid unpleasant, time-consuming and stressful legal complications.
* Careful checking and supervision of both medical and non-medical subordinates avoids much trouble.
* The need for meticulous clinical records can never be over-emphasized.
* Lastly, except when formally acting as a patient's adviser in a possible negligence suit, a doctor should avoid 'off-the-cuff' criticism of another doctor, dentist or hospital. All too often a hasty or ill-judged comment proves in restrospect to have been the starting-point of an unjustified complaint or claim; for example, the junior doctor makes a snap diagnosis of pneumonia when he sees a chest X-ray, inferring that the general practitioner should have recognized this, although no-one could have done so without an X-ray. Similar

aspersions occur with such statements as, 'why did your doctor not send you into hospital before?'. The last person to see the patient often has the advantage, for the diagnosis has become obvious due to the passage of time. Hence the proverb, 'Blessed is the physician who is called in last'.

A dilemma for doctors occurs when a patient's case has been mismanaged, and there is a margin between being honest and not letting another doctor down—a divided loyalty. Diplomacy is needed in explaining the situation without covering up for a colleague.

> *Patients are more anxious to find out what has gone wrong than to make money*
>
> *said a solicitor*

Improving communication between doctors and patients

Emphasis should be given to communication from the moment when the patient first enters hospital. 'Guidance for patients' is the title of one brochure about hospital life: it gives details of identity bracelets, laundry, meal-times, and so on. Medical information may hardly be mentioned. The following could be inserted:

> *Talking with your doctor.* Your doctor will want you to know about your tests, progress, illness and treatment; so do ask him anything. Some forget when the doctor comes, so you could write down any questions.

Patients generally do not feel that they can ask questions unless invited to; some are too embarrassed to ask and others do not want to waste the doctor's time; if the explanation is unclear, the risk of appearing ignorant or stupid prevents some from asking for more information. The method of asking patients to write down questions to be discussed on the next ward round can be most successful and none can then complain that they were not given a chance to talk. These (Figure 45) often raise points that are easily overlooked and can be discussed with the patients and junior staff.

Doctors, who are trained mainly to think of disease, can so easily ignore the patient: X-rays are scattered all over the bed and the consultant passes on without a reassuring word or, a situation which patients find worrying and impolite, a discussion in whispered tones takes place at the foot of the bed. The practice of doing rounds in two stages avoids this:

1 *The academic round* takes place in a side-room equipped with a viewing box

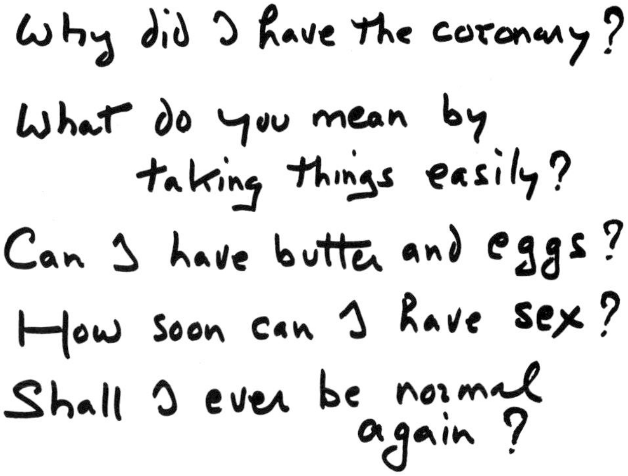

Why did I have the coronary?

What do you mean by
    taking things easily?

Can I have butter and eggs?

How soon can I have sex?

Shall I ever be normal
            again?

FIGURE 45. Questions written by a patient. Asking patients to write down queries can be a useful aid to communication.

and seats. The problems of each patient are discussed and most decisions taken.

2 *The personal round* consists just of talking to patients. Many can be seen in a separate room especially when ambulant, instead of being lined up by their beds. Then private matters can be discussed without other patients overhearing.

Case-notes should include what the patient is told as well as an account of his disease. The problem sheet [33], which lists all problems from indigestion to marital difficulties and treatment and is attached to the front of the notes, can have a compartment headed COMMUNICATION (Figure 46).

The need for written information. Talking is not enough. In no other field of life is the written word so neglected: when buying a car or radio, brochures and pamphlets are provided—whereas someone undergoing a major operation may be brushed off with a few words during a busy round. To expect anyone to understand and remember medical details after a brief talk is absurd. Lectures and seminars to medical students are supplemented by hand-outs and reading lists; seldom do they learn anything solely by listening, yet patients are hardly ever given anything in writing.

Written information is cheap and easy. No equipment is needed except a duplicator. Information leaflets and hand-outs supplement talking and could be available on every ward and actually prescribed for patients. Junior doctors might prepare these for their seniors, a chore which will impress them with the need to inform patients. Often all that is needed is for details of a consultation to

PROBLEM LIST

	ACTIVE PROBLEMS	DATE	SOLUTION	DATE	INACTIVE PROBLEMS
NAME		NO			AGE
1					
2					
3					
4					
5					
6					
7					
8					

COMMUNICATION WITH PATIENT

FIGURE 46. The problem sheet lists all the patient's problems, from indigestion to marital difficulties, and records treatment. The section 'Communication' was added so that everyone concerned knew what had been said to the patient.

be taped and edited later. A few hand-outs will cover most aspects of a specialist's work and can be used as follows:

* *To explain investigations.* For example, a leaflet about the barium meal helps co-operation (compliance); it avoids the patient coming with a full stomach and counteracts wrong information from others who, in the past, have swallowed a pint of barium in the pitch dark, instead of a few ounces in a dimly lit room.

* *Operation.* Information and relief of anxiety before operation reduces analgesic drugs needed afterwards. Details are needed about approximate length of time in hospital, reassurance about the anaesthetic, what operation is likely to be done and how soon a return to work is likely.
* *Information about the illness.* One leaflet written for patients suffering from a heart attack (coronary infarction) has proved useful in the author's experience. It explained the condition briefly and gave advice. The patient and spouse discussed it and the doctor answered any queries.
* *Guidance about drugs.* Patients are prescribed potentially dangerous drugs, often with no more information than the name written on the bottle, but this situation is changing due to the more active role of the community pharmacist (formerly called a retail chemist) who now meets the patient when dispensing the prescription; problems can arise if he says anything which is contradictory to the GP's advice. Hand-outs can guide and warn about side-effects. A further measure is for tablets to be put on cards with Sellotape, together with their names and objects (see Figure 22, page 126).

Too little use is made of the large amount of literature written for patients. The Health Education Index [34] lists booklets by nearly 400 voluntary organizations, and a list of those published by pharmaceutical firms was recorded in the *British Medical Journal* in 1984 [35]. Patients soon forget verbal information and the beneficial effect of leaflets—providing that they are clearly written in lay language—was described in a leader in the *British Medical Journal* itself [36]: information is more easily recalled when it is written, patients are more likely to take important drugs regularly, and the side-effects of drugs are more likely to be reported when these are written down rather than described by the doctor, also a more useful discussion can take place between doctor and patient. The Family Doctor booklets issued by the British Medical Association, which cover virtually every condition, and those available free from the Arthritis and Rheumatism Council, for example, provide patients with models of clear information written in a reassuring manner.

Tape recording could be used more often as many patients possess tape cassettes or have access to them. Consultations can be recorded especially when patients or relatives repeatedly ask the same questions. Also instructions can more easily be given to the blind and partially sighted.

In practice, much information for patients is provided by the paramedical staff, such as nurses and physiotherapists, so it is important for all to work as a team and not to give conflicting information. Their attitude is as important as that of the doctors. The first contact that a patient has with the GP is through the receptionist and a warm sympathetic manner is an invaluable aid. The same need applies to the out-patient department where most people have their first contact with the hospital. Patients should be addressed by the title 'Mr', 'Mrs' or 'Miss' instead of just calling for 'Smith' or 'Jones' and the receptionist and nurse must be taught, if necessary, to smile.

Much has been written about extra-verbal forms of communication. Touch is important [37]. One study of patients being treated for leukaemia in a sterile enclosure showed that the worst feature of this isolation was the lack of touch by a nurse or doctor. The American physician, Dr Robert Loeb, was once asked, when he shook hands with a patient on rounds at Bellevue Hospital, whether it was to determine the temperature, moisture, or strength of the arm. He replied, 'Gentlemen, the thing that I am doing is greeting another human being' [38].

Patient participation schemes help to solve problems of communication. One, organized in a general practice in Birchfield in Birmingham, is described by the patient [39] and a similar arrangement can be made in hospitals by having ward meetings between patients and staff [40]; most staff and patients considered these meetings to be valuable and they provided a way of making hospital more responsive to patients' concerns.

TEACHING MEDICAL STUDENTS

Education about these matters should start early and it is odd that the doctor–patient relationship is a subject usually missing from a medical student's curriculum. The student is expected to learn communication skills from the example of his seniors whose approach is often imperfect. To help remedy this defect, a seminar entitled Doctor–Patient Relationships was started [41]. The seminar began with a brief history of the bedside manner, a term frequently used in an ironical sense because it has been so exploited by doctors in the past. The qualities of this as needed today were then described: confidence, personal attention, sympathy, and salesmanship—a word used to describe the illness to the patient, the type of language to choose, the method of advising, and how to persuade the patient about the need for the drug. Next the students were addressed by the patient—often chosen because of their long experience of doctors due to a chronic illness. Others who attended these seminars were a ward sister, general practitioner, a member of the Patients' Association and always a doctor from the Medical Defence Union who described problems that can arise from bad relationships, and answered numerous questions from the students. A booklet is presented to all students in some medical schools called *Talking with Patients: A Teaching Approach* [42] as this covers the whole field and much of the literature on this subject (Figures 47 and 48 are reproduced from it).

Medical books should contain information about the needs of patients as

FIGURE 47. There is no better way of preventing patients from feeling free to talk than by appearing bored or concerned only with note-taking. (Reproduced by kind permission of The Nuffield Provincial Hospitals Trust and the artist Dr John Moll.)

FIGURE 48. Doctors sometimes talk to each other, or to a nurse, across a patient's bed, referring to him as a third person. (Reproduced by kind permission of The Nuffield Provincial Hospitals Trust and the artist Dr John Moll.)

well as treatment of their disease, and should also discuss ethical matters. Textbooks outline the treatment of the diseases described but as Dr A. M. Cooke wrote, 'physicians do not treat diseases, they treat human beings, all of whom differ from each other, with individual likes and dislikes, fears and prejudices, a unique set of genes, and widely differing environmental backgrounds. A patient is not merely an example of some disease described in the textbook, but is a fellow creature and emphatically not "a case". Used in this sense the word "case" should be expunged from the medical vocabulary' [43]. The following could routinely be included in textbooks:

* General problems for patients. The *Oxford Textbook of Medicine* [44] provides a model for any editor as it starts by describing the effects of admission to hospital: feelings of strangeness and helplessness; worry about relatives and dependants; worry about job and money matters; concern about the illness itself; fear of pain or of operation; and fear of death.

* Specific problems. These concern the effect of different conditions—glaucoma, coronary thrombosis, colostomy, abortion—upon the patient and his family.

* Ethics, for example, when it is kinder to stop resuscitation and allow a patient to die in peace and not 'to strive officiously to keep alive'.

* Medico-legal aspects. Students and doctors should be made aware of potential legal problems and high-risk areas.

KEEPING UP TO DATE

Keeping up to date is a Herculean task but it is essential both for the patient and in the event of a medico-legal problem; for a doctor's actions are judged in court according to the level of knowledge expected in his field. Plato said that 'education is a life-long business' and this applies especially to the profession of medicine. The problem is the torrent of new knowledge and how to get it to doctors as quickly as possible. Apart from medical meetings, journals, video-tapes, and abstracts, computer terminals in medical libraries now provide print-outs of recent and other literature and, in the USA, a medical information system is now developing under the aegis of the National Library of Medicine which, in the next decade, should 'lead American medicine into a network of communication that has not hitherto been dreamed of' [45].

Equally important is the need for doctors to keep in touch with new medico-legal problems and more could be done by the medical defence bodies to spotlight these. Their annual reports make interesting and anecdotal reading, but an example of an important new risk (such as drug interaction) is hidden amongst other perennial problems. An early-warning system is needed and measures are being taken to circulate doctors with this information. A diploma course in medical ethics and the law is available for anyone considering specializing in this subject: it is organized by Professor Ian Kennedy at King's College, London and lasts one year. In the USA, a hospital risk management course is run by William Curran, who has been called 'the father of legal medicine', and who is Professor of Legal Medicine at the Harvard University School of Public Health. A standard textbook is *Law and Medicine*, written by Professor Walter Wadlington and his colleagues Jon R. Waltz and Roger B. Dworkin (1980) [46].

MEDICAL AUDIT

The term 'audit' is unfortunate as it is more commonly associated with accountancy, implying numerical review by an outside investigator directed at, amongst other things, the prevention of fraud. More congenial synonyms are 'review' or 'monitoring'. To evaluate what we are doing is important although it is always more enjoyable to evaluate what others are doing.

Much audit is being done [47–52]. Indeed doctors belong to one of the most self-critical professions, which is constantly challenging traditional beliefs and assessing progress. The obstetricians pioneered audit with their studies of infant and maternal mortality. External scrutiny and peer review has been accepted: for example the Medical Research Council visitations, the University Grants Committee assessment of medical schools and the National Quality Control Scheme. Professor Ian McColl reviewed the various audits taking place at hospital level [53]. There are various targets: to assess patients' satisfaction, weekly 'death and complications' meetings to determine whether any could have been avoided, results of operations [54], comparison of the work load and the results of two hospitals in the same district [55]; and weekly ward meetings where all the staff attend and go through patients' case-notes, criticizing any unnecessary investigations or other alternatives. All these studies are sporadic but increasing.

One implication of audit is that doctors learn from their mistakes so as to avoid them in the future. Hiding mistakes, according to McIntyre and Popper, should be regarded as a deadly sin [56]. Some errors, they write, are inevitably revealed such as operating on the wrong patient or removing a wrong limb but other errors are not so easily exposed. Unfortunately it is not common clinical practice to keep full and systematic records of medical and surgical errors, so that without detailed records of wrong diagnoses and prognoses, of unpredicted side-effects, or of failure of effective treatment, the empirical basis needed for any adequate action is missing.

Perhaps the defence bodies, now that their information is computerized, will play a role in auditing medico-legal problems in the future: for example, in the analysis of factors responsible for mishaps, or the incidence of malpractice in different parts of the country.

Peer review has been less acceptable. Sir Douglas Black, former President of the Royal College of Physicians, stated: 'there are strong public and parliamentary pressures to bring medical practice under closer scrutiny, whether by the ombudsman, or in some other way. Some members of the profession maintain that such pressures are to be resisted, without argument and without compromise, and that we should have nothing to do with medical audit, quality control, or whatever' [57]. An encouraging sign, however, was the fact that it was the juniors who led the call for medical audit at the Annual Representative Meeting of the BMA in 1979, for 'the medical profession has been dilatory in setting up its own workable procedures for intraprofessional audit and if it did not do so control would pass to someone else'. The reactionary doctor will invoke the need for clinical freedom but this is often a cloak for ignorance and occasionally an excuse for prescribing obsolete treatment. Needless to say, any audit, especially if done by peers, must be carried out sympathetically and not vindictively.

Doctors in the United States of America are more willing to co-operate in peer review and similar procedures, whether as assessors or assessed, probably because of legislation which compels doctors working in the government-sponsored Medicaid or Medicare schemes to submit to this. The joint commission on Accreditation of Hospitals in the USA publishes a quarterly *Quality Review Bulletin* which documents the results of audit and peer review procedures.

'Doctors should not play God'

Medicine, wrote Rudolf Klein, provides 'an example of professional power in the extreme—and in some ways unique—form, if only in the last resort it deals with matters of life and death . . . There is not only the imbalance in technical knowledge common to every service based on any kind of expertise—whether of the doctor, the plumber or the car mechanic. There are also emotional and other factors special to medicine. On the whole, people are not anxious when taking a car to be repaired, even though the mechanic may well be able to blind them with technical detail. However, a visit to a doctor for anything except a minor complaint is a much more highly charged and intense experience. In the last resort an old car can be scrapped and replaced by a new one but this is not yet true of the human body' [15].

Arrogance in the doctor was implied by the statement of Sir John Donaldson when he said: 'the law will not permit the medical profession to play God. The law and the court cannot stand idly by if the profession, by an excess of paternalism, denies their patient a real choice . . .' This was at the Appeal trial of Mrs Sidaway [58] who alleged that she was not told of the risk of paralysis from an operation on the neck.

The Scottish playwright James Bridie, who qualified and practised as a doctor, wrote 'there is a temptation for any creature who seems obviously to be doing the work of the Almighty to imagine himself a god. This is particularly so in medicine, and an almost unavoidable error in the hospital physician or surgeon. He is surrounded by respectful and adoring acolytes, and he holds the power of life and death over helpless patients . . .' [59]. Fortunately, life in hospital has changed since that was written several decades ago: then the consultant was commonly autocratic and held himself at the apex of a pyramid whereas today most would view themselves more like the chairman of a committee, the committee being the junior staff and paramedical colleagues.

The late Dr Franz Ingelfinger, in a masterly essay on arrogance, wrote that 'although arrogance in some of its more nefarious meanings—vanity, insolence, and ruthlessness, for example—cannot, I believe, be identified as a general characteristic of the medical profession, the profession as a whole is affected by a brand of arrogance subsumed under lack of empathy. Doctors for various reasons find it difficult to put themselves in the patient's place; they do not sufficiently appreciate, or perhaps do not have the time to appreciate, how the patient feels and how he reacts to the medical information and procedures to which he is exposed' [60]. This is an erudite though poignant account as Dr Ingelfinger then knew that he was suffering from a carcinoma of the oesophagus—many colleagues had given him advice but eventually he found solace by being under his own general practitioner and wrote that 'if you agree that the physician's primary function is to make the patient feel better, a certain amount of authoritarianism, paternalism, and domination are the essence of the physician's effectiveness, then some degree of arrogance is a good thing'. He was speaking from experience.

Authoritarianism has to be put aside when dealing with the public concerning medical-social problems. The social climate has changed since the Duke of Edinburgh said in his Presidential Adress to the British Medical Association in 1959 'maintenance of the honour and respectability of the profession generally . . . This means that it was recognised from the start that the profession was responsible for its own ethics. This is really the crux of any professional organisation' [61]. Now the current view is that the public should have a say in many ethical matters in medicine. Ian Kennedy [10] writes

'a doctor has no more competence than you or I to decide, for example, which of competing candidates should have access to a kidney machine in the context of a scarcity of resources. The answer will be offered that the kidney machine goes to the patient most suited, but this is patently question-begging, partic

such factors as psychological stability and ability to comprehend and follow the necessary regime of food and behaviour are considered. Clearly, doctors must be the arbiters of those questions which are technical. Thereafter, the issue is an ethical one . . . It is in the resolution of such problems that a Code of Practice on medical ethics is so urgently required'.

Ethical dilemmas are one of the greatest problems for doctors and increase with the developments of medical technology; and, although the suggestion that 'a doctor has no more competence than you or I to decide . . .' seems debatable, most doctors would welcome constructive help and moral support from lay people in making such decisions.

References

1 Taylor J. Quoted by Strauss M.B., Ed. *Familiar Medical Quotations*. London: J. & A. Churchill, 1968, p. 394.
2 Proverb. *Ibid*: 179.
3 French proverb. *Ibid*: 397.
4 Jekyll J. *Ibid*: 395.
5 Bacon R. 'On the Errors of Physicians'. In *Essays on the History of Medicine*. Eds Singer Charles & Sigerist H. E. (MS transl by E. T. Withington). London, 1924, p. 149.
6 Voltaire. Quoted by Strauss M.B., Ed. *Familiar Medical Quotations*. London: J. & A. Churchill. 1968, p. 394.
7 Kant I. *Ibid*: 95.
8 Smith R. Medicine and the media. *British Medical Journal* 1 (1983): 1433.
9 Patients as consumers: wants and needs (annotation) *Lancet* 1 (1961): 927–8.
10 Kennedy I. *The Unmasking of Medicine: A Searching Look at Health Care Today*. London: Granada Publishing Limited, 1983.
11 Moore A.R. Personal view. *British Medical Journal* 2 (1978): 1363.
12 Means J.H. *Daedalus* 92 (1963): 701.
13 Editorial. *Lancet* 2 (1899): 416.
14 Mitchell J.R.A. Who needs clinical pharmacology? *British Medical Journal* 298 (1984): 1119–20.
15 Klein R.E. *Complaints Against Doctors*. London: Charles Knight, 1973.
16 GMC strengthens professional conduct procedure. *British Medical Journal*. 289 (1984): 1325–6.
17 Cartwright A. & Anderson R. *General Practice Revisited: A Second Study of Patients and Their Doctors*. London: Tavistock Publications, 1981.
18 Cartwright A. *Human Relations and Hospital Care*. London: Routledge & Kegan Paul, 1964.
19 Lawson R. Patients' attitude to doctors. *Journal of the Royal College of General Practitioners*. 30 (1980): 137–8.
20 Bonham Carter Lady Violet B. The power of words. *Lancet* 2 (1951): 997.
21 The Patients Association, 11 Dartmouth Street, London SW1H 9BN.
22 Hawkins C.F. Patients' reactions to their investigations: a study of 504 patients. *British Medical Journal* 2 (1979): 638–40.
23 Walton J. & McLachlan G. (Eds.) *Doctor to doctor: writing and talking about patients*; a collection of essays from a Nuffield Working Party on Communication. London: Nuffield Provincial Hospital Hospitals Trust, 1984.
24 Medicolegal. Dr Leonard Arthur: his trial and its implications (legal correspondent). *British Medical Journal* 283 (1981): 1340–1 & *The Times* 6 November (1981): p1, 12.

25 Dunea G. Squel rules in the nursery. *British Medical Journal* 287 (1983): 1203–4.

26 Culliton B.J. 'Baby Doe' regs. Thrown out by court. *Science* 220 (1983): 478–80.

27 Robb Barbara (Ed.) *Sans Everything. A Case to Answer.* Presented on behalf of AEGIS. London: Nelson, 1967.

28 Letter from Lord Strabolgi and others. *The Times.* 10 November (1965) p. 13 (col 6).

29 *Report: Findings and Recommendations following Enquiries into Allegations concerning the Care of Elderly Patients in Certain Hospitals.* London: Her Majesty's Stationery Office, 1968.

30 Wood B., Catford J.C. & Cogswell J.J. Confidential paediatric inquiry into neonatal deaths in Wessex, 1981 & 1982. *British Medical Journal* 288 (1984): 1206–8.

31 Simanowitz A. How large is the problem of medical negligence? *Ibid.* 288; 1460 and 1912 (address of AVMA is 135 Stockwell Road, London, SW9 9TN).

32 Cooke A. The doctor in society. *British Medical Journal* 283 (1981): 1652–5.

33 Weed L.L. *Medical Records, Medical Education and Patient Care: The Problem-Oriented Record as a Basic Tool.* Chicago: The Press of Case Western Reserve University, 1969.

34 Edsall B. *Health Education Index.* London: Edsall and Co Ltd, 1983.

35 Sloan P.J.M. Patient information booklets. *British Medical Journal* 288 (1984): 1694.

36 Drury V.W.M. Patient information leaflets (leader). *British Medical Journal* 288 (1984): 427–8.

37 Lee R.V. The generalist: a jaundiced view. *American Journal of Medicine* 73 (1982): 617–8.

38 Loeb R.F. Quoted by David Seegal in *Journal of the American Medical Association* 177 (1961): 641.

39 Birchfield Medical Centre Patients' Association. *British Medical Journal* 282 (1981): 2103–4.

40 Graffy, J. Ward meetings: a forum for patients' concerns. *British Medical Journal* 286 (1983): 371–2.

41 Hawkins C.F. Personal view. *British Medical Journal* 4 (1968): 640.

42 *Talking with Patients: A Teaching Approach.* Observations of a Working Party on Communications with Patients. London: The Nuffield Provincial Hospitals Trust.

43 Cooke A.M. In Introduction to *Oxford Textbook of Medicine.* p. 1.3–1.5. (see below).

44 Weatherall D.J., Ledingham J.G.G. & Warrell D.A. (Eds). *Oxford Textbook of Medicine.* Oxford University Press, 1983.

45 Davies N.E. Medicine in the United States (letter). *British Medical Journal* 288 (1984): 1913.

46 Wadlington W., Waltz J.R. & Dworkin R.B. *Law and Medicine.* United States of America: Foundation Press Inc., 1980.

47 Gough M.I.Y., Kettlewell M.G.W., Marks C.C.G., Holmes S.J.K. & Holderness J. Audit: an annual assessment of the work and performance of a surgical firm in a regional teaching hospital. *British Medical Journal* 281 (1980): 913–8.

48 Hoff W. Van't. Audit reviewed. A progress report. *Journal of the Royal College of Physicians of London* 16 (1983): 62–4. Audit reviewed: Value for money in medicine. *Ibid.* 17 (1983): 150–2.

49 Shaw C.D. Aspects of audit. *British Medical Journal.* 280 (1980): 1256–8; 1314–6; 1361–3; 1443–6; 1509–11.

50 Swansea Physicians Audit Group. Audit reviewed: Implementing audit in a division of medicine. *Journal of the Royal College of Physicians of London* 16 (1983): 252–4. Audit of clinical practice: Opportunities to rationalise the use of resources. *Ibid.* 1983; 17: 235–8.

51 Baron D.N. Can't audit won't audit! (leader). *British Medical Journal* 286 (1983): 1229–10.

52 Griffiths B.K. Audit reviewed: the view of the patient and the community. *Journal of the Royal College of Physicians of London* 16 (1983): 132–4.

53 McColl I. Medical audit in British hospital practice. *British Journal of Hospital Medicine* 22 (1979): 485–9.

54 Irving M., Temple J. Surgical audit: one year's experience in a teaching hospital. *British Medical Journal* 2 (1976): 746–7.

55 Gilmore O.J.A., Griffiths N.J., Connolly J.C., Dunlop A.W., Hart S., Thomson J.P.S. & Todd I.P. Surgical audit comparison of the work load and results of two hospitals in the same district. *British Medical Journal* 281 (1980): 1050–2.

56 McIntyre N. & Popper K. The critical attitude in medicine: the need for a new ethics. *British Medical Journal* 287 (1983): 1919–23.
57 Black Sir Douglas. Apples of discord. *Journal of the Royal Society of Medicine* 74 (1981): 92–100.
58 *Sidaway* v. *Board of Governors of the Bethlem Royal Hospital and the Maudsley Hospital and others.* Weekly Law Reports. 2 (1984): 778 and *British Medical Journal* 289 (1984): 325.
59 Bridie James. Quoted by Strauss M.B. (Ed.) In *Familiar Medical Quotations.* London: J. and A. Churchill, 1968, p. 384.
60 Ingelfinger F.J. Arrogance. *New England Journal of Medicine* 303 (1980): 1507–11.
61 Edinburgh, Duke of. Presidential Address to the British Medical Association. *British Medical Journal* II (1959): 839–40.

12

Epilogue

'I find the great thing in this world is not so much where we
stand as in what direction we are moving!' [1]
OLIVER WENDELL HOLMES (1809–1894)

Since 1885 the wind of change has profoundly affected doctor–patient relationships: more is expected of the doctor, the public are more critical, potential medico-legal problems abound and any mishap may result in the doctor appearing metaphorically naked in the spotlight of the mass media.

The image of doctors may have altered but fortunately, according to one editorial writer, it is still good [2]:

'When people are asked to say which professionals command the most respect they usually put doctors at the top of the list—above clergymen and lawyers. Asked for adjectives to describe doctors they will choose ones like honest, reliable, and trustworthy. This respect goes beyond an appreciation of the special technical skills of doctors; they are seen as men and women of good character, whose priority is—or should be—the good of their patients. This is why, for instance, doctors are allowed to sign passport forms and why a reference from a doctor is much valued. Such special respect is important to doctors not because it boosts their own esteem, which it undoubtedly does, but because it has practical value in their professional work. At the simplest level trust is essential for home visiting or gynaecological examination in general practice; more fundamentally a patient and his family need to believe their doctor when he or she says some course of action is essential'.

Generally, doctors have been a privileged class throughout history. Originally linked with religion, the medicine man had power over illness and the devils that were thought to cause it. A high ethical outlook and intellectual approach was shown by the physicians who wrote the Hippocratic collection and this set the standard for Western medicine. From time to time, however, fluctuations in the prestige of the doctor have taken place. For example, in the last century, the image of the doctor in the public mind was not always that of the beloved physician: one cartoon in *Punch* showed him as a pompous, frock-coated humbug, remote from the patient and blandly giving himself away: 'Oh doctor, I am afraid I am pretty well at death's door', says the patient. 'Don't you worry, my dear sir', replies the doctor, 'we will pull you through'. Considering the lack of medical knowledge and his impotence in treatment, it is amazing that the doctor did have so much prestige; perhaps this was due to his work for charity, his sincerity and selfless overwork, and the tendency for many diseases to get better by themselves whatever remedy was given. Today, the doctor's status in society is maintained because medicine is a dynamic, not static, subject, and the obvious progress over disease—as seen through television and other media—boosts the regard for our profession.

The status of the patient has been different. This, except in the wealthy minority, meant a depressed class and all that could be hoped for was charity. As in biblical days, 'the poor, and the maimed, and the halt and the blind' have been grouped together. The attitude of condescension in caring for the sick occurs throughout history. For some centuries in England, many sick would receive no treatment though some might be lucky and be treated by an apothecary. Our hospitals have often developed from Poor Law institutions; and the long wards have evolved from workhouse dormitories. Fortunately, the status of the patient today is being raised, and he is paying for the National Health Service and is not dependent upon charity. This betterment is long overdue and proceeding rapidly, as shown by the reports of various committees: the study of the patient's day in hospital with its suggestion that he is awoken at a civilized hour; the avoidance of noise in hospital; the treatment of expectant mothers in hospital, amongst others; and hospitals are being built for the needs of patients as well as their disease.

Lest all these assertions about the position of doctors appear complacent and presumptuous, I must point out that the quotation on page 295 was merely the start of an editorial in the *British Medical Journal* [2] which expressed worry about a decline of the doctor's status and listed various misdemeanours of a few doctors that are tending to tarnish the image of the rest. This has happened in the USA—but largely due to the commercial approach to medicine; some doctors there have had to accept that their huge earnings have resulted in their being seen as uncaring money-grabbers. Reducing the practice of the profession of medicine to a mere commercial transaction spoils the doctor–patient relationship and destroys the image of a caring profession. The National Health Service, with all its faults and failings, is preferable, and the patient benefits too, as his doctor's recommendation is likely to be what is best for him rather than what is best for the doctor's pocket [3]. Nevertheless there are other more subtle pitfalls for any doctor and, to take one example from those discussed in the *British Medical Journal*, 'patients and their relatives are worried and sometimes angry that doctors retreat behind technical and institutional barriers, giving the impression that the profession no longer cares for patients as individuals but sees them only as interesting or trivial or chronic cases.'

No doubt the best way to avoid misunderstandings is a partnership based on mutual respect. Doctor R. F. Loeb, the distinguished American physician, is alleged to have said that 'the patient should be managed the way the doctor or a member of his family would wish to be treated if he were that patient in that bed at that time' [4]—a laudable approach which, if adopted by everyone as well as the doctors, would result in some sort of Utopia. But a good rapport should, of course, be the aim of every doctor. Kindness, consideration and sensitivity are ingredients which ensure this, whereas an abrasive and insensitive attitude generates mistrust and misconception. However, a pleasant approach, sympathy and forbearance cannot be commanded by order or brought about by legislation. These qualities are partly infectious: hence the importance of those in authority—ward sisters, consultants, senior general practitioners and others—being endowed with them. Many doctors choose medicine because they like people and so possess such qualities, but a few will always lack a good 'bedside manner', or just manners, and probably should not have become clinicians in the first place.

High technology medicine with its expensive, complex and often alarming equipment can hinder close relations with patients, as the doctor's attention may be diverted by the possibilities of scientific investigation. The patient then becomes the duodenal ulcer in the end bed instead of Mr Robinson the window cleaner. The intensive therapy unit (Figure 49) where the patient lies like a physiological specimen on a life support system is a far cry from the personal approach of the last century (Figure 1). Then, the bedside approach with its reassurance was all that could be offered; indeed, charm, kindness and good manners were a necessity for high success and some of the practitioners of old had this in abundance—according to a fascinating article called 'My grandfather's practice', which described a doctor's life in the decade which is portrayed at the start of this book [5]. The letters TLC (tender loving care) are sometimes written in case-notes when nothing more can be done and the patient is expected to die, but TLC should be a positive art as important as treatment of the disease itself, as is illustrated by the care of the dying in the modern hospice [6]. Identification of 'my doctor' gives the patient a sense of security but this feeling can be lost when he is looked after by a team instead of a person. Hospitals can then become frightening and impersonal. The word 'hospital' was derived from the same Latin as 'hospitable' but the setting—take for example the scene in a busy out-patient department where patients may have to wait and wait—is hardly conducive to anyone feeling they are being received as a guest.

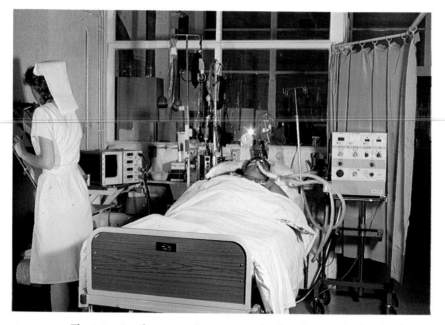

FIGURE 49. The intensive therapy unit—an example of modern medical technology where the patient who is sedated lies like a physiological specimen on a life support system.

The popularity of the seemingly new approach of 'holistic medicine'—the aim being to treat the whole person and not just the disease—appears to be the result of public and professional disenchantment with what is seen as a lack of caring on the part of doctors, coupled with the excesses of medical science. The term is not, however, new; holistic is derived from the Greek ὅλος (whole) and was used by Professor John Ryle [7] when lecturing to medical students in 1931 and many doctors have followed this principle.

Doctors have to be up-to-date technicians in treating organic disease but, in most conditions, there is also the psychological component. We have no means of measuring this; no biochemical tests to detect it—it can easily be missed in the complexities of advancing scientific medicine and cannot be treated by pills. To care for both the physical and the psychological parts of the patient together is surely the art of medicine and thus, in whatever sphere of the profession, we become the personal doctor to our patient. Moreover, the achievement of this also offers the best chance of avoiding some of the problems which have caused doctors to consult the experience and expertise gained by the Medical Defence Union over the last hundred years.

Epilogue

References

1 Holmes O.W. *Medical Essays: The Young Practitioner.* Boston: Houghton, Mifflin & Co, 1883.
2 The changing image of doctors (editorial). *British Medical Journal* 289 (1984): 1713–14.
3 Sandhu B. Personal view. *British Medical Journal* 289 (1984): 554.
4 Loeb R.F. quoted by David Seegal in *Journal of the American Medical Association* 177 (1961): 642.
5 Nicholls L. My grandfather's practice. *Lancet* 2 (1966): 1412–13.
6 Sauders C. & Baines M. *Living with Dying. The Management of Terminal Illness.* Oxford: Oxford University Press, 1984.
7 Ryle J.A. *The Natural History of Disease.* Oxford: Oxford University Press, 1936. p. 15.

Appendices

I Types of membership of the MDU

1 *Newly Qualified*

Special reduced rates have been arranged to assist members in the first four years after qualification.

2 *Full Membership*

Members are encouraged to maintain full membership if they need indemnity.

3 *Associate Membership*

Members who require only the advisory services may opt for this form of membership which has a reduced subscription. These members will not receive assistance in claims for medical negligence. They may, however, receive assistance in accordance with the benefits of membership in claims arising from attending a patient in a genuine emergency.

4 *Special Membership*

UK members who earn less than a certain sum and who have been with the Union for more than three years on the date when their subscription falls due may have the full benefits of membership at half the standard subscription. Full details are available from the London office.

5 *Honorary Life Membership*

Members who have contributed forty subscriptions are eligible to be elected Honorary Life Members by the Council. They will remain full members without payment of further subscriptions.

6 *Retired Membership*

Those who have not completed forty years as a member of the Union but who have retired from all professional work may apply for this form of membership. No subscription is payable. Members will continue to receive the Annual Report and may be assisted in respect of any claim arising out of attending a patient in a genuine emergency.

7 *Representative Membership*

The Union may assist, under the benefits of membership, the personal representatives of a deceased member in proceedings arising out of professional work. Should action for negligence be threatened or instituted against the estate of a deceased member, the Union should be notified immediately.

II The benefits of membership

1   Advice on any matter connected with medical or dental practice, whether in hospital, in private practice, or while serving in a public or other service.
2   Assistance in defending proceedings where a question of professional principle is involved.
3   Assistance in vindicating a member's professional interests, honour and character.
4   Assistance in proceedings brought by a patient arising from the act or omission of himself or of:

(a) a partner who is a member of any other defence or protection society with which a reciprocal arrangement has been effected;

(b) an assistant who is a member of any other defence or protection society with which a reciprocal arrangement has been effected;

(c) a locum tenens, whether or not a member of any defence or protection society;

(d) a subordinate medical or dental officer, including a house surgeon or similar hospital medical or dental officer, whether or not a member of any defence or protection society;

(e) an assistant or subordinate who is not a registered medical or dental practitioner, such as a nurse, dispenser, radiographer, physiotherapist, dental auxiliary or laboratory technician, etc.

The Council will not normally accept responsibility under this paragraph where a claim in respect of a non-medical or non-dental assistant or subordinate arises as a result of the engagement of the member in an activity outside the normal range of medical or dental practice, e.g. where he is the proprietor of a nursing home or a laboratory.
5   Assistance when damages and costs are awarded by a court or a settlement is made out of court.

III Educational material issued by the Medical Defence Union

BOOKLETS AVAILABLE ON REQUEST

Consent to treatment
Theatre safeguards*
~~Complaints to Family Practitioner Committees~~
Memorandum concerning signing of pathology reports
Guide for dental students and practitioners
'Damocles' (medical and dental editions)
Cautionary tales

FILMS AVAILABLE ON LOAN
(16mm colour optical sound)

A Chapter of Accidents. . . . . Accident and Emergency (28 mins)
Get it Right . . . . General Practice (20 mins)
Injection Errors† . . . . Medical and Dental (19 mins)
Ogden v. *Bell* . . . . Medical (22 mins)
Tom, Dick and Harriet† . . . . Dental (27 mins)
Without Due Care† . . . . Surgical (15 mins)
For the Record† . . . . General (15 mins)
First Patient Please† . . . . Dental (15 min)
Becoming an Associate† . . . . Dental (15 mins)
Doctors' Dilemmas† . . . . Accident and Emergency (25 mins)

IV Advice to members

The following is a combined version taken from the annual reports of both the Medical Defence Union and the Medical Protection Society:
∗ Do ensure that your subscription is paid on the due date—preferably by direct debit.
∗ Advise the Secretary of any change of address; this is important especially if moving to a country where a different rate of subscription applies. Also notify the Registrar of the General Medical Council, 44 Hallam Street, London W1N 6AE or of the General Dental Council, 37 Wimpole Street, London W1N 8DQ if you have moved.
∗ Report promptly to the Secretary any mishap affecting a patient or circumstances which could give rise to a complaint or claim.

* Published in co-operation with the other defence organizations, the Royal College of Nursing and the National Association of Theatre Nurses.

† Available on video cassette

* Do not reply to any letter of serious complaint, threats of proceedings or claims for compensation, or attend any conference with lawyers or administrators to discuss the treatment of patients without first consulting the Secretary. Early reporting in writing of possible legal trouble is recommended.
* Please refer to the guidelines (see Chapter 6) when preparing a report.
* Make and keep accurate, contemporaneous notes. They should be legible, objective and worthy of independent scrutiny.
* Do keep copies of all letters of introduction and reports about patients.
* Do not admit legal liability without reference to the defence association.
* Do not alter or tamper with case-notes if a patient has made a complaint or a legal claim concerning treatment. If it later becomes necessary to modify or add to an existing entry, a note that this has been done should always be inserted, signed and dated.
* Do not incur any legal expense in connection with a case without first consulting the Secretary. The responsibility for any legal or other expense incurred will not be accepted in the absence of the prior authority of the Secretary or the Council.
* Ensure that anyone to whom a task is delegated is competent, understands what is required and is encouraged to seek help if in difficulties.
* Criticism is easy with hindsight; avoid criticism of colleagues unless and until the full facts are made available in response to a formal request.
* Show professional courtesy at all times.

V The Declaration of Helsinki†

In the field of clinical research a fundamental distinction must be recognized between clinical research in which the aim is essentially therapeutic for a patient, and clinical research, the essential object of which is purely scientific and without therapeutic value to the person subjected to the research.

I BASIC PRINCIPLES

1   Clinical research must conform to the moral and scientific principles that justify medical research, and should be based on laboratory and animal experiments or other scientifically established facts.
2   Clinical research should be conducted only by scientifically qualified persons and under the supervision of a qualified medical man.

† *Dictionary of Medical Ethics* (Eds) A. S. Duncan, G. R. Dunstan & R. B. Welbourn. London: Darton, Longman and Todd, 1981, p. 132. Other ethical declarations are also recorded: Geneva; Sydney, a statement on death; Oslo on therapeutic abortion; Tokyo on torture; and Hawaii which provided ethical guidelines for psychiatrists.

3   Clinical research cannot legitimately be carried out unless the importance of the objective is in proportion to the inherent risk to the subject.

4   Every clinical research project should be preceded by careful assessment of inherent risks in comparison to foreseeable benefits to the subject or to others.

5   Special caution should be exercised by the doctor in performing clinical research in which the personality of the subject is liable to be altered by drugs or experimental procedure.

II CLINICAL RESEARCH COMBINED WITH PROFESSIONAL CARE

1   In the treatment of the sick person the doctor must be free to use a new therapeutic measure if in his judgment it offers hope of saving life, re-establishing health, or alleviating suffering.

If at all possible, consistent with patient psychology, the doctor should obtain the patient's freely given consent after the patient has been given a full explanation. In case of legal incapacity consent should also be procured from the legal guardian; in case of physical incapacity the permission of the legal guardian replaces that of the patient.

2   The doctor can combine clinical research with professional care, the objective being the acquisition of new medical knowledge, only to the extent that clinical research is justified by its therapeutic value for the patient.

III NON-THERAPEUTIC CLINICAL RESEARCH

1   In the purely scientific application of clinical research carried out on a human being it is the duty of the doctor to remain the protector of the life and health of that person on whom clinical research is being carried out.

2   The nature, the purpose, and the risk of clinical research must be explained to the subject by the doctor.

3   (a) Clinical research on a human being cannot be undertaken without his free consent, after he has been fully informed; if he is legally incompetent the consent of the legal guardian should be procured.

(b) The subject of clinical research should be in such a mental, physical, and legal state as to be able to exercise fully his power of choice.

(c) Consent should as a rule be contained in writing. However, the responsibility for clinical research always remains with the research worker; it never falls on the subject, even after consent is obtained.

4   (a) The investigator must respect the right of each individual to safeguard his personal integrity, especially if the subject is in a dependent relationship to the investigator.

(b) At any time during the course of clinical research the subject or his guardian should be free to withdraw permission for research to be continued. The investigator or the investigating team should discontinue the research if in his or their judgement it may, if continued, be harmful to the individual.

VI The Hippocratic Oath*

I swear by Apollo the physician, and Aesculapius and Health, and All-heal, and all the gods and goddesses, that, according to my ability and judgement, I will keep this Oath and this stipulation—to reckon him who taught me this Art equally dear to me as my parents, to share my substance with him, and relieve his necessities if required; to look upon his offspring in the same footing as my own brothers, and to teach them this Art, if they shall wish to learn it, without fee or stipulation; and that by precept, lecture and every other mode of instruction, I will impart a knowledge of the Art to my own sons, and those of my teachers, and to disciples bound by a stipulation and oath according to the law of medicine, but to none other. I will follow that system of regimen which, according to my ability and judgement, I consider for the benefit of my patients, and abstain from whatever is deleterious and mischievous. I will give no deadly medicine to anyone if asked, nor suggest any such counsel; and in like manner I will not give to a woman a pessary to produce abortion. With purity and with holiness I will pass my life and practise my Art. I will not cut persons labouring under the stone, but will leave this to be done by men who are practitioners of this work. Into whatever houses I enter, I will go into them for the benefit of the sick, and will abstain from every voluntary act of mischief and corruption; and, further, from the seduction of females, or males, of freemen or slaves. Whatever, in connection with my professional practice, or not in connection with it, I see or hear, in the life of men, which ought not be be spoken of abroad, I will not divulge, as reckoning that all such should be kept secret. While I continue to keep this Oath unviolated, may it be granted to me to enjoy life and the practice of the Art, respected by all men, in all times. But should I trespass and violate this Oath, may the reverse be my lot.

VII The Declaration of Geneva
(1948; amended 1968)†

At the time of being admitted as a Member of the Medical Profession:
  I solemnly pledge myself to consecrate my life to the service of humanity;

* This translation is the one adopted in *The Handbook of Medical Ethics*, published by the British Medical Association, 1981.

† The declaration was made in 1948 and the amendment of 1968 is shown in italics. For reference see page 303.

I will give to my teachers the respect and gratitude which is their due;

I will practise my profession with conscience and dignity;

The health of my patient will be my first consideration;

I will respect the secrets which are confided in me, *even after the patient has died*;

I will maintain by all the means in my power, the honour and the noble traditions of the medical profession;

My colleagues will be my brothers;

I will not permit considerations of religion, nationality, race, party politics or social standing to intervene between my duty and my patients;

I will maintain the utmost respect for human life from the time of conception; even under threat, I will not use my medical knowledge contrary to the laws of humanity;

I make these promises solemnly, freely and upon my honour.

VIII Glossary of abbreviations

AHA	Area Health Authority
AMA	American Medical Association
AR	Annual Report
BMA	British Medical Association
DHA	District Health Authority
DHSS	Department of Health and Social Security
EC	Ethical Committee
FPC	Family Practitioner Committee
GDC	General Dental Council
GMC	General Medical Council
GP	General Practitioner
HSC	Health Service Commissioner (Ombudsman)
MCQ	Multiple Choice Questions
MDDUS	Medical and Dental Defence Union of Scotland
MDU	Medical Defence Union
MPS	Medical Protection Society
NHS	National Health Service
RHA	Regional Health Authority
RTA	Road Traffic Accident
SHO	Senior House Officer
WMA	World Medical Association

Index of specific legal cases

Index

Index

Index

Index

Index

Index

Index